DICTIONARY **OF**
Slogans

NIGEL REES

HarperCollins*Publishers*

HarperCollins*Publishers*
P.O. Box, Glasgow G4 0NB

First published 1997

Reprint 10 9 8 7 6 5 4 3 2 1 0

© Nigel Rees

ISBN 0 00 472042 3

A catalogue record for this book is available from the British Library

Printed and bound in Great Britain by
Caledonian International Book Manufacturing Ltd, Glasgow G64

Contents

You can tell the ideals of a nation by its advertisements.
Norman Douglas, South Wind *(1917)*

All over London the lights flickered in and out, calling on the public to save its body and purse...Whatever you're doing, stop it and do something else! Whatever you're buying, pause and buy something different! Be hectored into health and prosperity! Never let up! Never go to sleep! If once you are satisfied, all our wheels will run down. Keep going – and if you can't, Try Nutrax for Nerves!
Dorothy L. Sayers, Murder Must Advertise *(1933)*

There's a difference between a philosophy and a bumper sticker.
Charles M. Schulz, quoted in 1979

Our major obligation is not to mistake slogans for solutions.
Edward R. Murrow, quoted in 1979

What passes for culture in my head is really a bunch of commercials.
Kurt Vonnegut, quoted in 1979

If you feed people with revolutionary slogans they will listen today, and they will listen tomorrow, they will listen the day after tomorrow, but on the fourth day they will say, 'To Hell with you!'
Nikita S. Khruschev, quoted in 1980

Introduction

This is the age of the slogan. They leap out at us from countless billboards, TV screens, T-shirts, bumper stickers and buttons. Politicians and minorities hector us with them; polishers of diamonds, makers of movies and slicers of bread use them to nudge and cajole. We even wear and bear slogans ourselves to proclaim beliefs and sexual preferences. They show what we stand for and what we will not stand for.

There is much feeble-minded puffery. There is also much that is lively, arresting and entertaining. Only occasionally do slogans achieve excellence or memorability or touch a popular chord. This book sets out to record a thousand or so notable examples, good *and* bad, long-lasting *and* ephemeral.

What is a slogan?

Richard Usborne defined a slogan as 'a form of words for which memorability has been bought' (in a 1964 letter to the editors of *The Penguin Dictionary of Quotations*). Indeed, few of the following phrases would have arisen without bidding. Unlike those phrases from entertainment which spontaneously catch on, the success of these slogans has been engineered and encouraged. In some cases, vast sums of money have been spent to keep them before the public. They rarely contain universal truths or profound insights. They may not be true at all. The distance between a copywriter's fancy and reality can be infinite. The common denominator is that all these phrases promote a product, a cause or an idea.

In strict advertising parlance, the slogan is the phrase which comes at the end of the ad and encapsulates the message. It has been said that it should never comprise more than seven words. The advertiser's devout wish is that the phrase will then continue to buzz around the consumer's head, further enforcing the message. There are, in addition, certain advertising phrases which are generally regarded as slogans because they are associated with specific products:

Good To The Last Drop   **It Beats As It Sweeps As It Cleans**
Pure Genius   **Does She ... Or Doesn't She?**

These phrases have the power of slogans even if they are not self-sufficient. The days are long gone when a perfect slogan was supposed to name and define a product as well as promising some benefit.

In short, this book is devoted to slogans in the broadest sense. It includes memorable lines and phrases, mottoes and catchwords, that stand out from advertising, political campaigns and promotions with a social purpose, and which may be said to have some of the force of full-blooded slogans.

How slogans originate

In trying to discover when and where all these different kinds of phrases were first used, together with some indication of how and by whom they were created, I was frequently told that their origins had been lost in the mists. Only a few commercial or political organizations have assembled archives recording their promotional activities. Even among those which have, few have bothered to record specifically who coined the phrases which have helped give enduring success or fame to their products.

There are some people in advertising who feel that this is only proper. One creative chief warned: 'If you are going to try and credit individuals with slogans, you are inevitably going to upset an awful lot of people. Slogans tend to evolve by some strange form of osmosis and normally more than one person can genuinely lay claim to having made a contribution.' Indeed, in advertising more than most professions, 'success has a hundred fathers and failure is an orphan'. But when it has been possible to get somewhere near the truth it has been thought worthwhile to point a finger.

A further complication is that advertising agencies are for ever splitting up, regrouping under ever more peculiar names, and occasionally they lose accounts in sudden-death situations which erase memories of even the proudest achievements. All this applies equally, if not more, to slogans carrying a social or political message. These often arise out of a popular mood and are snapped up before anyone has had time to record how they were formulated. So, inevitably, much of the information here gathered is incomplete. Corrections and suggestions for future editions will be warmly welcomed.

Their use and their popularity

Slogans can be either sharp or blunt instruments, even if it is hard to measure what they do to our minds by simplifying issues and purveying propaganda - or what they do to our language by relying so heavily on puns, alliteration, rhythm and balance. Accordingly, this book is a celebration of slogans, but one tempered with a certain irreverence. Occasional examples have been included of the way in which slogans have been alluded to or maltreated in other contexts. If manufacturers or even copywriters recoil, they should console themselves with the knowledge that they have at least contributed something to the language.

At one time everybody seemed to have a slogan. The crisp phrase was refreshing after the torrents of verbiage that characterized early advertising. Now, whether in press ads or on TV, there is a greater emphasis on the visual – sometimes almost to the exclusion of the verbal. One agency creative director commented: 'Slogans have to be brilliant to work, and actually say something rather than merely boast. If all that can be said is a bit of clever puff, we'd rather do without.'

What, then, makes a successful slogan? There is only one test - whether it promotes the product or cause effectively. **Votes For Women** is not notably clever or catchy but it achieved its purpose. On the other hand, there are plenty of phrases which have caught on but which have failed to promote the product or the cause.

Now the time has come to 'run this book up the flagpole and see if anyone salutes it' and to 'put it out on the porch and see if the cat eats it' – to use those phrases beloved of advertising folk. If the collective noun for the phrases that follow is a 'boast' of slogans, let the boasting begin.

Nigel Rees
London, 1997

Acknowledgements

Many people have helped me with my inquiries, on both sides of the Atlantic, and I am much indebted to them. My wife, Sue Bates, helped compile the original list of slogans. Helpful suggestions came from Ron and the late Pat Lehrman, Keith and Avril Ravenscroft, and especially Barry Day. Among the other individuals from advertising agencies and elsewhere who provided information were: Don Arlett; Paul Beale; John Bessant (Central Office of Information); Paul Best; Tony Brignull; Jill Craigie; Julian Bradley (New Scotland Yard); Donald Hickling; Maurice Drake; Alan Evans (Birds Eye Wall's Ltd); David Hall (Arthur Guinness Son & Co. (Park Royal) Ltd); Dany Khosrovani; David J. Kingsley; David Lamb (Rowntree Mackintosh Ltd); Derek Lamb; Terry Lovelock; Jane Maas; Charles Moss; Chris Munds; David McLaren; E.N. Monahan (Shell UK Oil); Roger Musgrave; John Paine; George MacDonald Ross; Valerie Simmonds; David Simpson (Action on Smoking and Health); Maurice Smelt; Edward Taylor; Royston Taylor; Peter Thomson (Advertising Standards Authority); Len Weinreich; Fay Weldon; David White (Start-Rite Shoes Ltd); Lois Wyse. These kind people helped me with my original book *Slogans* published by George Allen & Unwin (1982) and/or subsequently.

I am also most grateful to many companies and organisations for providing me with research facilities. Among them: Austin Reed Ltd; Bass Ltd; Bovril Ltd; British Rail; Carnation Foods Company Ltd; Design & Art Directors Association of London; Hoover Historical Center; John Haig & Co. Ltd; John Lewis Partnership Ltd; John Player & Sons Ltd; Leo Burnett USA; Hovis Ltd; Institute of Practitioners in Advertising; Kentucky Fried Chicken (Great Britain) Ltd; Mars Ltd; R. Paterson & Sons Ltd; A.& F. Pears Ltd; Prudential Assurance Company Ltd; RHM Foods Ltd; Jos. Schlitz Brewing Company; The J.M. Smucker Company; Tate & Lyle Ltd; Texaco Ltd; Wm Whiteley Ltd; F.W. Woolworth & Company Ltd.

How To Use This Book

The following terms have been used throughout the book. For a list of the most frequently cited sources, see page 285.

Types of slogan

- Bill-matter – a phrase used (often quirkily) to describe and promote an entertainer on a bill-poster or in some other form of advertisement.
- Corporate slogan – a relatively recent development through which (as with a corporate logo or livery) a large business or organization seeks to make the public view it in the best possible light. Often portentous and irritatingly feeble, such slogans have been dubbed 'corporate apologias' and 'corporate custard'.
- Fictional slogan – one devised for a novel or film but which may not have been used in real life.
- Informal/Unofficial slogan – by which I mean, a form of words that has been dreamt up by an individual (perhaps hand-written on a card in the simplest form of protest) in response to some state of affairs; but one which has not been crafted by a formal advertising or political agency.

Place and date of first use

- 'US' or 'UK' signifies no more than the country of origin – the slogan may well have been used elsewhere;
- 'by 1963' or 'current 1963' – documentary evidence is available of the slogan in use that year, though it probably arose earlier;
- 'from 1963' – the slogan was first used in that year;
- 'quoted 1963' – means no more than that; the slogan was most likely coined or current well before.

He wont be
happy
till he
gets it!

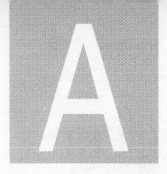

A.B.C. - Anyone But Carter
See TIME IS NOW

Abolish The Draft
Anti-draft slogans during the Vietnam War; US, 1960s. Also **Hell, No, We Won't Go**.

Abolition!
Political slogan of colonists; North America, c.1765. Demanding the repeal of the British Stamp Act. After repeal in 1766, the slogan was widely applied to the abolition of slavery. (Flexner, 1976)

Absolutely Pure
Royal Baking Soda (baking powder); US, current 1880s. The slogan was also used for Swan Soap in the US and Cadbury's Cocoa Essence in the UK.

Access Takes The Waiting Out Of Wanting
Access credit card; UK, c.1973. Withdrawn after protests about the ethics of the pitch and replaced by **Makes Sensible Buying Simple**. More recently: **Access – Your Flexible Friend** (UK; current 1981).

Ace Caff With A Nice Museum Attached, An
Victoria and Albert Museum, London; UK; current 1988.

Action Not Words – Vote Conservative
Conservative Party general election slogan; UK, 1966. It did not succeed in winning the election for the newly chosen leader of the party, Edward Heath.

Acts Twice As Fast As Aspirin
Bufferin; US, current 1950. (See over.)

Bufferin

TRADE-MARK

Acts twice as fast as aspirin!

New product for fast pain relief doesn't disagree with you!

Adopt, Adapt, Improve
National Association of Round Tables of Great Britain and Ireland;
UK, 1927–. Motto with the force of a slogan. The Prince of Wales
(later Edward VIII) had said in a speech at the British Industries
Fair in Birmingham (1927): 'The young business and professional
men of this country must get together round the table, adopt
methods that have proved sound in the past, adapt them to the
changing needs of the times and, whenever possible, improve
them.' The Round Table movement is a social and charitable organization for young professional and business men under the age
of forty (after which age Rotary takes over).

Advance Australia
Government campaign; Australia, current in 1982. The song
'Advance Australia Fair' by Peter Dodds McCormick was first
performed in Sydney in 1878, but the alliterative slogan 'Advance
Australia' had apparently already existed when Michael Massey
Robinson wrote in the *Sydney Gazette* (1 February 1826):
' "ADVANCE THEN, AUSTRALIA", / Be this thy proud gala / …
And thy watch-word be "FREEDOM FOR EVER!" ' 'Advance
Australia' then became the national motto of the Commonwealth
of Australia when the states united in 1901.
  In the 1970s and 1980s, as republicanism grew, the phrase
acquired the force of a slogan and was used in various campaigns
to promote national pride (sometimes as 'Let's Advance

Australia'). In 1984, the song 'Advance Australia Fair', slightly adapted, superseded 'God Save the Queen' as the national anthem:

> Australia's sons, let us rejoice,
> For we are young and free,
> We've golden soil and wealth for toil,
> Our home is girt by sea;
> Our land abounds in nature's gifts
> Of beauty rich and rare;
> In hist'ry's page, let ev'ry stage
> Advance Australia Fair,
> In joyful strains then let us sing
> Advance Australia fair.

The first line became 'Australians all let us rejoice ... ' and McCormick's second verse was mostly ignored:

> When gallant Cook from Albion sailed
> To trace wide oceans o'er,
> True British courage bore him on
> Till he landed on our shore.
> Then here he raised Old England's flag,
> The standard of the brave.
> With all her faults we love her still
> Britannia rules the wave.
> In joyful strains then let us sing,
> Advance Australia Fair.

Afore Ye Go
Bell's Scotch whisky; UK, undated. (Sunners)

After The Pill: Posturpedic
Sealy mattresses; US, undated. (Baker)

Ahh Bisto!
Bisto (gravy browning); UK, from 1919. The product name is said to be a hidden slogan, too. When the Cerebos company put it on the market in 1910, the product did not have a name. According to legend, the initial letters of the proposed slogan 'Browns, Seasons, Thickens In One' were rearranged to give the brand name. The

Bisto Kids, drawn by Will Owen, first appeared in 1919, sniffing a wisp of gravy aroma and murmuring, 'Ahh Bisto!' This is a phrase which has endured ever since and has been parodied in numerous cartoons over the years, providing almost a pocket history of the century – 'Ah! Ribso'; 'I Smell Bristowe!'; 'Ah,Blitzo!'; 'Ah, Bizerta'; 'Ah, Crippso!'; 'Ah! Winston!'; 'Ah! Coupon free!'; and 'Arrgh!'

Ah, Woodbine – A Great Little Cigarette
Woodbine cigarettes; UK, current 1957. TV ads used Norman Hackforth's celebrated voice to deliver the line.

Ain't No Reason To Go Anyplace Else
Wendy hamburger restaurants; US, 1981. 'Primary school pupils, often the target for ungrammatical TV advertising assaults are finally hitting back ... More than 200 protesting wrote in. One declared: "Violets are blue ... Roses are red ... I go to school ... But you should instead' (*Daily Mail*, 2 June 1981). See also WHERE'S THE BEEF?

Airline Run By Professionals, The
Delta airline; US, probably 1970s.

Alas! My Poor Brother
Bovril (meat extract); UK, current 1896. Bovril came on to the market in Britain when bold, modern advertising techniques were being applied for the first time. John Lawson Johnston, a Scot who emigrated to Canada, developed a way of blending meat extract with other raw materials. The product was first sold as Johnston's Fluid Beef in 1874. In London, S.H. Benson, a Johnston employee, set up his own business as an 'advertiser's agent' with Bovril as his first client. By the end of the century he had made Bovril a household name – and launched an advertising business that kept the Bovril account until the agency folded in 1969. 'Alas! My Poor Brother' is the most famous of the early Bovril captions, appearing with W.H. Caffyn's poster of a tearful bull eyeing a jar. **The Glory Of A Man Is His Strength** dates from this time, too. Coupled with the picture of a youth in a leopard-skin wrestling with a lion, it endured on the Bovril label for more than fifty years. **The Two Infallible Powers. The Pope And Bovril** is advertising chutzpah of the first order. It appeared in the late 1890s. **I Hear**

They Want More, spoken by one nervous bull to another in 1903, again pointed up the somewhat uncomfortable fact of where the product originated. **It *Must* Be Bovril** stemmed from an endorsement by Sir Ernest Shackleton, the explorer, in 1909. 'The question of the concentrated beef supply [on expeditions] is most important – it must be Bovril.' The phrase was still in use as late as 1936. **Give Him/Her/Them Bovril** appeared in the last campaign before the outbreak of the First World War. The Bovril airship bearing 'Give Him Bovril' on one side and 'Give Her Bovril' on the other made numerous flights over London at heights of between 100 and 1000 feet and engaged in mock battles with a biplane, anticipating the more realistic encounters to come. (Source: Peter Hadley, comp., *The History of Bovril Advertising*, 1970).

Bovril Prevents That Sinking Feeling, on H.H. Harris's cheery poster of a pyjama-clad man astride a jar in the sea, ushered in the post-war years in 1920, although the slogan had apparently been coined in a golfing booklet issued by Bovril in 1890 which included the commendation: 'Unquestionably Bovril ... supplies ... the nourishment which is so much needed by all players at the critical intermediate hour between breakfast and luncheon, when the sinking feeling engendered by an empty stomach is so distressing, and so fruitful of deteriorated play.' It is said that Bovril had intended to use this slogan earlier but withheld it because of the *Titanic* disaster. With updated illustrations the slogan endured until 1958. Examples of the way the phrase entered the language: 'He had had that sinking feeling before, and he knew what it meant. *He was hungry*' (A.A. Milne, *Winnie-the-Pooh*, 1926); 'As usual I had the sinking feeling which I always have when he leaves – for one day, he will go away and never return, the victim of some fanatic's aim' (Sir Henry Channon's diary for 6 December 1938); heading from *The Independent* (12 April 1989): 'Crucible challenge for a champion [Steve Davis, snooker player] who thinks rivals under the table before relishing that sinking feeling.'

Aunt Bovril Sandwiches Grandma? is one of numerous awful puns perpetrated in Bovril advertising, especially on the railways, in the 1920s and 1930s. Others included: **Bovril 2.40fy You; Scotch Express Great Faith In Bovril; If You've Mr Train Don't Miss Bovril; Noel Feelings To Bovril; Isn't The Milkmaid Attractive With Bovril?; To All In Tents Bovril Is As Good As A Blanket.**

Algérie Française [Algeria is French]
Political slogan; France, from May 1958. Right-wing opponents of
President de Gaulle objecting to Algerian independence. The
rhythm of the slogan was tooted on car horns and the actual
phrase often delivered as part of the longer chant, '*Vive l'Algérie
Française, Vive la République, Vive la France!*'

All Animals Are Equal, But Some Animals Are More Equal Than Others

Fictional slogan from George Orwell's novel *Animal Farm* (1945) –
a commentary on the totalitarian excesses of Communism. It had
been anticipated: Hesketh Pearson recalls in his 1956 biography of
Sir Herbert Beerbohm Tree that the actor-manager wished to
insert one of his own epigrams in a play called *Nero* by Stephen
Phillips (1906). It was: 'All men are equal – except myself.' In Noël
Coward's *This Year of Grace* (1928), there is this exchange – Pellet:
'Men are all alike' Wendle: 'Only some more than others'.

The saying alludes, of course, to Thomas Jefferson's 'All men are
created equal and independent', from the Preamble to the
American Declaration of Independence (1776). It has the makings
of a formula phrase in that it is more likely to be used to refer to
humans than to animals. Only the second half of the phrase need
actually be spoken, the first half being understood: 'You-Know-
Who [Mrs Thatcher] is against the idea [of televising parliament].
There aren't card votes at Westminster, but some votes are more
equal than others' (*The Guardian*, 15 February 1989).

All For One, And One For All [*Tous pour un, un pour tous*]

Fictional motto of Three Musketeers in the novel *Les Trois
Mousquetaires* (1844–5) by Alexandre Dumas. Earlier, Shakespeare
in his poem, *The Rape of Lucrece*, l. 141–4 (1594) had written:

> The aim of all is but to nurse the life
> With honour, wealth and ease, in waning age;
> And in this aim there is much thwarting strife
> That *one for all, or all for one* we gage [= pledge].

Compare **Each For All And All For Each**: Co-Operative
Wholesale Society; UK, date unknown.

All Human Life Is There
News of the World newspaper; UK, from c.1958. The only reference to this phrase in *The Oxford Dictionary of Quotations* is listed under Henry James. His *Madonna of the Future* (1879) contains the line: 'Cats and monkeys, monkeys and cats – all human life is there.' So, what is the connection, if any, with the steamy British Sunday newspaper? Maurice Smelt said (1981): ' "All Human Life Is There" was my idea, but I don't, of course, pretend that they were my words. I simply lifted them from *The Oxford Dictionary of Quotations*. I didn't bother to tell the client that they were from Henry James suspecting that, after the Henry James-Who-He? stage, he would come up with tiresome arguments about being too high-hat for his readership. I did check whether we were clear on copyright, which we were by a year or two. The agency I was then working for was Colman, Prentis & Varley. I do recall its use as baseline in a tiny little campaign trailing a series that earned the *News of the World* a much-publicised but toothless rebuke from the Press Council. The headline of that campaign was: ' "I've Been A Naughty Girl' Says Diana Dors". The meiosis worked, as the *News of the World* knew it would. They ran an extra million copies of the first issue of the series.'

All Over The World Good Mornings Begin With Gillette
Gillette razor blades; UK, current c.1952.

All Power To The Soviets
Petrograd workers' slogan; Russia, October/November 1917.

All Talking! All Singing! All Dancing!
Film, *Broadway Melody*; US, 1929. When sound came to the movies, this very first Hollywood musical – from MGM – was promoted with posters bearing the slogan:

> *The New Wonder of the Screen!*
> ALL TALKING
> ALL SINGING
> ALL DANCING
> *Dramatic Sensation*

Curiously enough, in the same year, two rival studios hit on the same selling pitch. Alice White in *Broadway Babes* (using Warners' Vitaphone system) was '100% TALKING, SINGING, DANCING'. And Radio's *Rio Rita*, with Bebe Daniels, was billed as 'ZIEGFELD'S FABULOUS ALL-TALKING, ALL-SINGING SUPER SCREEN SPECTACLE'. It was natural that the studios should wish to promote the most obvious aspect of the new sound cinema but it is odd that they should all have made use of much the same phrase.

Accordingly, the worlds of computing and finance have both inherited a phrase – 'all-singing, all-dancing' – whose origins are pure Hollywood. First, the computing use. From a report in *The Guardian* (3 October 1984) about a new police computer called 'Holmes': 'Sir Lawrence Byford is proud that Britain got there first. Holmes, he claims, is unique. "It should provide our detectives with unrivalled facilities when dealing with crimes such as homicides and serious sexual offences ... it's the all-singing all-dancing act." The only thing it can't do, it seems, is play the violin.' And from a special report on computers in the same paper (24 June 1985): 'I'm knocking these present notes together on the word-processor incorporated into Jazz, the all-singing, all-dancing "integrated" package from the Lotus Development Corporation.' Partridge/*Catch Phrases* dates the start of the computing use to about 1970.

The phrase is used every bit as much when writing about financial 'packages'. From a special report in *The Times* (8 November 1985): 'The City's financial institutions have been busily preparing themselves for the changes [i.e. Big Bang the following year]. Many of the large stockbroking firms have forged links with banks: conceding their independence but benefiting from the massive capital injection which many believe will be necessary to cope with the new look all-singing-and-dancing exchange.' From 'Family Money' in the same newspaper (31 May 1986): 'There are a number of all-singing, all-dancing and rather moderately performing plans on the savings and insurance market. They offer just about every financial service under the sun without necessarily distinguishing themselves in any one particular field.'

The meaning is reasonably clear. What you should anticipate getting in each sphere is a multipurpose something or other, with every possible feature, which may or may not 'perform' well. A dictionary of jargon (1984) goes so far as to give the general business meaning as 'super-glamorised, gimmicky, flashy', when referring to a version of any stock product.

All The Hits And More on 194
Capital Radio (station, London); UK, current 1981.

All The News That's Fit To Print
The New York Times newspaper; US, from 1896. This slogan was devised by Adolph S. Ochs when he bought *The New York Times* and it has been published in every edition since – at first on the editorial page, on 25 October 1896, and from the following February on the front page. It became the paper's war-cry in the 1890s battle against formidable competition from the *World*, *Herald* and *Journal*. It has been parodied by Howard Dietz as 'All The News That Fits We Print' and at worst sounds like a slogan for the suppression of news. However, no paper prints everything.

All The News That Fits
Rolling Stone Magazine; US, current in 1982.

All The Way With LBJ
Presidential election slogan for Lyndon B. Johnson; US, 1964. Also **USA For LBJ.** Gave him a landslide victory over the Republican challenger, Barry M. Goldwater, in the year following the Kennedy assassination. 'All The Way With LBJ' had first been used when Johnson was seeking the presidential nomination which eventually went to Kennedy in 1960. 'All through the fall and winter of 1959 and 1960,' wrote Theodore White, 'the noise-makers of the Johnson campaign ... chanted "All The Way With LBJ" across the South and Far West, instantly identifiable by their Texan garb, their ten-gallon hats (and, said their enemies, the cowflap on their boots).' (White, 1965) **In Your Heart You Know I'm Right** was the much-parodied Goldwater slogan. Come-backs included: 'In your guts, you know he's nuts' and 'You know in your heart he's right – far right'. **AuH2O = 1964** gave rise to the riposte 'AuH20 = H2S' and 'Gold-water in '64, Hot Water in '65, Bread and Water in '66'.

Almost A Gentleman

Bill-matter for Billy Bennett, the British music-hall comedian (1887-1942). The playwright John Osborne took it as the title of his second volume of memoirs (1991). Compare Daisy Ashford, *The Young Visiters*, Chap. 1 (1919): 'I am not quite a gentleman but you would hardly notice it but can't be helped anyhow.'

Always The Leader

Corporate slogan for Mack Trucks; US, current 1980.

America Cannot Stand Pat

Presidential election for Richard M. Nixon; US, 1960. His rival John F. Kennedy had quoted **Stand Pat With McKinley** as an example of Republican reaction. So Nixon countered with 'America Cannot Stand Pat' – until it was politely pointed out that he was married to a woman with that name. **America Cannot Stand Still** was rapidly substituted. (Safire) In *Before the Fall* (1975), William Safire gives a somewhat different version of this tale which, alas, is aprocryphal anyway.

America, Love It Or Leave It

Semi-official political slogan; US, current 1969. One of the few memorable patriotic slogans from the Vietnam War period. Hence, the 1970 graffiti joke: 'Greenland: love it or Leif it.' (Reisner)

America's Beloved Baritone

Bill-matter for the singer John Charles Thomas; US, probably 1940s.

America's Favorite British ...

See BRITAIN'S FAVOURITE ...

America's Most Famous Dessert

Jell-O; US, current 1900. Made by the Genesee Pure Food Company of Le Roy, New York.

America's Storyteller

Merrill Lynch bank; US, current 1980.

Amistad!
Political slogan; US, after 1839. In that year, fifty-four slaves aboard the Spanish schooner *Amistad* on a voyage from Cuba murdered the captain and three of the crew. They ordered the remaining crew to sail to Africa but instead found themselves taken to Long Island and imprisoned. Later, they were freed and returned to Africa. The cry was taken up by militants in the 1960s. (Flexner, 1976)

Anarchy Now
Anarchist slogan; UK, by 1979.

And All Because The Lady Loves Milk Tray
Cadbury's Milk Tray chocolates; UK, 1968–76. The pay-off line to action ads showing feats of daring of a James Bond kind and leading up to the presentation of a box of the chocolates (with calling card) to a suitably alluring female. Previously Milk Tray advertising had stressed the more romantic associations of chocolates with present-giving.

And Your Best Friends ...
See OFTEN A BRIDESMAID ...

Another Morris
Morris Motors; UK, undated. The first Morris car, the Oxford 'bullnose' was built by William Morris (later Lord Nuffield) in 1913. This low-key slogan endured for many years. Eventually Morris became part of the British Motor Corporation and then BL.

... Anyhow Have A Winfield
Winfield cigarettes; Australia, current 1975. From long-running TV campaigns featuring Paul Hogan came the distinctive pronunciation of 'anyhow' as 'ennyeeiaouww ... !'

Anything To Beat Grant
Presidential election slogan *against* Ulysses S. Grant; US, 1872. After one term, Grant had proved to be ill-suited to office despite a legendary military reputation gained in the Civil War. This was a slogan somewhat half-heartedly in support of his opponent, Horace Greeley. Grant was nonetheless re-elected.

Any Time, Any Place, Any Where
See RIGHT ONE

Arbeit macht frei [Work makes you free]
Motto/slogan over the entrance to the Nazi concentration camp at
Dachau; Poland, by 1933. Also later at Auschwitz.

Aren't You Glad You Use Dial ...
See PEOPLE WHO LIKE ...

Are You A Cadbury's Fruit And Nut Case?
Cadbury's Fruit and Nut chocolate; UK, current 1964. Or
'Everyone's A ...'

Are You Four-Square?
Religious slogan; US, 1930s/40s. Greeting of the followers of
Aimée Semple McPherson, the Canadian-born revivalist
(1890–1944). Used to mean, 'are you solid, resolute?' Being
'square', in this sense, dates from at least 1300. Angelus Temple in
Los Angeles was the centre of her 'Foursquare Gospel'.

Are You Getting It Every Day?
The Sun newspaper; UK, 1979–80. An inevitably nudging slogan
from TV ads.

Are You Ready, Eddie?
Today newspaper; UK, 1986. Not an immortal slogan, but worth
mentioning for what it illustrates about advertising agencies and
the way they work. *Today*, a new national newspaper using the latest production technology, was launched by Eddie Shah, hitherto
known as a union-busting printer and publisher of provincial
papers. In its collective wisdom, the Wight Collins Rutherford
Scott agency, charged with promoting the new paper's launch,
built the whole campaign round the above slogan. Why had they
chosen it? Starting with the name 'Eddie' – Mr Shah being thought
of as a folk hero in some quarters – the agency found that it
rhymed with 'ready'. So the man was featured in TV ads surrounded by his staff being asked this important question.

Unfortunately, the ad agency had zeroed in all too well on the most pertinent aspect of the new paper's launch. *Today* was *not* ready, and the slogan echoed hollowly from the paper's disastrous start to the point at which Mr Shah withdrew to lick his wounds.

The phrase had earlier been used as the title of a track on the Emerson, Lake and Palmer album *Tarkus* (1971), where it referred to the recording engineer, Eddie Offord (to whom it had, presumably, been addressed).

The same rhyme occurs in 'ready for Freddie', meaning 'ready for the unexpected, the unknown or the unusual' (according to *The Dictionary of American Slang*, 1960), and was a phrase that came out of the 'L'il Abner' comic strip in the 1930s. **Are You Ready for Freddy?** was also used as a slogan to promote the film *Nightmare on Elm Street – Part 4* (US, 1989) – referring to a gruesome character, Freddy Krueger.

Are You Ready To Take The Challenge?
See COME ALIVE ...

'Arf A Mo, Kaiser!
Army recruiting slogan; UK, 1915–16. A poster with this caption showed a British 'Tommy' lighting a pipe prior to going into action. Became a catchphrase and even surfaced again, on one occasion, in the Second World War as "Arf A Mo, Hitler!'

Arise! Go Forth and Conquer
See VOTES FOR WOMEN

Army Builds Men, The
Army recruiting slogan; US, by the 1960s. Unverified. **The Marine Corps Builds Men** certainly seems to have existed, given the graffiti parodies in Reisner – 'The Marine Corps builds Oswalds', etc. **Ask A Marine** was used in 1970.

Ars gratia artis [Art for art's sake]
Metro-Goldwyn-Mayer film company; US, from c.1916. Howard Dietz, director of publicity and advertising with the original Goldwyn Pictures company, had left Columbia University not long before. When asked to design a trademark, he based it on the

university's lion and added the Latin words underneath. The trademark and motto were carried over when Samuel Goldwyn retired to make way for the merger of Metropolitan with the interests of Louis B. Mayer. (Lambert) 'Goldwyn Pictures Griddle The Earth' is the no doubt apocryphal slogan said to have been suggested by Samuel Goldwyn himself.

Ask A Marine
See ARMY BUILDS MEN

Ask The Man From The Pru
See MAN FROM THE PRU

Ask The Man Who Owns One
Packard automobiles; US, from 1902. This slogan originated with James Ward Packard, the founder of the company, and appeared for many years in all Packard advertising and sales material. Someone had written asking for more information about his motors. Packard told his secretary: 'Tell him that we have no literature – we aren't that big yet – but if he wants to know how good an automobile the Packard is, tell him to ask the man who owns one.' A 1903 placard is the first printed evidence of the slogan's use. It lasted for more than thirty-five years. (Lambert)

As Long As Firestone Keeps Thinking About People, People Will Keep Thinking About Firestone

Corporate slogan for Firestone; US, quoted 1983 – in *Ogilvy on Advertising*. David Ogilvy goes on to slam all such lines: 'The copy in most corporate advertisements is distinguished by a self-serving, flatulent pomposity which defies reading, and agencies waste endless hours concocting slogans of incredible fatuity … all these bromides are interchangeable – any company could use any of them.'

At General Electric Progress Is Our Most Important Product
Corporate slogan for General Electric; US, by 1954–5. In that season, Ronald Reagan became host of the popular TV drama show *General Electric Theater*. Each edition ended with his intoning the line. At least, this corporate tag was closely linked to the name of the company.

At 60 Miles An Hour The Loudest Noise In This New Rolls-Royce Comes From The Electric Clock
Rolls-Royce motors; US, from 1958. The best-known promotional line there has ever been for an automobile. It was not devised by some copywriting genius but came from a car test of the 1958 Silver Cloud by the Technical Editor of *The Motor* magazine. David Ogilvy recalled presenting the headline to a senior Rolls-Royce executive in New York who shook his head sadly and said: 'We really ought to do something about that damned clock.' In fact, the idea turns out not to have been very original anyway – a 1907 review of the Silver Ghost in *The Autocar* had read: 'At whatever speed the car is driven, the auditory nerves when driving are troubled by no fuller sound than emanates from the 8-day clock.'

Rolls-Royce had initially advertised with the description **The Best Car In The World** (current 1929) – though this, too, was a journalist's accolade, having first appeared in *The Times* in 1908.

At The Sign Of The Black Horse
Lloyd's Bank; UK, current 1980. This slogan capitalizes upon the bank's black horse symbol, which dates back to 1666.

Auf nach Berlin [On to Berlin]
Nationalist slogan; Germany, current 1919-24.

AuH2O = 1964

See ALL THE WAY WITH LBJ
Aunt Bovril Sandwiches Grandma?
See ALAS! MY POOR BROTHER

Australians Wouldn't Give A XXXX For Anything Else
Castlemaine XXXX lager; UK, 1986. Suitably frisky, given the
product and the country of origin.

Avis – We Try Harder
See WHEN YOU'RE ONLY …

Avoid Five O'Clock Shadow
Gem razors and blades; US, current 1945. This slogan is apparently
the origin of the expression 'five o'clock shadow' to describe the
stubbly growth that some dark-haired men acquire on their faces
towards the end of the day. A 1937 Gem advert had warned: 'That
unsightly beard growth which appears prematurely at about 5 pm
looks bad.'

The most noted sufferer was Richard Nixon, who may have lost
the TV debates in his presidential race against John F. Kennedy in
1960 as a result. In his *Memoirs* (1978), Nixon wrote: 'Kennedy
arrived … looking tanned, rested and fit. My television adviser,
Ted Rodgers, recommended that I use television make-up, but
unwisely I refused, permitting only a little "beard stick" on my
perpetual five o'clock shadow.'

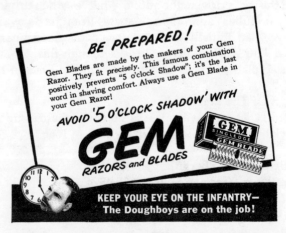

26

Avon Calling!
Avon cosmetics; US, 1886. The first Avon Lady, Mrs P.F.A. Allre, was employed by the firm's founder, D.H. McConnell, to visit and sell cosmetics in the home. It was still in use a century later. (Flexner, 1976)

Award Yourself The C.D.M.
Cadbury's Dairy Milk chocolate; UK, 1967–77. Devised by Dennis Auton at the Young & Rubicam agency, this campaign invited the public, through TV, posters and press ads, to nominate worthy recipients of an award. These people then had their citations published in a style parodying the British official honours lists. Recipients included 'Miss S. Pollak, Eton Villas, London SW3, "for walking in her mini-skirt within whistling distance of the building site" (nominated by Mr T. Taylor)' and Arkle, the Grand National Steeplechase winner.

Ayer's Sarsparilla Purifies The Blood, Makes The Weak Strong
Ayer's Sarsparilla (health drink); probably UK, date unknown. Advertisements featured the picture of a little girl. The drink was made from the sarsparilla plant which is an aphrodisiac to South Americans.

Babies Are Our Business
Gerber Products; US, current 1954.

Babies Love It
Cow & Gate milk food; UK, undated. (Sunners)

Back To Basics
Conservative Government unofficial slogan; UK, 1993. John Major, the Prime Minister, launched this ill-fated slogan in a speech to the Conservative Party Conference: 'The message from this Conference is clear and simple. We must go back to basics … The Conservative Party will lead the country back to these basics, right across the board: sound money, free trade; traditional teaching; respect for the family and the law.' A number of government scandals in the ensuing months exposed the slogan as hard to interpret or, at worst, suggesting rather a return to 'the bad old days'.

The alliterative phrase (sometimes 'back to *the* basics') may first have surfaced in the US where it was the mid-1970s slogan of a movement in education to give priority to the teaching of the fundamentals of reading, writing and arithmetic.

Back To Normalcy
Presidential election slogan for Warren G. Harding; US, 1920. Also **Return To Normalcy With Harding**. Both were based on his remark in a speech at Boston, Mass. (14 May 1920): 'America's present need is not heroics but healing, not nostrums but normalcy, not revolution but restoration, not agitation but adjustment, not surgery but serenity, not the dramatic but the dispassionate, not experiment but equipoise, not submergence in internationality but sustainment in triumphant nationality.' Out of such an alliterative bog stuck the word 'normalcy', a perfectly

good Americanism, though it has been suggested that Harding was actually mispronouncing the word 'normality'. He himself claimed that 'normalcy' was what he had meant to say, having come across the word in a dictionary.

Back To The Land

Political slogan; UK, by the 1890s. The cry was first heard when it was realized that the Industrial Revolution and the transfer of the population towards non-agricultural labour had starved farming of workers. At about this time, a Wickham Market farmer wrote to Sir Henry Rider Haggard, who was making an inventory of the decline, published as *Rural England* (1902): 'The labourers "back to the land". That is the cry of the press and the fancy of the people. Well, I do not think that they will ever come back; certainly no legislation will ever bring them. Some of the rising generation may be induced to stay, but it will be by training them to the use of machinery and paying them higher wages. It should be remembered that the most intelligent men have gone: these will never come back, but the rising generation may stay as competition in the town increases, and the young men of the country are better paid.'

The *OED2* cites an 1894 formulation of the idea, from *The Times* (25 October): 'All present were interested in the common practice that it was desirable, if possible, to bring the people back to the land.' By 1905, *The Spectator* (23 December) was saying: ' "Back-to-the-land" is a cry full not only of pathos, but of cogency.'

In the 1970s, a TV comedy series was called *Backs to the Land*, playing on the phrase to provide an innuendo about its heroines – 'Land Girls', members of the Women's Land Army conscripted to work on the land during the Second World War (though the WLA was first established in the First World War.)

Ban The Bomb

Political slogan; US, from 1953; not really until 1960 in the UK. One of the simplest and best-known alliterative slogans. The (British) Campaign for Nuclear Disarmament – whose semi-official slogan it became – was not publicly launched until February 1958. Richard Crossman referred rather to 'Scrap the Bomb' in a 1957 press article.

Bargain And Corruption

Presidential election slogan; US, 1828. No one candidate in the *previous* election had received a majority of the electoral vote although Andrew Jackson was in the lead. When that election came to be decided by the House of Representatives, John Quincy Adams struck a deal with fellow candidate Henry Clay (Speaker of the House) by which Adams won and Clay became Secretary of State. In 1828, using the slogan 'Bargain And Corruption', Jackson unseated President Adams. (Safire)

Bayonet Is A Weapon With A Worker At Each End, A

Pacifist slogan; UK, 1940. Quoted in *The Penguin Dictionary of Modern Quotations* (1971).

Beanz Meanz Heinz

Heinz baked beans; UK, current 1967. The kind of phrase that drives teachers into a frenzy because of its apparent encouragement of poor spelling. Johnny Johnson wrote the music for the jingle which went:

> A million housewives every day
> Pick up a tin of beans and say
> Beanz meanz Heinz.

'I created the line at Young & Rubicam,' said Maurice Drake (1981). 'It was in fact written – although after much thinking – over two pints of bitter in the Victoria pub in Mornington Crescent.'

Beaujolais Nouveau est arrivé!, Le

Beaujolais Nouveau (wine); UK, from the early 1970s (also used elsewhere, including the Netherlands and Belgium). Selling Beaujolais during the first year of a vintage became a marketing ploy in Britain. For a number of years, a race was held to see who could bring the new stock most quickly over from France to Britain.

Be Careful How You Use It!

Hai Karate deodorant or after-shave; US, undated. (Atwan)

Because You Are The Very Air He Breathes
Veto deodorant; US, quoted 1958. Norman B. Norman of the
Norman, Craig, Kummel agency asked: 'Why advertise what
everybody expects? Of course it should stop perspiration, people
expect that. We gave them a slogan with empathy, that gets at the
very heart of the matter.' (Mayer)

Beecham's Pills Make All The Difference
See WORTH A GUINEA A BOX

Beer That Made Milwaukee Famous, The
Schlitz; US, from c.1895. The Jos. Schlitz Brewing Company has its
roots in an operation begun in Milwaukee in 1849. By 1871, the
year of the great Chicago fire, it was a thriving concern. The fire left
Chicago thirsty. The city was desperately short of drinking water
and its breweries had virtually been destroyed. So Joseph Schlitz
floated a shipload of beer down Lake Michigan to refresh his
parched neighbours. They liked and remembered the Milwaukee
beer long after the crisis passed. It is not known who coined the
phrase but this is the incident which led to it. The slogan was incorporated in a label, registered in 1895 and has been in use ever since.

Claude C. Hopkins, one of advertising's immortals, was once
engaged on a campaign for Schlitz. He was taken on a tour of the
brewery to give him ideas. He saw the malt and the hops but his
enthusiasm for the steam bath, in which the bottles were washed
before being filled with beer, was unbounded. As the client was at
pains to point out, this method was standard in all breweries, but
Hopkins realised that the point had never been used in ads before.
Hence the slogan: **Our Bottles Are Washed With Live Steam.**

Before You Invest – Investigate
The National Better Business Bureau Inc.; US, current 1941.
Suggested by S.P. Halle, President of Halle Brothers, while a mem-
ber of the Cleveland Better Business Bureau. Designed to warn
prospective investors. (Lambert) Also used in the UK by the
Lambeth Building Society, c.1960.

Be Like Dad, Keep Mum
Security slogan from the Ministry of Information; UK, c.1941. The

security theme was paramount in UK and US wartime propaganda. Civilians as well as military personnel were urged not to talk about war-related matters lest the enemy somehow got to hear. Also **Keep Mum, She's Not So Dumb** (illustrated by an elegant un-Mum-like blonde being ogled by representatives of the three services).

Be My Guest
Hilton hotels; US and elsewhere, probably 1950s. *American Speech* in 1955 had 'be my guest' as a way of saying 'go right ahead; do as you wish'. Hilton hotels may also have used 'be my guest' as a slogan at some time. Certainly, *Be My Guest* was the title of a book (1957) by the company's founder, hotelier Conrad Hilton.

Be Prepared
Motto of the Boy Scout movement; UK, from 1908. Based on the initials (BP) of its founder Sir Robert Baden-Powell. Also used as an advertising slogan by Pears' Soap and, as a motto, by police in South Africa.

Berlin By Christmas
Unofficial anti-German slogan; UK, 1914. Quoted in Partridge/ *Catch Phrases*. Initially, it was thought that the war with Germany would not last very long. The phrase 'All Over By Christmas' was used by some optimists as it had been in several previous wars – none of which was over by the Christmas in question.

Best By Taste Test
Royal Crown Cola; US, current 1944. Quoted in Partridge/*Catch Phrases*.

Best Car In The World, The
See AT 60 MILES AN HOUR ...

Best For Less
See PILE IT HIGH ...

Best Sherry In The World, The
Harvey's Bristol Cream; UK, current 1981. When challenged

about the basis for this claim (in the *Sunday Express*, 19 July 1981), a spokesperson said: 'No, there hasn't been a competition as such, but we've been using the slogan for nearly 20 years – in press adverts, posters and commercials. And we think it is justified.'

Best Tobacco Money Can Buy, The
Rothman's cigarettes; UK, current 1981. With equal modesty: **The Greatest Name In Cigarettes** and **The World's Most Popular King Size Filter Cigarette**.

Best To You Each Morning, The
Kellogg's corn flakes and other breakfast cereals; US, from 1953.

Better, Oh, Better, Very Much Better. Better Smoke 'Capstans'. They're Blended Better
Capstan cigarettes; UK, 1920s/30s. Quoted in Janet Hitchman, *Such A Strange Lady* (1975) as an example of a slogan of the period. Also: **Have A Capstan**; UK, current 1930s.

Better Red Than Dead
Nuclear disarmament slogan; UK, from c.1958. In that year, Bertrand Russell wrote: 'If no alternative remains except communist domination or the extinction of the human race, the former alternative is the lesser of two evils.' *Time* Magazine (15 September 1961) gave 'I'd rather be Red than dead' as a slogan of Britain's Campaign for Nuclear Disarmament. The counter-cry **Better Dead Than Red** may also have had some currency. (In the film *Love With a Proper Stranger* (US, 1964) Steve McQueen proposed to Natalie Wood with a picket sign stating 'Better Wed Than Dead'.)

Better Things For Better Living ... Through Chemistry
Corporate slogan for Du Pont Corporation – various products; US, current 1958. The danger in all sloganeering is that people will remember your slogan but not the cause or product that it promotes. Nowhere is this danger greater than in the field of 'corporate apologias' – institutional advertising where we are made to think of the Du Pont Corporation not as 'Merchants of Death' but as providing 'Better Things ... ' (Boorstin)

The Dow Chemical Company also appears to have used the

line **Better Living Through Chemistry.** Graffiti cited by Reisner include 'Dow – better murder through chemistry' and (in 1968) 'Acid – better living through chemistry'.

Better To Die On Your Feet Than To Live On Your Knees, It Is
Republican slogan in Civil War; Spain, 1936. Dolores Ibarruri ('La Pasionaria') said it in a radio speech from Paris calling on the women of Spain to help defend the Republic (3 September 1936). According to her autobiography (1966), she had used these words earlier, on 18 July, when broadcasting in Spain. Emiliano Zapata (c.1877–1919), the Mexican guerilla leader, had used the expression before her in 1910: 'Men of the South! It is better to die on your feet than to live on your knees! [… *mejor morir a pie que vivir en rodillas*]'. Franklin D. Roosevelt picked up the expression in his message accepting an honorary degree from Oxford University (19 June 1941): 'We, too, are born to freedom, and believing in freedom, are willing to fight to maintain freedom. We, and all others who believe as we do, would rather die on our feet than live on our knees.'

Better Yet Connecticut
Connecticut state tourism; US, from 1981. From *The New York Times* (22 April 1981): 'Connecticut came forth today with its official slogan … It was created by Joseph Roy, a 45-year-old graphic artist … "We had thought of 'I Love New York, But Better Yet Connecticut,' but it was too long," said Richard Combs, chairman of the Governor's Vacation Travel Council as he announced at a news conference that Mr Roy's slogan was "the winner of a block-buster contest."'

'John J. Carson said the slogan would adorn T-shirts and be displayed in banks and on billboards and bumper-stickers. Both state officials and Vacation Travel Council members voiced confidence that their slogan could vie in the marketplace with such tourism precursors as I LOVE NEW YORK, **Make It In Massachussetts** and **Virginia Is For Lovers**.

'Asked to describe the creative process that went into formation of the phrase, Mr Roy replied: "I went to bed thinking about it and when I woke in the morning I had it." The runner-up was "Connecticut Is a Whale of a State." '

Betty Ford's Husband For President
Informal presidential election slogan; US, 1976. This was the best-selling button of the campaign in which Gerald Ford tried to hold on to the White House to which he acceded after the resignation of Richard Nixon. The slogan represented the high regard in which Betty Ford was held. Quoted in Barry Day, *It Depends On How You Look At It...* (1978).

Bet You Can't Eat Just One
Lay's potato chips; US, quoted 1981.

Bet You Can't Eat Three
Shredded Wheat breakfast cereal; UK, current 1982. TV ads with this line featured cricketer Ian Botham.

Beware Of Imitations
General use, particularly in wordy, old-style ads. For example, Dobbins' Electric Soap used it; US, 1888.

Beware of Imitations.

INSIST upon **Dobbins'** Electric. Don't take Magnetic, Electro-Magic, Philadelphia Electric, or any other fraud, simply because it is cheap. They will ruin clothes, and are dear at any price. Ask for

—··◇·◁ **DOBBINS' ELECTRIC** ▷·◇·—

and take no other. Nearly every grocer from Maine to Mexico keeps it in stock. If yours hasn't it, he will order from his nearest wholesale grocer.

READ carefully the inside wrapper around each bar, and be careful to **follow directions** on each outside wrapper. You **cannot afford** to wait longer before trying for yourself this old, reliable, and truly wonderful

Dobbins' ✦ Electric ✦ Soap.

Bewdy Newk!
See LIFE. BE IN IT

Big Brother Is Watching You
Fictional slogan from George Orwell, *Nineteen Eighty-Four* (1949). In a dictatorial state, every citizen is regimented and observed by a spying TV set in the home. The line became a popular catchphrase following the sensational BBC TV dramatization of the novel (1954). Aspects of the Ministry of Truth in the novel were derived not only from Orwell's knowledge of the BBC (where he worked) but also from his first wife Eileen's work at the Ministry of Food, preparing 'Kitchen Front' broadcasts during the Second World War (c.1942–4). One campaign there used the slogan **Potatoes Are Good For You** and was so successful that it had to be followed by **Potatoes Are Fattening**.

Big Fry
Fry's chocolate bars; UK, from the mid-1960s. Playing on the phrase 'small fry', TV ads featured a 'beefcake Santa Claus with the muscle power to carry wooden crates crammed with chocolate bars to wherever the lucky recipients waited – on clifftops, mountain sides, harbours – to greet him with a delighted "Big Fry!" ' (Source: Jo Gable, *The Tuppenny Punch and Judy Show*, 1980). The character was played by the Australian actor George Lazenby who graduated (briefly) to playing James Bond in *On Her Majesty's Secret Service* (1969).

Biggest Daily Sale On Earth
See FORWARD WITH THE PEOPLE

Bill, The Whole Bill ...
See VOTES FOR WOMEN

Birds* Is Coming!, *The
Film, *The Birds*; US, 1963. Supposedly created by the film's director, Alfred Hitchcock. This probably derives ultimately from the cry 'The Circus is coming!' In the early years of the twentieth century the new Camel cigarettes were launched with a teaser campaign using the words **The Camels Are Coming!** Possibly, there is

also an echo here of the old Scottish song, 'The Campbells are comin', oho, oho' (1745).

Black Is Beautiful
·Black civil rights slogan; US, from 1966. Martin Luther King launched a poster campaign round this slogan in 1967 but Stokely Carmichael had used the phrase at a Memphis civil rights rally the year before. The phrase had also appeared in the journal *Liberation* (N.Y.) on 25 September 1965. It may have its origins in The Song of Solomon 1: 1: 'I am black, but comely.'

Black Power
Black civil rights slogan; US, from 1966. This became an all-purpose slogan encompassing just about anything that people wanted it to mean, from simple pride in the black race to a threat of violence. The Harlem Congressman Adam Clayton Powell junior said in a baccalaureate address at Howard University in May 1966: 'To demand these God-given rights is to seek black power – what I call audacious power – the power to build black institutions of splendid achievement.' On 6 June, James Meredith (the first black to integrate the University of Mississippi in 1962), was shot and wounded during a civil rights march. Stokely Carmichael, heading the Student Non-violent Coordinating Committee, continued the march, during which his contingent first used the shout. Carmichael used the phrase in a speech at Greenwood, Mississippi, the same month. It was also adopted as a slogan by the Congress for Racial Equality. However, the notion was not new in the 1960s. Langston Hughes had written in *Simple Takes a Wife* (1953): 'Negro blood is so powerful – because just *one* drop of black blood makes a coloured man – one drop – you are a negro! ... Black is powerful.' (Flexner, 1976; Safire)

Blonde In Every Pond, A
Political slogan (informal); US, 1980. When Edward Kennedy sought to win the Democratic nomination from the incumbent President, Jimmy Carter, in the 1980 election, jokes were mobilized to remind voters of his shaky record. Principally, attention was drawn to his part in the 1969 Chappaquiddick incident in which a female assistant had drowned in Kennedy's car. In fact,

Kennedy failed to wrest the nomination from Jimmy Carter who was, in turn, defeated by Ronald Reagan. Also from that campaign: **A Reactor Is A Safer Place Than Ted Kennedy's Car** (window-sticker, 1979); **More Lives Were Lost At Chappaquiddick Than At Harrisburg** (ditto); **Reagan For President, Kennedy For Chauffeur**; **Re-Elect Carter, Free Joan Kennedy**.

Blood And Fire, (Through)

Salvation Army; UK, from c.1880. General William Booth had founded his Christian army in 1878. The conjunction of blood and fire has appropriate biblical origins. In Joel 2: 30, God says: 'And I will shew wonders in the heavens and in the earth, blood, and fire, and pillars of smoke.'

Blow Some My Way

Chesterfield cigarettes; US, from 1926. Used – some said suggestively – when a woman made her first appearance in US cigarette advertising. **I'll Tell The World – They Satisfy** was current the same year.

BOAC Takes Good Care Of You

See WE'LL TAKE MORE CARE OF YOU

Body Count Continues, The

Film, *Friday 13th Part II*; US, 1981. This was one of a series of horror suspense films. The term 'body count' came out of the Vietnam War, referring to the number of enemy dead (in use by 1968). From *Time* Magazine (15 April 1985): 'In the field, the Americans were encouraged to lie about their "body counts" (measuring progress in the war by lives taken, not land taken).' Later, it became used, less literally, to describe the number of people (not necessarily dead) in a specific situation.

Bombs Away With Curt Lemay!

Unofficial slogan; US, 1967. General Curtis E. Lemay (1906–90) was an Air Force chief who became famous for his gung-ho methods in the Vietnam War. He said of the North Vietnamese in *Mission with Lemay* (1965): 'My solution to the problem would be to tell them frankly that they've got to draw in their horns and stop their aggression, or we're going to bomb them back into the Stone Age.' This slogan was a popular criticism of his approach used by US anti-war demonstrators.

Born 1820 – Still Going Strong
Johnnie Walker whisky; UK, from 1910. There *was* an actual John Walker but he was not born in 1820 – that was the year he set up a grocery, wine and spirit business in Kilmarnock. In 1908, Sir Alexander Walker decided to incorporate a portrait of his grandfather in the firm's advertising. Tom Browne, a commercial artist, was commissioned to draw the founder as he might have appeared in 1820. Lord Stevenson, a colleague of Sir Alexander's, scribbled the phrase 'Johnnie Walker, Born 1820 – Still Going Strong' alongside the artist's sketch of a striding, cheerful Regency figure. It has been in use ever since.

Born Of The Age We Live In
Sun newspaper; UK, 1964. Aiming at affluent young people, this was the paper's original pitch at its launch. It was not a success. This enabled Rupert Murdoch to take over in 1969.

Bounty – The Taste Of Paradise
Bounty candy bar; UK, probably 1960s.

Bovril Prevents That Sinking Feeling
See ALAS! MY POOR BROTHER

Bowen's Beer Makes You Drunk
See MAKES YOU DRUNK

Boy! Do We Need It Now!
Film, *That's Entertainment*; US, 1974. Perhaps this was intended to reflect the fact that this compilation of Hollywood musicals came out in the wake of an oil crisis and as the Watergate crisis rocked American government.

Boys in the Band is *Not* A Musical, *The*
Film; US, 1970. A helpful indication of the film's content. It was about homosexuals and nothing to do with a musical band.

Brandy Of Napoleon, The

Courvoisier brandy; UK, from 1909. Napoleon really did drink it. When the former French Emperor gave himself up to the British in 1815 and was sent into exile on St Helena, a supply of the best cognac from Jarnac, selected by Emmanuel Courvoisier, travelled with him. Originally it had been intended to accompany him on a projected escape to the United Slates. British officers who escorted Napoleon to St Helena had many opportunities to taste the exile's cognac. In this way, Courvoisier came to be known, in English, as 'The Brandy Of Napoleon'.

Bread Wi' Nowt Taken Out

Allinson Wholemeal bread; UK, current 1985.

Breakfast Of Champions

Wheaties; US, current 1950. A series of ads featuring sporting champions showed, for example, 'Jackie Robinson – one of the greatest names in baseball ... this famous Dodger star is a Wheaties man: "A lot of us ball players go for milk, fruit and Wheaties," says Jackie ... Had your Wheaties today?' Kurt Vonnegut used the phrase as the title of a novel, 1973.

Breed Apart, A

See MERRILL LYNCH IS BULLISH ...

Bridge That Gap With Cadbury's Snack

Cadbury's Snack (confectionery); UK, current 1967. Coined by Mogens Olsen 'in the middle of the night – I was there too' (source: Fay Weldon letter, 1981).

Bright Lights Taste, The

Cinzano; UK, quoted 1981.

Bring Back The Cat

Unofficial political slogan; UK, probably 1950s. The cat-o'-nine-tails was the nine-thong whip once used to enforce discipline in the Royal Navy. This phrase has long been the cry of corporal punishment enthusiasts demanding its return. Usually associated with right-wing 'hangers and floggers' in the Conservative Party.

Bring On The *Real* Thirst-Quencher
See FRESHEN UP WITH 7-UP

Bring Our Boys Home
Anti-Vietnam War slogan; US, current 1972.

Brings The World To The World
Gaumont-British cinema newsreel; UK, from the 1930s.

Britain Can Take It
Morale-boosting slogan from the Ministry of Information; UK, 1940. Slogans rained down upon the hapless British as profusely as German bombs during the Second World War. The Ministry of Information, in blunderbuss fashion, fired away with as much material as possible in the hope of hitting something. Some of the slogans were brilliant, others were quite the reverse – like this one. 'While the public appreciated due recognition of their resolute qualities, they resented too great an emphasis on the stereotyped image of the Britisher in adversity as a wise-cracking Cockney. They were irritated by propaganda which represented their grim experience as a sort of particularly torrid Rugby match.' Hence the Ministry's abandonment of this slogan in December 1940. (McLaine)

Britain's Favourite American Performers
Bill-matter for the American vaudeville act Kimberley & Page; UK, 1940s. Curiously, in the US, they were billed as **America's Favorite British Performers**. They also used the bill-matter 'Love Laffs'.

Britain Will *Win* With Labour
Labour Party; UK, 1974. Used from August onwards in the second general election of that year, which secured Labour's majority for a further four-and-a-half years.

British Is Best
See MADE IN ENGLAND

British Made
See MADE IN ENGLAND

Brits Out
Irish republican slogan in Northern Ireland; current by 1981.

Britvic – Simply The Best There Is
Britvic fruit juice; UK, current 1980.

Brook Street Bureau Got Big By Bothering
Brook Street Bureau (secretarial agency); UK, current 1980s.

Buck Stops Here, The
Unofficial presidential slogan; US, late 1940s. President Harry S. Truman had a sign on his desk bearing these words, indicating that the Oval Office was where the passing of the buck had to cease. The phrase seems to have been of his own making. When President Nixon published his memoirs, people opposed to its sale went around with buttons saying: 'The book stops here.'

Buck Well Spent On A Spring-Maid Sheet, A
Springmaid sheets; US, undated.

Build Not Burn
Students For A Democratic Society; US, from the late 1960s. Quoted in Barbara Rowes, *The Book of Quotes* (1979).

Build Up Your Ego, Amigo
Adler Elevated Shoes; US, current 1940s. Coined by Shirley Polykoff.

Burger King – The Home Of The Whopper
Burger King hamburger chain; US, current 1981. Also **It Takes Two Hands To Hold A Whopper**; UK, undated.

Burn, Baby, Burn!
Black extremists' slogan; US, from 1965. Coinage came about the time of the August riots in the Watts district of Los Angeles when thirty-four people were killed and entire blocks burned down. The 1974 song with the title by Hudson-Ford had other connotations. Indeed, it has been suggested that the phrase arose as a joke expression of sexual encouragement a year or so *before* the Watts

riots. Popularized by the black disc jockey Magnificent Montague, it was called out by audiences to singers and musicians. The graffito, 'Earn, Baby, Earn' was recorded in Florida. (Reisner)

Burn Your Bra
Women's Liberation movement slogan; US, current by 1972. The *OED2* has 'bra-burning' by 1971 – by analogy with burning a draft-card as a protest against the Vietnam War. There is some doubt whether any feminists actually did burn their bras. It may have been a figure of speech only.

Business As Usual
General use; US and UK, by 1914. The standard declaration posted when a shop has suffered some misfortune like a fire or is undergoing alterations. However, in the First World War, the phrase was employed in another sense. H.E. Morgan (later Sir Herbert Morgan) was an advertising man working for W.H. Smith & Sons, who promoted this slogan which had quite a vogue until it was proved to be manifestly untrue and hopelessly inappropriate. Morgan was an advertising consultant to H. Gordon Selfridge, who consequently also became associated with the slogan. On 26 August 1914, Selfridge said: ' "Business As Usual" must be the order of the day.' In a Guildhall speech on 9 November, Winston Churchill said: 'The maxim of the British people is "Business as usual".'

Buy British
See MADE IN ENGLAND

Buy Some For Lulu
See WOT A LOT I GOT

Call A [Spade] A [Spade] And Branson's Coffee Perfection

Branson's Coffee; probably UK, quoted 1952. Pictures of two spades were inserted instead of the words. 'When this design was first propounded, the manufacturer was dubious. "They'll think we sell spades," he said. It was hailed as ... an effective poster ... The slogan is still used today.' (Turner)

Call For Philip Morris

Philip Morris cigarettes; US, current 1941. The jingle went: 'You get all the flavour and you get it mild/When you call for Philip Morris cigarettes.'

Camel – Where A Man Belongs

See I'D WALK A MILE FOR A CAMEL

Candy Mint With The Hole

See MINT WITH THE HOLE

Can't Be Beat

Broken Drum vegetables; US, undated. (Mayer) In 1927, Australian Chemical Products Co. of Melbourne was using this slogan together with the picture of a ram putting its feet through the skin of a drum.

Can't Pay, Won't Pay

Informal political slogan; UK, 1990. Adopted by those objecting to the British government's Community Charge or 'poll tax' in 1990 and by other similar protest groups. *Can't Pay, Won't Pay* was the English title of the play *Non Si Paga! Non Si Paga!* (1974) by Dario Fo, as translated by Lino Pertile (1981).

Can You Survive *The Texas Chain Saw Massacre* **... It Happened!**
Film; US, 1974. Bloody movie inspired by real events.

Can You Tell Stork From Butter?
Stork margarine; UK, from c.1956. One of the earliest slogans on British commercial TV – endlessly alluded to at the popular level. Housewives in TV ads were asked to take part in comparative tests between pieces of bread spread with real butter and with Stork.

Careless Talk Costs Lives
Security slogan; UK, from mid-1940. This became the most enduring of the security slogans, especially when accompanied by Fougasse cartoons – showing two men in a club, for example, one saying to the other ' ... strictly between four walls' (behind them is a painting through which Hitler's head is peeping), or two women gossiping in front of Hitler wallpaper.

Carry On, Roosevelt
See LAND LANDON ...

Carter. A Leader, For A Change
See HE'S MAKING US ...

Carter's Little Liver Pills
See HELPS YOU BREAK ...

Carthage Must Be Destroyed
See *DELENDA EST CARTHAGO*

Cast Of 125,000, A
Film promotional line for *Ben Hur*; US, 1927. It may have been the origin of 'cast of thousands'.

Castrol. Liquid Engineering
Castrol motor oil; UK, from 1977 – 'Oil is too small a word for it.' Royston Taylor commented (1981) that Castrol was one percentage point ahead of Duckhams but was prevented by the advertising rules from referring to itself as brand leader or knocking the

competition. So the Dorland agency looked at the terminology of oil itself and the result was that Castrol left Duckhams way behind. This was attributed solely to the advertising. Compare Bovril being referred to as **Liquid Life**; UK, current 1900.

Casual Comedian, The
Bill-matter for the entertainer Geep Martin; US, probably 1940s. In fact, according to Dick Vosburgh (1981), his hands shook so much you could hear his script rattling at the microphone ...

Cerebos ...
See SEE HOW IT RUNS!

Chases Dirt
Old Dutch Cleanser; US, from 1905. Still in use in 1941. The ad showed a Dutch woman with a stick, literally chasing dirt away.

Cheeky Chappie, The
Bill-matter for the British comedian Max Miller; UK, from the 1940s. Miller (1895–1963) advanced the cause of the *double entendre*. Sometimes billed as 'The Pure Gold of the Music Hall'. See also ONE AND ONLY.

Chicken In Every Pot
See HOOVER AND HAPPINESS ...

Children Cry For It
Fletcher's Castoria (medicine); US, current by the 1880s.

Children's Shoes Have Far To Go
Start-Rite children's shoes; UK, current 1946. The idea of the boy and girl 'twins' walking up the middle of a road between rows of beech trees came to the company's advertising agent as he drove back to London from a meeting at Start-Rite's Norwich offices. He was reminded of the illustration in Kipling's *Just So Stories* of 'the cat who walked by himself' and developed the idea from there – despite many subsequent suggestions from the public that walking down the middle of the road would not enable children, or their shoes, to go very far.

Chile Out
Informal slogan; UK, c.1978. 'Out of what?' one might ask. This sort of slogan (compare BRITS OUT) was neatly mocked by another on a Martello tower near Dublin which said 'Napoleon Out'.

Chock Full O'Nuts Is That Heavenly Coffee
Chock Full O'Nuts coffee; US, current 1950s. Included in a jingle by Shirley Polykoff.

Chocolate Coloured Coon, The
Bill-matter for the British entertainer G.H. Elliott (1884–1962); UK, 1920s/30s. In the innocent days before political correctness, Elliott blacked up to impersonate a nigger minstrel (as one was allowed to call them in those days).

Chocolates With The Less Fattening Centres
Maltesers; UK, current 1965.

Citi Never Sleeps, The
Citibank 24-hour banking service; US, 1977. Clearly echoing the film title *City That Never Sleeps* (US, 1953). Compare WE NEVER SLEEP.

Cleanliness Is Next To Godliness
Pears' Soap; UK/US, 1880s. Although this common phrase appears in one of John Wesley's sermons, it is within quotation marks and without attribution. The British advertising agent Thomas J. Barratt (1842–1914) could hardly have been expected to leave it alone. On a visit to the US in the 1880s, he sought a testimonial from a man of distinction. Shrinking from an approach to President Grant, he ensnared the eminent divine, Henry Ward Beecher. Beecher happily complied with Barratt's request and wrote a short text beginning: 'If cleanliness is next to Godliness … ' and received no more for his pains than Barratt's 'hearty thanks'. (Turner)

Cleans Round The Bend
Harpic lavatory cleaner; UK, from the 1930s. Playing upon rather than coining the expression 'round the bend' meaning 'mad'

(which was especially popular from the Second World War on). The *OED2* cites F.C. Bowen's description of the expression in *Sea Slang* (1929) as, 'an old naval term for anybody who is mad'.

Cleans Your Breath While It Cleans Your Teeth
Colgate Dental Cream; US, current 1946. Every toothpaste can do it but none had made the claim before. Also **The Colgate Ring Of Confidence** (by 1967).

Clown Prince Of Wales, The
Bill-matter for the Welsh entertainer Wyn Calvin; UK, current in the 1950s/60s. Calvin dropped it in deference to Prince Charles at the time of his investiture as Prince of Wales in 1969. Also billed as 'The Welsh Prince of Laughter'.

Clunk, Click, *Every* Trip
Road-safety/seat-belt campaign; UK, 1971. Echoing the sound of a car door being closed and a seat-belt being fastened. Used in road safety TV ads featuring Jimmy Savile. In 1979, someone wrote the slogan on a museum cabinet containing a chastity belt.

C'mon, Aussie, C'mon!
Slogan supporting the Australia cricket team; Australia, 1981. A song with this title had already been recorded in 1979.

C'mon Colman's, Light My Fire
Colman's mustard; UK, current 1979. Accompanying the picture of a voluptuous woman on a tiger rug who is clearly in no need of any such encouragement. A clear borrowing of the title of the Doors/Jim Morrison song '(Com' On, Baby,) Light My Fire' (1967).

Coke Adds Life
See DRINK COCA-COLA

Coke Is It!
See DRINK COCA-COLA

Colgate Ring Of Confidence
See CLEANS YOUR BREATH ...

Come Alive – You're In The Pepsi Generation

Pepsi Cola; US, from 1964. This slogan presented certain problems when translated for overseas markets. In German it came out as 'Come alive out of the grave', and in Chinese 'Pepsi brings your ancestors back from the dead'.

Pepsi Cola is now consumed in as many countries as its great rival Coca-Cola and has achieved this in a shorter time and, for many years at least, with considerably less expenditure on advertising. Often its slogans have stressed value for money: **Twice As Much For A Nickel, Too** (US, current 1930s) – Walter Mack is credited with writing this 'first advertising jingle in history' (it was sung to the tune of 'John Peel'), which was much used on American radio in the 1930s – indeed, an estimated six million times. After the Second World War, the value-for-money principle went out of the window and the price of Pepsi had to be raised to six and then seven cents. Consequently, the jingle had to be revised to **Twice As Much And Better, Too**. (Source: J.C. Louis and Harvey Yazijian, *The Cola Wars*, 1980). **You've Got A Lot To Live, Pepsi's Got A Lot To Give** (US, current 1960s) – James B. Somerall, Pepsi's President at the time of the Vietnam War, claimed that this slogan drew attention to America's new national pastime – 'living, and making every second count.' **Lipsmackin thirst quenchin (ace tastin motivatin good buzzin cool talkin high walkin fast livin ever givin cool fizzin) Pepsi** (UK, from 1974) – a jingle written by John Webster at Boase Massimi Pollitt (though Chris Wilkins and Dave Trott have also been credited with it). 'Lipsmackin' Rock 'n' Rollin', a record based on this reached the British pop charts in 1977, sung by Peter Blake.

Are You Ready To Take The Challenge? was a phrase used by Diet Pepsi (UK, 1990) when consumers took part in comparative tests with Diet Coke. **Taste The Difference** was the Diet Pepsi slogan at about this time.

Come And Talk To The Listening Bank

Midland Bank; UK, from 1980. A slogan that turned sour when a twenty-year-old student was *arrested* when she went to see her manager about her overdraft. Also: **Together We Make A Great Team**.

Come Home To A Real Fire
National Coal Board; UK, probably 1970s. Sometimes recalled as having 'coal' before the 'fire'.

Come Home To Birds Eye Country
Birds Eye frozen vegetables, etc.; UK, current early 1960s.

Come On ...
See C'MON ...

Come To Jamaica. It's No Place Like Home
Jamaica tourist board; UK, quoted 1982.

Come To Where The Flavor Is. Come To Marlboro Country
Marlboro cigarettes; US, current from mid-1950s. Originally devised by the Leo Burnett agency in Chicago as a means of shifting the appeal of Marlboro from women to men – by showing it in use by rugged cowboy types. Hence, also, **Man-Sized Flavour** but, hedging the bet, **A Man's Cigarette That Women Like Too**.

Completely New Experience Between Men And Women!, A
Film, *The Men*; US, 1950. It was about paraplegic war veterans.

Complete Satisfaction Or ...
See CUSTOMER IS ALWAYS RIGHT

Computers Help People Help People
Corporate slogan for IBM; US, quoted 1976.

Concern For The Future, A
Corporate slogan for PPG Industries; US, current 1980.

Connally Will Do Something About The State We're In
Political slogan for John B. Connally Jr in Texas gubernatorial elections; US, 1972. His father, John B. Connally, a former Governor was now moving towards seeking a presidential nomination. The pun resurfaced in the UK as the title for Will Hutton's book *The State We're In* (1995).

Constantly Imitated – Never Equalled
Onyx Hosiery; US, from 1908.

Cool As A Mountain Stream
Consulate cigarettes; UK, current early 1960s. Also **Menthol-Fresh, Cool, Clean, Consulate** which was changed following the 1963 cancer scare to **Cool, Fresh, Consulate**.

Cool, Calm And Collect It
See GUINNESS IS GOOD FOR YOU

Coolidge Or Chaos
See KEEP COOL WITH COOLIDGE

Corn And Cluck For A Buck
See IT'S FINGERLICKIN' GOOD

Coughs And Sneezes Spread Diseases
Ministry of Health slogan; UK, from c.1942. Coupled with the line 'Trap The Germs In Your Handkerchief'.

Country Fit For Heroes, A
See LAND FIT FOR HEROES

Courier Express. Today's Delivery Problems Solved Tomorrow
Courier Express delivery service; UK, current 1981. A well-meaning slogan, but ...

Course You Can, Malcolm
Vick's Sinex (nasal spray); UK, 1970s. One of those TV advertising phrases that, for no accountable reason, catches on for a while. In February 1994, after the ads had been relaunched starring the original 1970s cast, the manufacturers released a record single telling the adventures of Malcolm, the congested youth in the TV commercials. It was called 'Course You Can, Malcolm', of course, but failed to reach the charts.

Courtesy And Care
Automobile Association (motoring breakdown service); UK, since

c.1912. Actually, the Association's motto, devised by Viscount Brentford, its chairman (1910–22), and included in its armorial bearings. See also FOURTH EMERGENCY SERVICE.

Crane's Peppermint Life Savers For That Stormy Breath
US, until 1913.

Craven 'A' – It's Kind ...
See FOR YOUR THROAT'S SAKE ...

Crime Doesn't Pay
General use; US, by 1927. Used variously by the FBI and by the cartoon character Dick Tracy. 'Crime never pays, not even life insurance benefits' – Zelda Popkin, *No Crime For a Lady* (1942).

Crowdstopper
Durex condoms; UK, quoted 1981.

Curse of Frankenstein Will Haunt You Forever (Please Try Not To Faint), *The*
Film; UK, 1957.

Customer Is Always Right, The
General use; US/UK, by 1900. The hotelier César Ritz (1850–1918) was being quoted by 1908 as saying, *'Le client n'a jamais tort* [The customer is never wrong]'. The earliest citation in *The Concise Oxford Dictionary of Proverbs* is from Carl Sandburg's *Good Morning, America* (1928), introduced by the words, 'Behold the proverbs of a nation'. These may have been anticipated by Gordon Selfridge (1856–1947), an American, who after a spell with Marshall Field & Co. in Chicago came to Britain and introduced the idea of the monster department store. It was he who said 'the customer is always right' and many another phrase now generally associated with the business of selling through stores. He may have invented the notion of so many **Shopping Days To Christmas** – at least, when he was still in Chicago he sent out an instruction to Marshall Field's heads of departments and assistants: 'The Christmas season has begun and but twenty-three

more shopping days remain in which to make our holiday sales record.'

The store which he opened in Oxford Street, London, in 1909, gave rise to the slogans **This Famous Store Needs No Name On The Door** (because it had none – in about 1925 Selfridge removed the name-plates). His publicity director, George Seal, thought up this rhyme and it was used on the firm's notepaper as a caption to a picture of the building (there was no other heading); and **Complete Satisfaction Or Money Cheerfully Refunded**. Selfridge apparently made this the text of one of his staff sermons and added: 'If a customer wants to try on fourteen pairs of gloves and then decides not to buy – why, that's all right by me.' (Source: A.H. Williams, *No Name On The Door*, 1957)

Cymru am byth [Wales for ever]
Motto of the Welsh Guards; UK, from 1915. But also used as a kind of slogan for the principality as a whole.

Daddy, What Did *You* Do In The Great War?
Army recruitment slogan; UK, from c.1916. Accompanying the picture of an understandably appalled family man puzzling over what to reply to the daughter on his knee. This became a catchphrase in the form 'What did you do in the Great War, Daddy?' and gave rise to such responses as 'Shut up, you little bastard. Get the Bluebell and go and clean my medals.' (Partridge/*Catch Phrases*)

Daily Mail, Million Sale
Daily Mail newspaper; UK, 1920s/30s. (Turner) Said to have been invented by the proprietor, Lord Northcliffe. Compare **Sunday Dispatch, Best Of The Batch**. Unverified.

DANGER: H.M. GOVERNMENT HEALTH DEPARTMENT'S WARNING: CIGARETTES CAN SERIOUSLY DAMAGE YOUR HEALTH
UK, 1980s. The basic slogan 'Cigarettes Can Damage Your health' is believed to have originated at the Central Office of Information in the early 1960s. It was certainly current by 1971, on all cigarette advertising and packs. The 'seriously' was added in 1977, the 'Danger' in 1980.

David Simpson, Director of ASH (Action on Smoking and Health), commented (1981): 'There is no law that the words should be on the packs but it is one provision of the "voluntary" agreement which the tobacco industry has entered into with the Department of Health as a preference to the possibility of legislation. For a product which will kill one in four of those who smoke twenty a day all their lives, the warnings are hopelessly inadequate.'

Numerous – and increasingly stronger – warnings have been added since. These include: **Think First – Most Doctors Don't Smoke** (1981). Compare: WARNING ...

Death With Dignity
The Hemlock Society; UK, by 1990. The Society promotes voluntary euthanasia. Compare **Dignity In Destiny**, name of a pre-paid funeral arrangement but also used as a slogan by Hodgson Holdings (funeral directors); UK, from 1989.

Decide For Christ
Evangelistic slogan; US, from 1943. Used widely by Dr Billy Graham (1918–) in his 'crusades'.

Deeds, Not Words
See VOTES FOR WOMEN

Deep Down Clean
See TIDE'S IN, DIRT'S OUT

Delenda Est Carthago [Carthage must be destroyed]
Roman political slogan. Cato the Elder (or 'the Censor'), politician and orator (234–149 BC), punctuated or ended his speeches to the Roman Senate with this slogan for eight years, c.157 BC, realizing the threat Carthage posed to the state. It worked – Carthage was destroyed (in 146 BC) and Rome reigned supreme, though Cato did not live to see the effect of his challenge. He did have the decency to precede the slogan with the words '*ceterum censeo* [in my opinion]'.

Delta Is Ready When You Are
Delta Airlines; US, by 1968. Or just **Ready When You Are**.

Designed By Computer. Silenced By Laser. Built By Robot
Fiat Strada motor car; UK, 1970s. Hence, the graffito addition: '... Driven by moron' (by 1978). Also **If It Were A Lady, It Would Get Its Bottom Pinched** – Fiat 127 Palio (by 1982).

Desperation, Pacification, Expectation, Acclamation, Realization
Fry's chocolate; UK, current by the 1920s. Ads featured the faces of the famous 'five boys' anticipating a bite.

Deutschland über Alles [Germany before/beyond everything]
National slogan; Germany, by 1900. Originally the title of an 1841

poem by August Heinrich Hoffman (1798–1874). Sung to Haydn's tune for the Austrian national anthem, it was Germany's national anthem (1922–45). It was reinstated in 1950 without the *über Alles*.

Diamond Is Forever, A

De Beers Consolidated Mines; US, from 1939. It is odd, at first glance, that diamonds should need advertising. Are they not their own best advertisement? But in 1939 the South Africa-based De Beers launched a campaign to promote further the diamond engagement ring tradition. It was devised by the N.W. Ayer agency of Chicago and the original copy was written by B.J. Kidd. The idea was not new. Anita Loos in her novel *Gentlemen Prefer Blondes* (1925) enshrined it in: 'Kissing your hand may make you feel very, very good but a diamond and safire bracelet lasts for ever.' Later, Ian Fleming gave a variation of the phrase as the title of his 1956 James Bond novel *Diamonds Are Forever*.

Technically speaking, however, diamonds are *not* forever. It takes a high temperature, but, being of pure carbon, they will burn.

Didjavagoodweekend?/No, I forgot the Aerogard

Aerogard insect repellent; Australia, early 1980s. The question, said with a strong Aussie accent, passed into the language Down Under – not least because it was the sort of thing which people would naturally ask in conversation anyway.

Did You Maclean Your Teeth Today?

Maclean's toothpaste; US, current 1934.

Difficult We Do Immediately, The Impossible Takes A Little Longer (The)

US Army Service Forces; US, 1940s. But not original to that organization. In the form 'The difficult is what takes a little time; the impossible is what takes a little longer', it was attributed to Fridtjof Nansen, the Norwegian explorer – in *The Listener* (14 December 1939). The idea has also been traced back to Charles Alexandre de Calonne (1734–1802), who said: '*Madame, si c'est possible, c'est fait; impossible? cela se fera* [if it is possible, it is already done; if it is impossible, it will be done]' – quoted in J. Michelet,

Historie de la Révolution Française (1847). Henry Kissinger once joked: 'The illegal we do immediately, the unconstitutional takes a little longer' (quoted in William Shawcross, *Sideshow*, 1979).

Dig For Victory

Ministry of Agriculture slogan; UK, from 1939. Shortage of foodstuffs was an immediate concern upon the outbreak of war. On 4 October, the Minister of Agriculture, Sir Reginald Dorman-Smith, said in a radio broadcast: 'Half a million more allotments properly worked will provide potatoes and vegetables that will feed another million adults and one and a half million children for eight months out of twelve ... So, let's get going. Let "Dig For Victory" be the motto of everyone with a garden and of every able-bodied man and woman capable of digging an allotment in their spare time.' As a result, the number of allotments rose from 815,000 in 1939 to 1,400,000 in 1943. In the US, there was the equivalent slogan **Garden For Victory**.

Dignity In Destiny

See DEATH WITH DIGNITY

Ditch The Bitch

Unofficial political slogan; UK, 1981. An anti-Margaret Thatcher slogan when she was British Prime Minister, though it is not clear with whom it originated. The *Daily Mail* (16 June 1981) carried a report saying that it had been condemned as sexist by the National Conference of Labour Women.

Does She ... Or Doesn't She?

Clairol hair colorant; US, from 1955. In her book entitled *Does She ... Or Doesn't She?* (1975), Ms Polykoff commented on her creation: 'This seemingly non-acceptable phrase turned a non-acceptable commodity into the highly respected industry that hair-coloring is today.' It appears that the real inspiration for the line was Polykoff's mother-in-law twenty years previously: 'I had just met George ... when he invited me to Passover dinner in Reading, Pa ... it was tantamount to a proposal of marriage ... I could hardly wait to start the drive home to find out how I had done ... "She (George's mother) says you paint your hair. Well, do you?" I merely scrunched down on my side of the car. I could hear his mother thinking as she cleared away the dishes: "Zee paint dos huer? Odder zee paint dos nicht?" Freely translated that means, "Does she ... or doesn't she?" '

When the Clairol account moved to Foote Cone & Belding in the mid-1950s, Polykoff was assigned to it and suffered the customary creative block that preceeds many a great coinage. As she tells it, she was at a party with George, now her husband, when in came a girl with flaming red hair. Polykoff involuntarily uttered the line.

Next morning she wrote a memo to the head art director, giving two lines to be rejected and the one she wanted accepted to be followed by the phrase 'Only her mother knows for sure!' or 'So natural, only her mother knows for sure'. She felt she might have to change 'mother' to 'hairdresser' so as not to offend beauty salons – and **Only Her Hairdresser Knows For Sure** was duly chosen. First reaction to the headline was that the double meaning in the words 'Does she ... or doesn't she?' would have the line rejected out of hand. Indeed, initially, *Life* Magazine would not take the ad. But subsequent research at *Life* failed to find a single female staff member who admitted seeing a double-meaning in it, and the phrases were locked into the form they had for the next eighteen years. ('J' underlines the double-meaning implicit in the slogan with this comment from *The Sensuous Woman*: 'Our world has changed. It's no longer a question of "Does she or doesn't she?" We all know she wants to, is about to, or does.' A New York graffito, quoted 1974: 'Only his hairdresser knows for sure.')

Then came **Is She ... Or Isn't She?** Harmony hair-spray; UK, current 1980. Not by Shirley Polykoff, but a deliberate echo. 'Harmony has a ultra-fine spray to leave hair softer and more natural. She is wearing a hairspray but with Harmony it's so fine you're the only one that knows for sure.'

Does You Does Or Does You Don't Take Access?

Access credit card; UK, current c.1990. Credited to Dave Trott. Based on 'Is You Is Or Is You Ain't My Baby?', the 1943 song by Billy Austin and Louis Jordan.

Dog Is For Life, Not Just For Christmas (A)

National Canine Defence League; UK, probably from the late

1980s. Hence, from *The Independent* (1 February 1997): 'Repudiating a suggestion that a future Conservative government would abolish the Scottish parliament ... Mr Forsyth said: "A Scottish parliament is not just for Christmas; it's for life".'

Dog Litter – An Issue You Can't Sidestep
Political slogan; US, mid-1970s. Corny, but a candidate for local office in Washington won with it. (Safire)

Doing What We Do Best
Corporate slogan for American Airlines; US, current 1980. Also **Fly The American Way** (current 1961–81).

— Do It —
Informal and semi-official slogans for any number of organizations and groups; UK, from 1979. On 26 April 1979, the British *Sun* newspaper was offering a variety of T-shirts with nudging 'do it' slogans inscribed upon them. The craze was said to have started in the US. Whatever the case, scores of slogans 'promoting' various groups with this allusion to performing the sexual act appeared over the next several years on T-shirts, lapel-buttons, bumper-stickers and car window-stickers. In my *Graffiti* books (1979–86), I recorded some seventy, among them: 'Builders do it with erections'; 'Windsurfers do it standing up'; 'Printers do it and don't wrinkle the sheets'; 'Donyatt Dog Club does it with discipline and kindness'; 'Linguists do it orally'; 'Footballers do it in the bath afterwards'; 'City planners do it with their eyes shut'.

All this from simple exploitation of the innuendo in the phrase 'do it', which had perhaps first been seized on by Cole Porter in the song 'Let's Do It, Let's Fall in Love' (1928):

> In shady shoals, English soles do it,
> Goldfish in the privacy of bowls do it...

and then in a more personal parody by Noël Coward (in the 1940s):

> Our leading writers in swarms do it
> Somerset and all the Maughams do it...

Much later came the advertising slogan YOU CAN DO IT IN AN MG (quoted in 1983).

Domestos Kills All Known Germs (In One Hour)
Domestos bleach; UK, by 1959. The domestic cleaning agent and disinfectant appears to have used several versions of this slogan: **Domestos Kills Ninety-nine Per Cent Of All Known Germs** (undated and unverified – though BBC radio's *Round The Horne*, 13 March 1966, had: 'Ladies and gentlemen – the programme that contains ninety-nine per cent of all known jokes ... ') Orson Welles intoned the TV ad version **Domestos Kills All Known Germs - Dead!** in 1967.

Don't Ask A Man To Drink And Drive
Road safety slogan; UK, 1964. Created for the Central Office of Information.

Don't Ask The Price, It's A Penny
Marks & Spencer stores; UK, by 1900. The great British retail institution had its origins in a stall set up in Leeds market in 1884 by a 21-year-old Jewish refugee from Poland, Michael Marks. His slogan has become part of commercial folklore. It was written on a sign over the penny section – not all his goods were that cheap. He simply hit upon the idea of classifying goods according to price.

Don't Be A Paleface
See TAN – DON'T BURN

Don't Be Misled
See READY, AYE, READY

Don't Be Vague – Ask For Haig
Haig whisky; UK, since c.1936. The origin of this slogan is to some extent shrouded in a Scotch mist because many of the John Haig & Co. archives were destroyed during the Second World War. However, the agency thought to be responsible was C.J. Lytle Ltd. An ad survives from 1933 with the wording 'Don't Be Vague, Order Haig', another from 1935 with 'Why Be Vague? Ask for

Haig', and it seems that the enduring form arose in about 1936. (In 1981, a graffito in a Belfast Protestant slum declared: 'Don't Be Vague – Starve A Taig' – 'taig' being slang for a Catholic.) It has been jocularly suggested that Haig's premium brand, Dimple, which is sold as Pinch in North America, should be promoted with the slogan 'Don't Be Simple, Ask For Dimple'.

Don't Blame Me, I'm From Massachussetts
Informal political slogan; US, December 1972. Comment on snarled peace negotiations with the North Vietnamese. The state had voted for George McGovern in the November election. He had promised immediate peace. (Reisner) Earlier, in the UK, after the Conservatives had won the 1970 General Election, came the instant slogan **Don't Blame Me, I Voted Labour**.

Don't Call Me Babe
Film, *Barb Wire*; US, 1996. From a line spoken in the picture by Pamela Anderson as a no-nonsense agent of some description.

Don't Die Of Ignorance
AIDS awareness slogan; UK, 1987. The main line from the first British government campaign. In no time, a graffito was reported added to a poster: 'Don't Die Of Ignorance – *Sun* readers do.' Also, in the autumn of that year, **It Only Takes One Prick To Give You Aids** – aimed at drug addicts.

Don't Do It, Di!
Informal feminist slogan; UK, 1981. On badge prior to the royal wedding between Prince Charles and Lady Diana Spencer. A warning which, unfortunately, went unheeded.

Don't Forget The Fruit Gums, Mum
Rowntree's Fruit Gums; UK, 1958–61. Coined by copywriter Roger Musgrave at S.T. Garland Advertising Services. Market research showed that most fruit gums were bought by women but eaten by children. One Friday evening, Kenneth Gill, who was in charge of the campaign, gave Musgrave this information. Over the following weekend Musgrave conceived these words as part of a jingle which was used, word for word, as written. Later on,

the phrase fell foul of advertising watchdogs, who were keen to save parents from nagging. So 'mum' was amended to 'chum'.

Don't Forget The *TV Times*
TV Times (listings journal); UK, from the 1960s on. Long-running slogan, also as a jingle, joined in the 1970s by **I Never Knew It Had So Much In It**.

Don't Give Away The Ending. It's The Only One We Have
Film, *Psycho*; US, 1960.

Don't Just Say Brandy, Say R.G.B.
Ronyer Guillet Brandy; UK, undated. (Sunners)

Don't Leave Home Without It
American Express credit card; US, current 1981. Bob Hope once did a parody on a TV special in which he appeared as the Pope carrying his Vatican Express card ('Don't leave Rome without it'). In the UK in the late 1970s, **That'll Do Nicely, (Sir)! –**, a fawning line from an Amex TV ad which became a catchphrase. See also DO YOU KNOW ME?

Don't Let Them Take It Away
Presidential election slogan; US, 1948. Fears that a Republican President might re-enter the White House after sixteen years of Democratic rule gave rise to this unofficial slogan. It worked this time for Harry S Truman's re-election but not when the slogan was revived in 1952. At the beginning of the 1948 campaign Truman told Alben Barkley, his running mate, 'I'm going to fight hard. I'm going to give them hell.' So **Give 'Em Hell, Harry** also became a semi-official battle-cry.

Don't Pronounce It – See It!
Films, *Ninotchka*; US, 1939; and *Phffft!*; US, 1954.

Don't Say Brown – Say Hovis
Hovis bread; UK, current from mid-l930s. Originally called Smith's Patent Germ Bread and created by Richard Smith in the

1880s, Hovis takes its name from the Latin 'hominis vis' (strength of man). In the 1930s one of the firm's paper bags showed a radio announcer saying: 'Here's a rather important announcement ... I should have said Hovis and not just "brown".' The slogan was used in its final form from 1956 to 1964. It still reverberates: in May 1981, when a British golfer Ken Brown was deserted by his caddie during a Martini championship, a *Sunday Mirror* headline was: 'Don't Say Brown, Say Novice'. Compare DON'T JUST SAY ...

Don't Wear Ondine Unless You Mean It
Ondine perfume; US, undated. Preceded by the copy: 'Save it for the real men in your life. Men who want you all to themselves ... and keep you out too late ... ' (Baker)

Don't Write – Telegraph
Western Union Telegraph Co.; US, from 1920 – though the words first appeared unofficially written up on office windows of various branches in 1917–19. (Lambert)

Don't You Just Love Being In Control?
British Gas; UK, from 1991. This soon acquired catchphrase status, not least because of its scope for sexual innuendo. From *The Independent* (19 October 1992): 'England signally failed to achieve their stated [rugby union] goals. Perhaps disarranged by their new surroundings, England, who just love being in control, were frustrated by the resilience and organisation of the Canadians.' From *The Daily Telegraph* (5 April 1993): 'Most annoying of all is the circle of fire [in a National Theatre production of *Macbeth*], like a giant gas ring, which whooshes into jets of flame at certain key moments. It is ludicrously obtrusive and sometimes it doesn't seem to be working properly, adding to the viewer's sense of fretful alienation. As Alan Howard stands in the middle of it, looking haggard, you suddenly wonder if the whole dire production is actually an advertisement for British Gas. Will he suddenly flick his thumb and say "Don't you just love being in control?" '

Originally, the control element came from the fact that a gas appliance responds more quickly to its operator's demands than does an electrical one.

Double Diamond Works Wonders, A

Double Diamond beer; UK, from 1952. Double alliteration may have something to do with it, but it was surely the singing of this slogan to the tune of 'There's a Hole in my Bucket' that made it one of the best known of all beer slogans. In 1971, a visiting American copywriter, Ros Levenstein, at the Young and Rubicam agency, came up with the phrase **I'm Only Here For The Beer**. This passed into the language as an inconsequential catchphrase - somewhat detached from the particular brand – and Mo Drake commented (1981): '[She] really had no idea of what she had created.' In September 1971, the Duke of Edinburgh attended a champagne reception at Burghley. 'Don't look at me,' he was quoted as saying, 'I'm only here for the beer.' A.J.P. Taylor, the British historian, was quoted by Peter Vansittart in *Voices 1870–1914* (1984) as having said: 'In my opinion, most of the great men of the past were only there for the beer – the wealth, prestige and grandeur that went with the power.'

Double Your Pleasure, Double Your Fun

Wrigley's Doublemint chewing gum; US, by 1959. However, about the same time, in the UK, the signature tune of ITV's *Double Your Money* quiz included the line, 'Double your money, and double your fun'. That show was first transmitted in 1955.

Do You Know *Me*?

American Express credit card; US, since 1975. Celebrities like authors James Michener, Robert Ludlum and Stephen King – known for what they *did* but not for how they *looked* – explained that relative celebrity could have its drawbacks ... but not when you carried the card.

Do You Know Uneeda Biscuit?

Uneeda soda crackers; US, from 1898.

Drinka Pinta Milka Day

Milk; UK, from 1958. The target was to get everyone drinking one pint of milk a day and the slogan was a piece of 'bath-tub inspiration' that came from the client, namely Bertrand Whitehead, Executive Officer of the National Milk Publicity Council of

England and Wales. Francis Ogilvy, Chairman of Mather & Crowther, apparently insisted on it being used over the protests of the creative department, which wanted it strangled at birth. It was the sort of coinage to drive teachers and pedants to apoplexy, but eventually 'a pinta' achieved a kind of respectability when accorded an entry in *Chambers' Twentieth Century Dictionary* and others (the *OED2* in due course).

Drink Camp – It's The Best
See READY, AYE, READY

Drink Canada Dry
See EMIGRATE TO CANADA DRY

Drink Coca-Cola
Coca-Cola; US, since the late 1880s. Coca-Cola bids fair to be the most widely advertised product in the world. It would be hard to find a country unfamiliar with the logo and this simple injunction (in whatever language). Dr John Pemberton invented the drink in 1886. By 1890 the company was spending $11,000 a year on advertising. The drink was first sold outside the US in 1899. In 1981, Coca-Cola had a yearly advertising spend of $184 million worldwide. Over the years, much of the emphasis has been on driving away competitors, among them: Caro-Cola, Fig Cola, Candy Cola, Cold Cola, Cayola, Koca-Nola, Coca, Cola, Coca-Kola, Kora-Nola, Kola Nola, KoKola, Co Kola, Coke Ola, Kos Kola, Toca-Cola, Soda Cola. (Source: J.C. Louis and Harvey Yazijian, *The Cola Wars*, 1980).

Hence, the continuing necessity to maintain that 'Coke' is 'the real thing'. This idea appeared in 1942 as **The Only Thing Like Coca-Cola Is Coca-Cola Itself.** Later **It's The Real Thing** followed in 1970. Pepsi Cola is the only major rival.

Some of the scores of other slogans that have been used: **Thirst Knows No Season** (from 1922); **The Pause That Refreshes** (from 1929); **It's The Refreshing Thing To Do** (current 1937); **Things Go Better With Coke** (from 1963); **I'd Like To Buy The World A Coke** (from 1971) – the jingle became a hit in its own right when retitled 'I'd Like to Teach the World to Sing'; **Coke Adds Life** (from 1976); **Have A Coke And A Smile** (current 1980); **Coke Is It!** (from 1982).

Translating some of these slogans into foreign languages has caused certain problems. When Coca-Cola started advertising in Peking, **Put A Smile On Your Face** was translated as 'Let Your Teeth Rejoice'. Odder still, 'It's The Real Thing' came out as 'The Elephant Bites the Wax Duck'.

Drink More Milk
UK, quoted 1928. A later campaign from the Milk Marketing Board drew a response from the British Medical Association in January 1938 – an ad headed 'Is *All* Milk Safe To Drink?' (suggesting that milk should be tested for tuberculosis). The BMA had to modify this 'knocking copy' to 'Drink Safe Milk'.

Drink Tizer, The Appetizer
Tizer; UK, current from 1920s.

Dr Williams' Pink Pills For Pale People
US, current 1870s; UK, current 1900. 'The artful alliteration ... may have done much to build up the £1,111,000 fortune which George Taylor Fulford acquired from this property.' (Turner)

Dull It Isn't
Metropolitan Police recruitment; UK, 1972. The day after the brief TV and poster campaign using this slogan started, it was apparent that the phrase was catching on. A young policeman went to break up a fight at White Hart Lane football ground. Having seized a young hooligan, the constable emerged, dishevelled but triumphant, from the melee. A voice from the crowd cried out:

'Dull it effing isn't, eh?' The format sometimes recurs: *'Casualty* it isn't' – from the front cover of *Radio Times* (16 April 1994). It may derive ultimately from a Yiddish construction. In *The Joys of Yiddish* (1968), Leo Rosten has the phrase 'smart he isn't... '

Dynamic Tension
See YOU TOO CAN HAVE A BODY ...

Each For All And All For Each
See ALL FOR ONE ...

East Is Red, The
Chinese Cultural Revolution slogan; China, from 1966. Used notably in a song:

> The East turns red, day is breaking,
> Mao Tse-tung arises over Chinese soil ...

When the first Chinese space satellite was launched in April 1970, it circled the earth, broadcasting the message: *'Tung fang hung – Mao Tse-tung* [The east is red – Mao Tse-tung]'.

Eat More Fruit
British Fruit Trades Federation; UK, from 1923. The Federation launched a well mounted broadside 'stressing the enjoyment and good health to be derived from eating fruit. Fortuitously, an influenza epidemic broke out, enabling the promoters to point out how fruit fortified the human frame against illness' (Turner). The campaign was a great success and paved the way for rival 'Eat More' and 'Drink More' campaigns.

The reverse form of this kind of approach was contained in the First World War slogan **Eat Less Bread**. A poster of c.1917 explained: 'The sinking of foodships by German submarines and the partial failure of the World's wheat crop have brought about a scarcity of wheat and flour which makes it imperative that every household should at once reduce its consumption of BREAD. The Food Controller asks that the weekly consumption of Bread throughout the Country should be reduced by an average of 4 lbs. per head.'

Effect Is Shattering, The
See I THOUGHT ...

Eight Out Of Ten Cats Prefer It
Whiskas cat food; UK, 1980s. Unverified.

Ein Reich, Ein Volk, Ein Führer [One realm, one people, one leader]
Nazi slogan; Germany, 1934. First used at the Nuremberg rally in
September of that year.

Eleanor Start Packing, The Wilkies Are Coming
Unofficial presidential election slogan; US, 1940. Wendell Wilkie
challenged the incumbent President, Franklin D. Roosevelt, but
did not succeed in dislodging either him or his wife, Eleanor, from
the White House. (Safire)

Elizabeth Arden Is Real
Elizabeth Arden cosmetics; US, undated.

'Ello, Tosh, Got A Toshiba?
Toshiba electrical products; UK, quoted in 1990. Credited to Dave
Trott – and with catapulting Toshiba's brand awareness to equal
Sony's and Hitachi's.

Emancipation!
Unofficial political slogan; US, 1850s. The Fugitive Slave Act of
1850 attempted to stop people helping escaped slaves and
allowed owners to pursue them even into free states. Abolitionists
adopted the cry to reflect a broader concern beyond a straightfor-
ward abolition of slavery. (Flexner, 1976)

Emigrate To Canada Dry (For The Sake Of Your Scotch)
Canada Dry tonics and mixers; UK, current 1980. An earlier version of the slogan was used in his act by the American comedian
Pat Henning: 'He was a drinkin' man, my fadder. One day he's
standin' onna banks of the river, wonderin' what the hell folks can
do with all that water, when suddenly he sees a great sign on the
other side **Drink Canada Dry**. [Pause.] So he went up there.'
Compare: 'I saw a notice which said "Drink Canada Dry" and I've

just started' – attributed to Brendan Behan in *The 'Quote ... Unquote' Book of Love, Death and the Universe* (1980), but probably just a joke ascribed to any famous drinker. Canada Dry was originally the name of a Pale Ginger Ale which appears to have been introduced to the US market in the early 1920s.

End Is Nigh, The

Traditional doom-laden slogan of placard-bearing religious fanatics; UK, undated. Although 'nigh' is a biblical word, this phrase does not occur as such in the Authorized Version. See, however, 'The end of all things is at hand' (1 Peter 4: 7); 'The day of the Lord ... is nigh at hand (Joel 2: 1); 'the kingdom of God is nigh at hand' (Luke 21: 31).

End Of The Plain Plane, The

Braniff airline; US, from 1965. Created by Charlie Moss and Phil Parker at the Wells, Rich, Greene agency. Jane Maas commented (1981): 'You probably remember the stir that was caused when at Mary Lawrence's suggestion the planes were painted in bright colors, and the hostesses were dressed in Pucci outfits.'

Enemy Ears Are Listening

See WALLS HAVE EARS

England Expects That Every Man Will Do His Duty And Join The Army Today

Recruiting slogan; UK, during the First World War. An obvious extension of Lord Nelson's message to the British fleet before the Battle of Trafalgar in 1805. The original form of that slogan was 'Nelson Confides That Every Man Will Do His Duty' but it was suggested to him that it would be better to substitute 'England' for 'Nelson'. The signals officer, Lieutenant Pasco, also pointed out that if 'expects' was substituted for 'confides' he need only run up one flag instead of seven (as 'expects' was a common enough word to be represented by one flag in the signals book).

Enlist Today

Army recruitment phrase; UK, during the First World War. A poster addressed to employers of male servants, read: 'Have you a Butler,

Groom, Chauffeur, Gardener or Gamekeeper serving *you* who at this moment should be serving your King and Country? ... Have you a man digging your garden who should be digging trenches?' It concluded: 'Ask your men to enlist TO-DAY.' (Turner)

Enosis [One]
Political slogan; Cyprus, from c.1952. Referring to the proposed union of Cyprus with mainland Greece.

Enter A Different World
See EVERYTHING LONDON

Epic Love Story In Which Everybody Has A Great Role And A Big Part, The
Film, *Joseph Andrews*; UK, 1977. Based on Henry Fielding's novel. What a cheek.

E pluribus unum [One out of many]
The motto of the United States, with the force of a slogan; US, from 1776. A line from Virgil's *Moretum* was chosen by Benjamin Franklin, Thomas Jefferson and John Adams. It appears on the Great Seal of the United States and on all coins and banknotes, although 'In God We Trust' was formally adopted by Congress as the country's motto in 1956.

Equal Pay For Equal Work
Feminist slogan; UK, from the 1970s. Echoing a cry of teachers' organizations in the late nineteenth century. The phrase 'equal pay' on its own was known by 1923.

Equal Rights
Political slogan; UK, early nineteenth century. As a rallying cry for all forms (Roman Catholic/Protestant, animals/man etc.) this phrase was recorded in 1815. With specific application for women with equal rights to vote it was known by 1891. In a 1912 ad for the International Time Recording Company of New York, 'Equal Rights! – Sure!' was the headline over patronising copy which suggested that female employees were more interested in their hairdos than with their jobs and would benefit from clocking on

and clocking off. The culmination of this move was the Equal Rights Amendment (ERA) in the US (1981).

Essence of Eccentricity, The
Bill-matter of the British music-hall entertainer Nellie Wallace (1870–1948). A comedienne from about 1900.

Esso Sign Means Happy Motoring, The
Esso motoring fuel; UK, current 1950s. The line occurred in what has been described as the 1950s' 'longest-running jingle', written by David Bernstein at McCann-Erickson.

Europe – Or Bust
Confederation of British Industry slogan; UK, c.1975. This was at time of the British referendum on membership of the European Community. The origin of informal slogans ending ' ... or bust' is unclear (compare ' ... or die'), though the word 'bust' = burst was in used by the early nineteenth century. *Monte Carlo Or Bust* was the British title of the comedy film known elsewhere as *Those Daring Young Men in Their Jaunty Jalopies* (1969) (about contestants in the Monte Carlo Rally). It is particularly the type of slogan put on a vehicle taking part in some expedition: 'John O'Groats Or Bust!', 'Benidorm Or Bust!' and such like.

Eventually – Why Not Now?
Gold Medal Flour; US, from c.1880. The story has it that when Benjamin S. Bull, advertising manager of the Washburn Crosby company, requested members of his department to suggest catch-phrases to be used in support of Gold Medal Flour, nobody came up with anything worthwhile. Mr Bull demanded: 'When are you going to give me a decent slogan?' His underlings staved him off by saying, 'Eventually.' 'Eventually!' thundered Mr Bull, 'Why not now?' (Lambert)

Even Your Best Friends ...
See OFTEN A BRIDESMAID ...

Ever-Open Door, The
Dr Barnado's Homes; UK, by the 1910s. The first of the homes for

destitute children founded by Dr Thomas John Barnardo (1845–1905) was the East End Mission in Stepney (1867). Over the door was inscribed 'No Destitute Boy or Girl Ever Refused Admission' As a number of other homes followed in the greater London area, this motto was shortened to **No Destitute Child Ever Refused Admission**. The 'Ever-Open Door' theme seems to have caught on rather later. There was a play with the title in 1913 and *Punch* had a political cartoon with it as the caption (26 November 1913). However, I can recall it being applied to the insatiable mouth, representing the appetite of an un-orphaned youth (me) in the 1950s. A correspondent recalls a mother calling her son (b. 1900), 'the ever-open door'. And note this, from Alexander Pope's translation of the *Iliad*, vi.14 (1715–20):

> He held his seat; a friend to human race
> Fast by the road, his ever-open door
> Obliged the wealthy and relieved the poor.

In the 1980s, both the above slogans had long been abandoned. The current one was **Help Barnardo's Help A Child**.

Every Day And In Every Way I Am Getting Better And Better (though sometimes found as **Every Day In Every Way ...** or **Day By Day In Every Way ...**)
The slogan of Couéism – a system of 'Self-Mastery Through Conscious Auto-suggestion' which had a brief vogue in the 1920s. The French psychologist Émile Coué was the originator. His patients had to repeat this phrase over and over and it became a popular catchphrase of the time, though physical improvement did not noticeably follow. Couéism died with its inventor in 1926. (It gave rise to this joke: a woman became pregnant and went to Coué to ask how she could ensure that her child grew up with good manners. She was told to say many times every day: 'My Child Will Be Polite And Good-Mannered', or words to that effect. Nine months passed and no child was born. Years went by and still no child appeared. Eventually, the lady, now quite old, died and a post-mortem was held. As the body was opened, there stood two tiny old men with long white hair and beards, saying to each other: 'Après vous, m'sieur'; 'Non, non, après vous.')

Every Father's Daughter Is A Virgin!
Film, *Goodbye Columbus* (US, 1969). The offspring of two Jewish families grope towards a relationship.

Every Home Should Have One
General-purpose advertising line; probably originating in the US; from the 1920s/30s. Used as the title of a British film about an advertising man in 1970. Against the American origin, and the 1920s/30s dating, is the fact that *Punch* (18 October 1905) had a cartoon whose caption contained the variation: 'The Portable Gramophone ... no country house should be without it.'

Everyman A King ...
See SHARE THE WEALTH

Every Penny You Spend Will Help The World Wildlife Fund's Tropical Rain Forest Campaign ...
World Wildlife Fund; UK, c.1992. The WWF, as it was then called, had the bright idea of putting this slogan on wrappers. Contributed to BBC Radio *Quote ... Unquote* (9 November 1992) by Phyllis M. Teage of Devon.

Every Picture Tells A Story
Doan's Backache Kidney Pills; UK, current 1904. The picture showed a person bent over with pain. Probably a proverbial expression before this. In 1847, Charlotte Brontë had placed the same thought in *Jane Eyre*: 'The letter-press ... I cared little for ... Each picture told a story.'

Everything London
Harrods store; UK, undated. The one-time telegraphic address of the famous department store had the strength of a slogan. **Harrods For Everything** was an actual promotional slogan quoted in 1925. The Harrods motto is also said to be *Omnia omnibus ubique* [Everything for everyone everywhere]. Other slogans have included **Harrods Serves The World** (this was pre-1881) and **Enter A Different World** (current in the 1980s).

Everything You Want From A Store And A Little Bit More
Safeway supermarkets; UK, by 1980.

Export Or Die, We Must
Informal slogan of the British Labour government in 1945–6. It arose out of a severe balance of payments problem.

Exporting Is Fun
Informal slogan of the British Conservative government; UK, 1960. The phrase was included in an address to businessmen by the Prime Minister, Harold Macmillan, but when he came to the passage he left out what was later considered to be a rather patronizing remark. The press, however, printed what was in the advance text of the speech as though he had actually said it.

Eye It – Try It – Buy It!
Chevrolet automobiles; US, current 1940.

Eyes And Ears Of The World, The
Paramount News (cinema newsreel); UK, from 1927 to 1957.

Fair Day's Wages For A Fair Day's Work, A

Political slogan; UK, nineteenth century. T. Attwood in a speech in the House of Commons (14 June 1839) said: 'They only ask for a fair day's wages for a fair day's work.' Benjamin Disraeli had the slogan in his novel *Sybil* (1845). Charles Dickens in *Our Mutual Friend*, Bk. I, Chap. 13 (1864–5), had: 'A fair day's wages for a fair day's work is ever my partner's motto.'

Fair Deal, (The)

Presidential slogan; US, 1949. From President Truman's State of the Union message: 'Every segment of our population and every individual has a right to expect from this government a Fair Deal.' Proposals included legislation on civil rights and fair employment practices.

Fair Shares For All Is Labour's Call

Labour Party slogan in the Battersea North by-election; UK, June 1946. It was apparently devised by the candidate, Douglas Jay, who won.

Family That Prays Together Stays Together, The

Roman Catholic Rosary Crusade; US, from 1947. Devised by Al Scalpone. The crusade began in 1942 and the slogan was first broadcast on 6 March 1947, according to Father Patrick Peyton, *All For Her* (1967). The slogan is quoted in Joseph Heller, *Catch-22* (1961) which is set in the period 1944–5, but this may simply be an anachronism. It has been the inspiration of many humorous variants: 'The family that shoots together loots together', 'The family that slays together stays together' etc.

Fiddling And Fooling

Bill-matter for the British comedian Ted Ray; UK, from c.1930. Ray

(1906–77) was also a violinist and, throughout his life, would play the instrument in his act.

Fidelity, Bravery, Integrity
Federal Bureau of Investigation; US, undated. Motto, with the strength of a slogan, based on the initials F.B.I.

Fifty-Four Forty Or Fight
See WHO'S POLK?

Fills The Stage With Flags
Bill-matter for the music-hall entertainer Kardomah; UK, 1920s/30s. This told you precisely what his act consisted of.

Fine Sets These Ferguson's
Ferguson radios; UK, 1950s. The advertisments carried what looked like a wood-cut of a pipe-smoking man listening to one of the sets.

Firestone. Where The Rubber ...
See WHERE THE RUBBER ...

First Thing Every Morning Renew Your Health With ENO's
Eno's fruit salts laxative; UK, current 1927.

First Time Is Never The Best, The
Campari; US, current 1981.

Fit Dunlop And Be Satisfied
Dunlop tyres; UK, quoted 1925. From *Graffiti 2* (1980): 'Fit Dunlops and be satisfied' (seen on contraceptive ad, Hereford).

Flat Out On Ethyl
Joke suggested slogan; UK, 1920s/30s. Ethyl was a type of petrol which was derived from tetraethyl lead. It is no longer available. In fact, this was probably just a joke riposte to the question, 'What's better than 50 mph on Shell?' Esso Ethyl was, however, promoted (September 1935) in an advertisement featuring Sir Malcolm Campbell, then world land-speed record holder, with the slogan, **301 Miles An Hour On Special Esso Ethyl!**

Flavour Of The Month

Originally a generic advertising phrase aimed at persuading people to try new varieties of ice cream and not just stick to their usual choice (in the US, as 'flavor', by 1946). Latterly, it has become an idiom for a fad, craze or person that is quickly discarded after a period of being in demand. From the *Longman Register of New Words* (1989): 'The metaphorical possibilities of the word *ambush* are catching on in several areas of activity in the USA, making it the lexical flavour-of-the-month in American English.'

Flick Your Bic

Bic lighters; US, from 1975. Coined by Charlie Moss, the original usage occurred in an ad that showed how smart, sophisticated people did not use lighters – they simply 'flicked their Bics'. The line became a household word in the US and was picked up by many comedians. During the energy crisis, Bob Hope said: 'Things are getting so bad that the Statue of Liberty doesn't light up any more. She just stands there and flicks her Bic.'

Flower Power

Hippie slogan; US and elsewhere, from 1967. Inspired no doubt by 'Black Power'. Flowers were used as a love symbol.

Fly Now, Pay Later

See GO NOW, PAY LATER

Fly The American Way

See DOING WHAT WE DO BEST

Fly The Flag

See WE'LL TAKE MORE CARE OF YOU

Fly The Friendly Skies Of Your Land, The

United Air Lines; US, by 1973. Also **Fly The Friendly Skies Of United**.

Food For Strong And Weak

See GRATEFUL AND COMFORTING ...

Food Shot From Guns
Quaker Puffed Wheat and Puffed Rice; US, probably from 1900 onwards. From Claude C. Hopkins, *My Life in Advertising* (1927): 'I watched the process where the grains were shot from guns. And I coined the phrase. The idea aroused ridicule. One of the greatest food advertizers in the country wrote an article about it. He said that of all the follies evolved in food advertizing this certainly was the worst – the idea of appealing to women on "Food Shot From Guns" was the theory of an imbecile. But the theory proved attractive. It was such a curiosity rouser that it proved itself the most successful campaign ever conducted in cereals.'

For An A1 Nation Beer Is Best
Brewers Society; UK, from 1933. Part of a campaign which was aimed at restoring the pub's status as a social centre and to 'publicize the goodness of beer produced from prime barley and full-flavoured hops':

> On working days
>   or holidays
> On dismal days
>   or jolly days -
> Beer is best.

The temperance variant was: 'Beer is best – left alone'.

Forged By God, Foretold By A Wizard, Found By A King
Film, *Excalibur*; UK, 1981. Arthurian legends.

For God's Sake Care, Give Us A Pound
Salvation Army; UK, 1968. Created by the KMP Partnership. David Kingsley remembered (1982): 'This was a product of a team led by myself. The truth is, I put up "For God's Sake, Give Us A Pound" to the then General of the Salvation Army and he and I revised it to "For God's Sake Care … " for obvious reasons.'

For Halitosis, Use Listerine
See STOPS HALITOSIS

For Hands That Do Dishes
Fairy Liquid washing-up soap; UK, by 1981. From 1965 there had been: **Now Hands That Do Dishes Can Feel Soft As Your Face** ('with mild green Fairy Liquid').

For Mash Get Smash
Smash instant mashed potato; UK, 1967. Product made by Cadbury-Typhoo. Chiefly famous through a TV jingle with music by Cliff Adams.

For Men Of Distinction
Lord Calvert custom-blended whiskey; US, current 1945. 'For years', the copy ran, 'the most expensive whiskey blended in America, Lord Calvert [has been] intended especially for those who can afford the finest.' Marshall McLuhan wrote in *The Mechanical Bride* (1951): 'Snob appeal might seem to be the most obvious feature of this type of ad, with its submerged syllogism that since all sorts of eminent men drink this whiskey they are eminent because they drink it. Or only this kind of whiskey is suited to the palate of distinguished men, therefore a taste for it confers, or at least displays an affinity for, distinction in those who have not yet achieved greatness.'

For People Who Can't Brush Their Teeth After Every Meal
Gleem; US, quoted 1957. Research showed that many people felt guilty about not brushing their teeth after every meal. So a slogan was coined which gave these people the perfect excuse not to do so. (Packard)

For The Man Who Has Everything
General-use slogan; US; probably since the 1920s/30s. Promoting some odd luxury gift-item, inessential and over-priced. A salesman at the eponymous jewellery store in *Breakfast at Tiffany's* (film US, 1961) produces something, 'For the lady and gentleman who has everything'.

Forty Acres And A Mule
See TEN ACRES AND A MULE

Four-Square
See ARE YOU FOUR-SQUARE

Forward With The People
Daily Mirror newspaper; UK, from c.1935 until 1959. This slogan appeared on the paper's mast-head, though some who thought the paper had a way of anticipating the inevitable said the slogan ought to have been '*Sideways* With The People'. Later, **Forward With Britain**. Also **Biggest Daily Sale On Earth** (5.2 million copies was the figure in 1966).

For Years We've Been Making …
See PRICELESS INGREDIENT …

For Your Throat's Sake, Smoke Craven "A" – They Never Vary
Craven "A" cigarettes; UK, current 1920s and 1930s. A quite incredible sales pitch as viewed now, but at the time there were others, too: **Smoke Craven "A" – Will Not Affect Your Throat** and **Craven "A" – It's Kind To Your Throat** and **Made Especially To Prevent Sore Throats**.

Four More Years
General purpose presidential slogan in the US when the President is up for re-election. It was certainly used to support Richard Nixon in 1972. The transcript of Ronald Reagan's 'Remarks on Accepting the GOP Presidential Nomination, Dallas, Texas, August 23, 1984' is punctuated with: '*The Audience*. Four more years! Four more years! Four more years!' (*Speaking My Mind by Ronald Reagan: Selected Speeches*, 1989).

Fourth Emergency Service, The
See TO OUR MEMBERS …

Freedom Is In Peril – Defend It With All Your Might
National government morale-building slogan; UK, 1939. Selected by George Orwell at the end of the Second World War as an example of a 'futile slogan obviously incapable of stirring strong feelings or being circulated by word of mouth … One has to take into

account the fact that nearly all English people dislike anything that sounds high-flown or boastful. Slogans like THEY SHALL NOT PASS, or BETTER TO DIE ON YOUR FEET THAN LIVE ON YOUR KNEES, which have thrilled continental nations, seem slightly embarrassing to an Englishman, especially a working man.' To which Angus Calder added (*The People's War*, 1969): 'It was partly from the desensitized prose of most of the British press during the war, from the desertion of subtleties of meaning in favour of slogans, that George Orwell derived the notion of Newspeak, the vocabulary of totalitarianism' in *Nineteen Eighty-Four*.'

Freedom Is Slavery; Ignorance Is Strength; War Is Peace
Fictional slogans from the novel *Nineteen Eighty-Four* (1949) by George Orwell. They belong to the Ministry of Truth.

Freedom Now!
Civil rights slogan; US, early 1960s. A black litany went:

> Q. What do you want?
> A. Freedom!
> Q. Let me hear it again – what do you want?
> A. Freedom!
> Q. When do you want it?
> A. Now!

The format may have arisen from a petition to Alabama's Governor Wallace in March 1965. On this occasion Martin Luther King Jr and other civil rights leaders led some 3000 people in a 50-mile march from Selma to Montgomery. The petition began: 'We have come to you, the Governor of Alabama, to declare that we must have our *freedom now*. We must have the right to vote; we must have equal protection of the law, and an end to police brutality.' (Safire)

Free Lung Cancer With Every Packet
ASH Campaign for Freedom from Tobacco; UK, 1996. On spoof advertisement for a brand of cigarette called 'Emphysema'.

Free Soil, Free Men, Free Speech, Frémont
Presidential election slogan; US, 1856. The new Republican

Party's first candidate was John C. Frémont, a soldier and explorer. When formed two years before, the party had absorbed abolitionists including the Free Soil Party (which was dedicated to free land for settlers as well as to the abolition of slavery) who used the slogan **Free Soil, Free Speech, Free Labour, And Free Men**, which the Republicans adapted. Meanwhile, the American (Know Nothing) Party which supported ex-President Fillmore in the race used the slogan **Peace At Any Price** to mean that they were willing to accept slavery for blacks in order to avoid a civil war. Neither Frémont nor Fillmore won. James Buchanan did. It has been suggested that the phrase had been coined earlier (in 1820 or 1848) by Alphonse de Lamartine, the French foreign affairs minister in his *Méditations Poétiques* as '*La paix à tout prix*'. However, the Earl of Clarendon quoted an 'unreasonable calumny' concerning Lord Falkland in his *History of the Rebellion* (written in 1647): 'That he was so enamoured on peace, that he would have been glad the king should have bought it at any price.' When Prime Minister Neville Chamberlain signed his pact with Hitler in 1938, many praised him for trying to obtain 'peace at any price.'

Free The —
Protest slogan format; US and elsewhere, since the 1960s. Usually completed with a place and number. Hence, 'Free the Chicago 7' (charged with creating disorder during the Democratic Convention in 1968), 'Free the Wilmington 10', and so on. Dignifying protesters with a group name incorporating place and number began with the 'Hollywood 10' (protesters against McCarthyite investigations) in 1947.

The format has now become a cliché of sloganeering. Various joke slogans from the late 1970s demanded: 'Free the Beethoven 9/the Heinz 57/the Intercity 125/the Chiltern Hundreds/the Indianapolis 500/the Grecian 2000.'

Freshen-Up With 7-Up
7-Up; US, current 1962. Alternatively, **Bring On The *Real* Thirst-Quencher!** and **The Un-Cola**. 7-Up was first sold as an 'anti-acid' hangover remedy and in the early 1930s had the slogan **Takes The 'Ouch' Out of Grouch**.

Fresh To The Last Slice
Sunblest bread; UK, current early 1960s. Probably inspired by
GOOD TO THE LAST DROP.

Friday Night Is Amami Night
Amami hair products; UK, current 1920s. Presumably this gave
rise to the title of the long-running BBC radio show *Friday Night Is
Music Night*, from 1953.

**From Each According To His Ability, To Each According To His
Needs**
Marxist slogan; nineteenth century. Usually attributed to Karl
Marx, but from neither *Das Kapital* nor *The Communist Manifesto*.
The slogan appears in his *Critique of the Gotha Programme* (1875) in
which Marx says that after the workers have taken power, capi-
talist thinking must first disappear. Only then will the day come
when society can 'inscribe on its banners: from each according to
his ability, to each according to his needs'.

John Kenneth Galbraith commented in *The Age of Uncertainty*
(1977): 'It is possible that these ... twelve words enlisted for Marx
more followers than all the hundreds of thousands in the three
volumes of *Das Kapital* combined.'

There is some doubt whether Marx originated the slogan or
whether he was quoting Louis Blanc, Morelly or Mikhail Bakunin.
The latter wrote: 'From each according to his faculties, to each
according to his needs' (declaration, 1870, by anarchists on trial
after the failure of their uprising in Lyons).

Also, Saint-Simon (1760–1825), the French reformer, had earlier
said: 'The task of each be according to his capacity, the wealth of
each be according to his works.' And, much earlier, Acts 4: 34–35
had had: 'Neither was there any among them that lacked: for as
many as were possessors of lands or houses sold them, and
brought the prices of things that were sold, and laid them down
at the apostles' feet: and distribution was made unto every man
according as he had need.'

From Those Wonderful Folks Who Gave You Pearl Harbor
Joke suggested slogan for Panasonic electronics; US, 1960s. In a
book (1970) which has this slogan as title, Jerry Della Femina (b.

84

1936), the advertising executive, recounted how: 'Everybody sat around thinking about Panasonic, the Japanese electronics account. Finally I decided what the hell, I'll throw a line to loosen them up … "The headline is, the headline is: From Those Wonderful Folks Who Gave You Pearl Harbor." Complete silence.'

FTA (Fuck The Army)

Protest slogan, much used in the US Army, especially as graffiti. *The Dictionary of American Slang* (1975 ed.) adds that it has been used, 'Since c.1960, as a counter expression to disliked orders, rules etc.' *F.T.A.* was the title of an anti-Vietnam War film made by Jane Fonda in 1972.

The 'initial' strategy has also been used regarding the Pope (**FTP**) and the Queen (**FTQ**) especially in Northern Ireland (both types recorded in Belfast, 1971). (Reisner)

Full Dinner Pail, The

Presidential election slogan; US, 1900. A phrase which helped secure the re-election of the Republican President McKinley in 1900. Prosperity of this type was plainly more appealing to the average voter than William Jennings Bryan's call to secure **Immediate Freedom For The Philippines**. A remark made by McKinley supporter Senator Mark Hanna, 'We will stand pat', gave rise to the idea that 'Stand Pat With McKinley' was used as a slogan in this election but this appears to be a fallacy.

Full Metal Packet

See LOIN KING

Full Of Eastern Promise

Fry's Turkish Delight; UK, current late 1950s. Used in one of the longest-running series of British TV ads, appealing to escapist fantasies. One of the first showed a male slave unrolling a carpet containing a woman captive before an eastern potentate. The phrase was still in use on wrappers in 1981. From the *Independent on Sunday* (5 April 1992): 'Benny Hill was fired by Thames [TV] in 1989 when ratings slumped after decades of … the Crimplene eroticism of Hill's Angels – those willing young ladies with the bee-stung mouths, full of East End promise.'

Full Of Natural Goodness
Milk; UK, current 1980. A model was photographed wearing a T-shirt with 'I'm full of natural goodness' over her breasts. Subtle, eh?

Future's Bright, The Future's Orange (The)
Orange mobile phones; UK, current 1996.

Gable's Back And Garson's Got Him
Film, *Adventure*; US, 1945. Coined by Howard Dietz.

Garbo Laughs!
Film, *Ninotchka*; US, 1939. Coined by Howard Dietz. Garbo is supposed to have chided him for this, asking: 'How can you ever forgive yourself?' Earlier, Dietz had coined: **Garbo Talks!** for *Anna Christie*; US, 1930.

Garden For Victory
See DIG FOR VICTORY

Gauloises à rouler, OK
See VIRGINIAN ROLLS OK

Gentle Giant, The
General use; UK/US, undated. The alliteration is important and the application to any tall, strong person (or institution) has become a journalistic cliché. A policeman killed by an IRA bomb outside Harrods store in London (December 1983) was so dubbed. Terry Wogan, the disc jockey, used the expression allusively in the early 1980s to describe the BBC's Radio 2 network (whose official slogan about that time was **Two's Company**) Larry Holmes (b. 1950), former world heavyweight boxing champion, is another to whom the label has been affixed, as also James Randel Matson (b. 1945), the US track and field champion.

In 1967, there was an American film entitled *The Gentle Giant*. The film was about a small boy in Florida who befriends a bear which later saves the life of the boy's disapproving father. In the 1930s, Pickfords Removals were promoted with the following rhyme:

A note from you, a call from us,
The date is fixed, with no worry or fuss,
A Pickfords van, a gentle giant,
The work is done – a satisfied client.

Going back even further, the British journalist William Howard Russell wrote of Dr Thomas Alexander, a surgeon who served in the Crimean War, as a 'gentle giant of a Scotchman'.

George Davis Is Innocent

Informal protest slogan; UK, 1975. George Davis had been given a 17-year prison sentence after being found guilty of taking part in a robbery and for wounding with intent to avoid arrest. Those who believed in his innocence wrote 'Free George Davis now' and 'George Davis is innocent, OK' all over the East End of London and carried out other forms of protest quite widely. The campaign gathered strength and in May 1976 Davis was released from prison but not pardoned. In July 1978 he was sentenced to 15 years' gaol for his part in a subsequent bank robbery, which must have given the protesters something to think about. 'FREE GEORGE DAVIS' and the scribbled addition 'with every packet of cornflakes/gallon of petrol' was included in *Graffiti Lives OK* (1979).

George Washington Slept Here

See QUEEN ELIZABETH SLEPT HERE

Gertcha!

Courage Best Bitter; UK, c.1980. This exclamation (acquiring the force of a slogan) had a burst of popularity when used in TV ads which showed various grim-faced drinkers sitting around in an East End pub. They shouted it out during breaks in the music. Dave Trott, the copywriter responsible for using the word, suggested it derived from 'Get out of it, you!' This is supported by Partridge/*Slang*. He was on to it – as 'gercher' – in 1937. The *OED2* has 'get away/along with you' as a 'derisive expression of disbelief'. The line got into the commercial from a song composed by the Cockney singers Chas and Dave. They originally pronounced it 'Wooertcha'.

Getaway People, The
National Benzole; UK, from 1963. Bryan Oakes of London Press Exchange commented: 'They were the jet set, clean-limbed beautiful girls, the gods and goddesses who did exotic things. We used expensive cars – E-type Jaguars and Aston Martins – and the promise was that, if you get this petrol, you're aligning yourself with those wonderful people, midnight drives on the beach and so on. Of course, it's tough luck – you don't happen to have a Jag just yet, or a girl like that, but any day now ...' (Pearson)

Get Good Mileage For Your Money With Shell Economy
Shell Economy motor fuel; UK, 1969–70. This was spoken by the reporter (me) in several TV ads featuring the Shell Mileage tests. Members of the public were given one gallon of the petrol and drove round and round a race track or along country lanes until they stopped. I then burst out of the undergrowth and told Mr Lewis of Leicester, for example, that he had managed 52 miles in his Morris 1100. 'Fantastic. I'd never have believed it possible', replied he. Then I delivered the line. These mileage tests had the privilege of being parodied in the *Morecambe and Wise Christmas Show* (1970).

Get Into Fellas
Fellas men's underwear; New Zealand, current 1981.

Get Our Country Moving Again
See LET'S GET AMERICA ...

Gets Rid Of Film On Teeth
Pepsodent; US, current early 1900s. Another of Claude C. Hopkins's great coups – to claim something that every toothpaste could claim and get away with it. In *My Life in Advertising* (1927) he commented: 'People do not want to read of penalties. They want to be told of rewards ... People want to be told the ways to happiness and cheer'... I resolved to advertise this toothpaste as a creator of beauty.'

Get The Abbey Habit
Abbey National Building Society; UK, current late 1970s.

Getting Bigger By Being Better
Corporate slogan for Amoco; UK, current in 1981.

Getting People Together
Corporate slogan for Boeing aircraft; US, current in 1977.

Getting There Is Half the Fun ... Being There Is All Of It
Film, *Being There*; US, 1980. Clearly this builds upon the basic view that 'getting there is half the fun' which may be said to sloganize Robert Louis Stevenson's remarks 'I travel not to go anywhere, but to go' and 'to travel hopefully is a better thing than to arrive'. Then there is 'the journey not the arrival matters' (an expression used as the title of an autobiographical volume by Leonard Woolf, 1969). 'Getting there is half the fun' may possibly have been used to advertise Cunard steamships in the 1920s/30s.

In *Up the Organisation* (1970), Robert Townshend opined of getting to the top: 'Getting there isn't half the fun – it's all the fun.'

Girls Can We Interest You In A Package Holiday?
Club 18–30; UK, 1995. Accompanying a shot of a man's well-filled underpants, as also did the line **Pack Your Trunks**. After protests, the poster was withdrawn from display on hoardings but continued to appear in youth and style magazines.

Girl Who Made Vaudeville Famous, The
Bill-matter of the American musical entertainer Eva Tanguay (1878–1947); US, 1910s/20s. Mitzi Gaynor played her in a biopic, *The I Don't Care Girl* (US, 1953) – named after her one of her songs.

Girl With The Summer-Hot Lips ...
See MEAN! MOODY! ...

Give 'Em Hell, Harry
See DON'T LET THEM TAKE ...

Give Him/'Em A Guinness
See GUINNESS IS GOOD FOR YOU

Give Him A Right Good Hemeling Tonight
Hemeling lager; UK, by 1981. Also **Wouldn't You Rather Be Hemeling?**

Give Him Bovril
See ALAS! MY POOR BROTHER

Give The Presidency Back To The People
Presidential election slogan; US, 1968. Eugene McCarthy's cry, seeking the Democratic nomination, without success.

Give Whitman's Chocolates ...
See WOMAN NEVER FORGETS ...

Glass And A Half In Every Half Pound, A
Cadbury's Milk chocolates; UK, origination undated. Revived in 1976 and 1981.

Glaxo Builds Bonny Babies
Glaxo (dried, skimmed milk); UK, from 1913. The slogan 'swept the country', prompting the music-hall quip about the young husband who asked: 'Who takes it – me or the wife?'

Glory Of A Man Is His Strength, The
See ALAS! MY POOR BROTHER

Glow To It
See GO TO IT

God Created Woman – But The Devil Created Brigitte Bardot
Film, *And God Created Woman*; France, 1957 – when promoted in the UK.

Go For (The) Gold
General-purpose slogan; US/UK, 1980s. Meaning, literally, 'aim for a gold medal', this was probably first used by the US Olympic team at the Lake Placid Winter Olympics in 1980, as is alluded to in this report on ice hockey in *The Times* (16 February 1980): 'The

United States, now encouraged by the legend "shoot for the gold", took a grip of the game thereafter.' *Going for Gold* became the title of an Emma Lathen thriller set in Lake Placid, published in 1981. Other teams had taken it up by the time of the 1984 Olympics at Los Angeles – the British team recorded a song called 'Go for Gold' (accompanied by the Pangbourne Digital Silver Band). In his stump speech for re-election in that year, Ronald Reagan repeatedly said: 'And like our Olympic athletes, this nation should set its sights on the stars and go for the gold … ' A US TV movie *Going for the Gold* in 1985 was not connected to the Olympics, however. A BBC TV quiz called *Going for Gold* began in 1987.

Just to show, as always, that there is nothing new under the sun: in 1832, there was a political slogan 'To Stop the Duke, Go for Gold' – which was somehow intended, through its alliterative force, to prevent the Duke of Wellington from forming a government in the run up to the Reform Bill. The slogan was coined by a radical politician, Francis Place, for a poster, on 12 May 1832. (It was intended to cause a run on the Bank of England – and succeeded.)

Go For It!
General-purpose slogan; US/UK, from the early 1980s. Lisa Bernbach in *The Official Preppie Handbook* (1980) pointed to a possible US campus origin, giving the phrase as a general exhortation meaning 'Let's get carried away and act stupid'. At about the same time, the phrase was used in aerobics. Jane Fonda in a workout book (1981) and video (c.1983), cried, 'Go for it, **Go For The Burn!**' (where the burn was a sensation felt during exercise). There was also a US beer slogan (current 1981), 'Go for it! Schlitz makes it great'. Media mogul Ted Turner was later called a 'go-for-it guy', and so on. The phrase has become widely used as an exhortation in business and selling.

In June 1985, President Reagan's call on tax reform was, 'America, go for it!' Victor Kiam, an American razor entrepreneur, entitled his 1986 memoirs *Going For It!*; and 'Go for it, America' was the slogan used by British Airways in the same year to get more US tourists to ignore the terrorist threat and travel to Europe.

Partridge/*Slang* has 'to go for it' as Australian for being 'extremely eager for sexual intercourse' (c.1925).

Going! Going!! Gone!!! Too Late For Herpicide

Newbro's Herpicide; US, current from c.1900. Coined by Dr Newbro for his dandruff germ remedy. Accompanied by the cartoon logo of a man looking at the hairs coming out on his comb. (Lambert)

Gone For A Burton

Bass 'Burton' Ale; UK, 1930s. Unverified. Folk-memory suggests that this phrase was originally used to promote a Bass brew known in the trade as 'a Burton' (though, in fact, several ales are brewed in Burton-upon-Trent). However, research has failed to turn up more positive proof. Early in the war, the phrase was adopted as an idiom to describe what had happened to a missing person, presumed dead, especially in the RAF. There are, however, other theories as to the origin of this expression which do not link it to the putative ale.

Go Now, Pay Later

Unverified travel slogan; US, probably 1940s/50s. Daniel Boorstin in *The Image* (1962) makes oblique reference to travel advertisements using the line 'Go now, pay later'. Was hire purchase ever promoted with 'Buy now, pay later'? It seems likely. These lines – in the US and UK – seem to be the starting point for a construction much used and adapted since. Compare: **Pay As You Ride** (Maxwell Cars; US, 1916) which 'introduced the widespread buying of cars on credit or paying by instalments. Later phrases reminiscent of this slogan were to include **Pay As You Go**, for federal income withholding taxes since 1958, and **Fly Now, Pay Later** in airline and travel ads of the 1950s and 60s.' (Flexner, 1982)

Live Now Pay Later was the title of Jack Trevor Story's 1962 screenplay based on the novel *All on the Never Never* by Jack Lindsay. As a simple graffito, the same line was recorded in Los Angeles (1970), according to Reisner. The same book records a New York subway graffito on a funeral parlour ad: 'Our layaway plan – die now, pay later.' A 'Book now, pay later' ad was in the programme of the Royal Opera House, Covent Garden, in 1977.

Good Bacon Has Danish Written All Over It
Danish bacon; UK, 1960s. In fact, this brand had the word
stamped, literally, all over it. In 1985, the WCRS agency revived
the slogan, noting that Danish 'had a great asset they were sitting
on', also calling it a 'historical advertising property.'

Good For Life!
Dr Pepper soft drink; US, by 1937.

Good For Man Or Beast
Dr Hitchcock's Kickapoo Indian Oil; US, early 1870s. (Flexner,
1982)

Good Housekeeping **Seal Of Approval, The**
Good Housekeeping Magazine; US, undated. Originally an endorsement offered by the magazine to any advertiser who bought at
least two pages a year. Has become an all-purpose catchphrase.

Good Morning! Have You Used Pears' Soap?
Pears' soap; UK, current 1888 (still in use 1928); US, current 1880s.
Thomas J. Barratt (1842–1914) has been dubbed, with good reason,
the 'father of modern advertising', in the UK at least. With
remorseless energy and unflagging invention he flooded the
country with ads for Pears' soap from 1875 onwards. 'Any fool
can make soap,' he said. 'It takes a clever man to sell it.' Some of
his work also appeared in the US. Early on, Barratt 'decided he
must have a catch-phrase which would make the whole country
say "Pears' Soap". His staff were invited to nominate the com-
monest phrase in daily use. Inevitably, somebody suggested
"Good morning". The result was the notorious "Good Morning!
Have You Used Pears' Soap?" which scourged two continents.

'There were many who never forgave Thomas Barratt for debas-
ing this traditional, friendly greeting. The sensitive shrank from
saying "Good morning", knowing that it would only spark off the
exasperating counter-phrase in the mind of the person addressed.'
(Turner)

How Do You Spell Soap? Why P-E-A-R-S, Of Course; UK, current 1880s – can hardly have been a less trying catchphrase.

Good Name Is Better Than Promises
See THERE'S A FORD ...

Good To The Last Drop
Maxwell House coffee; US, from 1907. President Theodore Roosevelt was visiting Joel Cheek, perfector of the Maxwell House blend. After the President had had a cup, he said of it that it was 'Good ... to the last drop'. This has been used as a slogan ever since, despite the various smart-alecs who have inquired 'What's wrong with the last drop then?' Professors of English have been called in to consider the problem and have ruled that 'to' can be inclusive and not just mean 'up to but not including'. (Lambert) In 1982, Maxwell House in the US was still using a logo of a tilted coffee cup with the last drop falling from it. Also **Taste As Good As It Smells** – a slogan that attempts to remedy the age-old complaint, 'Why does coffee never taste as good as it smells?' Undated.

Gordon Liddy Doesn't Bail Them Out, He Puts Them In
Congressional nomination slogan; US, 1968. The candidate, lawyer G. Gordon Liddy (later the mastermind behind Watergate), lost narrowly.

Go To It
National government slogan; UK, summer of 1940. The Minister of Supply, Herbert Morrison, called for a voluntary labour force in a way that echoed the public mood after Dunkirk. On 22 May, he concluded a radio broadcast with these words and they were sub-sequently used as a wall-poster slogan – in vivid letters – in a campaign run by the S.H. Benson agency (which later indulged in self-parody on behalf of Bovril, with **Glow To It** in 1951–2). 'Go to it', meaning 'to act vigorously, set to with a will', dates from the early nineteenth century at least. In Shakespeare, *King Lear* (IV.vi.112), it means something else:

> Die for adultery! No:
> The wren goes to't, and the small gilded fly
> Does lecher in my sight.

Go To Work On An Egg

British Egg Marketing Board; UK, from 1957. Fay Weldon, later known as a novelist and TV playwright, was a copywriter on the 'egg' account at the Mather & Crowther agency. She took the trouble (in 1981) to put the record straight over her involvement in creating one of the more memorable British slogans: 'I was certainly in charge of copy at the time "Go To Work On An Egg" was first used as a slogan as the main theme for an advertising campaign. The phrase itself had been in existence for some time and hung about in the middle of paragraphs and was sometimes promoted to base lines. Who invented it, it would be hard to say. It is perfectly possible, indeed probable, that I put those particular six words together in that particular order but I would not swear to it. Mary Gowing, a very creative and talented advertising copywriter, was in charge of the account before I took over. She died, suddenly, when I was working under her and I, as the phrase goes, stepped over the cook; that is, I took over because there was nobody else to do it. If she wrote "Go To Work On An Egg" I don't want to claim it, but I can't be sure. I certainly devised, along with the art director, Ruth Gill, **Happiness Is Egg Shaped** and **You Can Rely On The Lion** but I think **There Is A Lion On My Egg** was Mary Gowing's.' (The lion device was stamped on eggs as a kind of hallmark. Another headline, in 1957, was **Was There A Lion On Your Egg This Morning?** But after all this effort, campaigns on behalf of eggs went out of favour.)

Gott strafe England! [God punish England]

Propaganda slogan; Germany, during the First World War. It apparently originated, or at least made an early appearance, in a book called *Schwert und Myrte* (1914) by Alfred Funke. Mocked in *Punch* (12 May 1915).

Go Well – Go Shell

Shell motor fuel; UK, current from late 1940s. Had the follow-on line **Keep Going Well – Keep Going Shell**. Both were featured in early TV commercials, most notably with Bing Crosby singing the jingle in 1962 and Sammy Davis junior in 1964. See also THAT'S SHELL ... and GET GOOD MILEAGE ...

Grace ... Space ... Pace
Jaguar cars; UK, by 1951.

Graded Grains Make Finer Flour
Homepride flour; UK, current
1968. The tag-line of a series of popular TV ads featuring the Homepride flour graders, a likeable race of bowler-hatted men.

Grateful And Comforting Like Epps's Cocoa
Epps's cocoa; UK, from c.1900. In Noël Coward's play *Peace In Our Time* (1947), a character says: 'One quick brandy, like Epps's Cocoa, would be both grateful and comforting.' When asked 'Who is Epps?' he replies: 'Epps's Cocoa – it's an advertisement I remember when I was a little boy.' Also, **The Food For Strong and Weak**. (Source: Christopher Baglee and Andrew Morley, *Street Jewellery: A History of Enamel Advertising Signs*, 1978).

Great Crusade, The
Presidential election slogan; US, 1952. Dwight Eisenhower called for one of these during his successful campaign.

Greater Than *Ivanhoe*
Film, *Julius Caesar*; US, 1953.

Greatest Motion Picture Ever Made, The
Film, *Gone with the Wind*; US, 1939.

Greatest Name In Cigarettes, The
See BEST TOBACCO MONEY ...

Greatest Show On Earth, The
Barnum & Bailey's circus; US, 1881. Name given by Phineas T. Barnum (1810–91) to the circus formed by the merger with his rival, Bailey's. Still the slogan of what is now Ringling Bros and Barnum & Bailey Circus. Used as the title of a Cecil B. De Mille circus movie, 1952.

Great Lager, Shame About The ...
Hofmeister lager; UK, by 1982. The year before, Listerine had

used the line '... shame about the breath'. Both were drawing on a catchphrase format 'nice —, shame about the —' which derived from 'Nice Legs, Shame About Her Face', the title of a briefly popular song recorded by The Monks in 1979. Compare these other uses of the format: a take-off by TV's *Not the Nine O'Clock News* team – 'Nice video, shame about the song' (1982). Headline to an *Independent* piece on the hundredth birthday of the 'The Red Flag': 'Good tune, shame about the words' (9 February 1989). Headline from *The Observer* (9 April 1989): 'Nice prints, shame about the books'. Also used loosely: 'Victoria Wood is almost perfect. Lovely lady, pity about the voice' (*Cosmopolitan*, February 1987); headline to an *Observer* report on puny car horns (January 1989): 'NICE CAR, BUT WHAT A VOICE!'

Great Society, The
Presidential slogan; US, 1964. After tentatively trying out this phrase several times, President Lyndon B. Johnson elevated it to capital letters in a speech at the University of Michigan in May 1964 – 'In your time we have the opportunity to move not only towards the rich society and the powerful society but upward to the Great Society.'

In 1967, Governor George Romney put it all in a nutshell: 'There was the NEW DEAL of Franklin Roosevelt, the FAIR DEAL of Harry Truman, and the ordeal of Lyndon Johnson.'

Great Stuff This Bass!
Bass beer; UK, current 1928. A character called 'Bill Sticker' was shown in advertisements plastering up this slogan in various unlikely places.

Great Way To Fly, A
Singapore Airlines; US, current 1980.

Grin Will Win, The
See HE'S MAKING US PROUD AGAIN

Guinness Is Good For You
Guinness; UK, from 1929. After 170 years without advertising,

Arthur Guinness Son & Company decided to call in the image-makers. Oswald Greene at the S.H. Benson agency initiated some consumer research (unusual in those days) into why people were drinking Guinness. 'We spent an awful lot of time in an awful lot of pubs,' recalled a colleague. Wherever they went they found that people thought Guinness did them *good*. Greene spotted the potential in this approach, though the slogan was nearly rejected as being too ordinary and not clever enough. The claim also conflicts with the fact that most drinkers drink for social reasons rather than for health.

The slogan has been revived only once since being discontinued in 1941 because claims for the health-giving powers of alcohol are frowned upon nowadays. The Advertising Standards Authority says that, technically, Guinness has never fallen foul of it because the 'Good For You' claim has not been made during the Authority's existence, adding: 'It is not certain it would offend.'

There is a story Guinness people like to tell about the man who questioned the amount of money they were spending each year telling him to drink the stuff. 'The only reason I drink Guinness', he said, 'is because it's good for me.'

Ask any British person to give an example of an advertising slogan and he is more than likely to say 'Guinness is good for you'. It is etched on the national consciousness to such an extent that although the slogan has not been used since 1963 people remember it as though they saw it yesterday.

Guinness Gives You Strength first appeared in 1929 as 'Guinness Is So Strengthening' and ran until 1959. It achieved its most memorable form in the 1934 poster by John Gilroy which shows a man carrying an iron girder on his fingertips.

As for **My Goodness, My Guinness**, Dicky Richards, Benson's art director, got the idea of a zoo-keeper chasing a sealion which had stolen his Guinness after he had paid a visit to the circus at Olympia. This led to a whole menagerie of animals being associated with the product between 1935 and 1958 – ostriches, lions, kinkajous and, above all, toucans. These last are said to have been the brainchild of Dorothy L. Sayers, the novelist, who was a copywriter at Benson's – but, in fact, she had left before they were introduced:

If he can say as you can
Guinness is good for you,
How grand to be a Toucan
Just think what Toucan do.

As for **Give Him/'Em A Guinness**, this marked the removal to the J. Walter Thompson agency of the Guinness account in 1969. Ironically, the form of the slogan had been used by Benson's many years previously to promote *Bovril*. It was followed by **7 Million Every Day And Still Going Down** in 1971 (which seems quite modest beside the 1955 Coca-Cola jingle **Fifty Million Times A Day**) and the pointed line **I've Never Tried It Because I Don't Like It** in 1973. In addition, there was a string of puns: **Tall, Dark And Have Some**; **Cool, Calm And Collect It**; **Hop Squash**; **Pint Sighs**; and, in Jubilee Year, **We've Poured Through The Reign**. None of these quite rose to the depths, however, of the old Benson line, **Pour Encourager Les Huîtres**.

More recent Guinness slogans have included **Not Everything In Black And White Makes Sense**; UK, 1996. See also PURE GENIUS.

Gung-Ho
Semi-official slogan of the US Marines; US, during the Second World War. Lt. Gen. Evans F. Carlson is said to have chosen it; in 1943, a film about the Marines had the title *Gung Ho!* Meaning 'enthusiastic, if carelessly so', the phrase derives from Chinese *kung* plus *ho* meaning 'work together'. In Geoff Chapple, *Rewi Alley of China* (1980), it is stated that the phrase was coined in 1938 and used as the motto of the Chinese Industrial Co-operatives Association.

Guns And/Or/Before Butter
Nazi political slogan; Germany, 1930s. When a nation is under pressure to choose between material comforts and some kind of war effort, the choice has to be made between 'guns *and* butter'. Some will urge 'guns *before* butter'. From the translation of a speech given by Joseph Goebbels in Berlin (17 January 1936): 'We can do without butter, but, despite all our love of peace, not without arms. One cannot shoot with butter, but with guns.' Later that same year, Hermann Goering said in a broadcast, 'Guns will make

us powerful; butter will only make us fat', so he may also be credited with the 'guns or butter' slogan. But there is a third candidate. Airey Neave in his book *Nuremberg* (1978) stated of Rudolf Hess: 'It was he who urged the German people to make sacrifices and coined the phrase: "Guns before butter".'

Guns Don't Kill People, People Kill People
National Rifle Association; US, current 1981, but of much earlier origin. Compare the 1970 graffito 'Puns don't kill people, people kill people.' (Reisner)

Had Enough?
See I LIKE IKE

Ham What Am, The
Armour & Co. meat products; US, current 1917. Accompanied by
the logo of a negro chef. Latterly used as a trademark for all the
company's meat products, not just the ham.

Hands Off —
Informal political slogan; UK and elsewhere, mid-twentieth century. A slogan formula demanding withdrawal of intervention
from any place or institution the speaker chooses. 'Hands Off
Vietnam' was common during the Vietnam War. 'Hands Off
Socialist Vietnam' (referring to the Chinese invasion) featured in
the 1980 May Day parade in Moscow. From a parliamentary
report in *The Times* (16 July 1981): 'Mr Brown strode to the Mace
... and placed ... a small red and black placard bearing the slogan:
"Hands off Lothian".'

Hang The Kaiser
Anti-German slogan; UK, 1918. Said originally to have been a dis-
missive phrase among British soldiers in the First World War who
would say, 'Oh, hang the Kaiser!' when bored with all the talk
about Kaiser Wilhelm II (1859–1941). However, in due course, it
became an unofficial political slogan. During the Versailles Peace
Conference and for some time afterwards, Britain's Northcliffe
newspapers and others kept up the cry in its literal sense. At the
1918 General Election, candidates are said to have lost votes if
they did not subscribe to the policy. In the Treaty of Versailles
(signed 28 June 1919), the Allies committed themselves to trying
the, by now, ex-Kaiser – but the Government of the Netherlands

refused to hand him over for trial in June 1920. The ex-Kaiser died, unhanged, in 1941.

Happiness Is —
General advertising formula; US, from the mid-1960s onwards. Taking their cue from *Happiness is a Warm Puppy*, the title of a 1962 Peanuts book by Charles M. Schulz, sloganeers went nuts on the 'Happiness is …' theme, gradually watering down the original: **Happiness Is Egg Shaped** (UK, selling eggs – see GO TO WORK ON AN EGG); **Happiness Is A Quick-Starting Car** (US, Esso); **Happiness Is A Cigar Called Hamlet** (UK, by 1970); **Happiness Is Being Elected Team Captain – And Getting A Bulova Watch** (US); **Happiness Is A $49 Table** (US, Brancusi Furniture); **Happiness Is Giving Dad A Terry Shave Coat For Christmas** (US, Cone Sporterry); **Happiness Is The Sands** (US, Las Vegas hotel); **Happiness Is A Bathroom By Marion Wieder** (US, decorator); **Happiness Can Be The Color Of Her Hair** (US, Miss Clairol); **Happiness Is Being Single** (bumper sticker, seen in NYC, 1981); **Happiness Is Slough In My Rear-View Mirror** (car sticker, seen in London, 1981).

No wonder Lennon and McCartney wrote a song called 'Happiness is a Warm Gun'.

Hard In, Soft Out
Campaign for Real Bread; UK, by 1977. Possibly more of an unofficial observation. I heard it from an official of the campaign in December 1977 after I had commented on the hardness of a sample of 'real bread'.

Hard Man Is Good To Find, A
Soloflex (body-building equipment); US, 1985. Ads showed the hand of a woman touching the bodies of well-known brawny athletes. Also, a remark sometimes attributed to Mae West. An inversion of the proverbial expression 'a good man is hard to find' – title of a song by Eddie Green (1919). Is this the same as 'Good men are scarce' found in 1609 by *The Concise Oxford Dictionary of Proverbs*?

Harmless As Water From The Mountain Springs
Hostetter's Stomach Bitters; US, current in the 1840s.

'Recommended for the shakes, dyspepsia, colic, dysentery, nervousness, and gloom – and containing 44 percent alcohol!' (Flexner, 1982)

Harpic Cleans Round The Bend
See CLEANS ROUND THE BEND

Harp Puts Out The Fire
Harp Lager; UK, from c.1976. Keith Ravenscroft, who coined the phrase at the Ayer Barker agency, commented in 1981 that he was surprised that no one had remarked on the detumescent promise inherent in this otherwise successful slogan.

Harrods For Everything
See EVERYTHING LONDON

Hasn't Scratched Yet!
Bon Ami cleansing powder; US, from c.1890; still current 1941.

Have A Banana
Unofficial slogan for bananas; UK, 1900s. Britain became 'banana-conscious' in the early years of the twentieth century following the appointment of Roger Ackerley as chief salesman of Elders & Fyffes, banana importers, in 1898. The phrase 'Have A Banana', never a slogan as such, was popularly interpolated at the end of the first line of the song 'Let's All Go Down The Strand', published in 1904. It had not been put there by the composer but was so successful that later printings of the song always included it. Every time it was sung the phrase reinforced the sales campaign, free of charge.

Other banana songs followed. In 1922, a further Elders & Fyffes campaign benefited from the song 'Yes, We Have No Bananas' – supposedly a remark the composer claimed to have heard from the lips of a Greek fruit-seller and which *Punch* described as 'the latest catchword' on 1 August 1923. Fyffes cooperated with the music publishers and distributed 10,000 hands of bananas to music-sellers with the inscription **Yes! We Have No Bananas! On Sale Here.**

The title of the next song, 'I've Never Seen A Straight Banana' –

like the line 'I had a banana/With Lady Diana' from the earlier 'Burlington Bertie from Bow' underlined the sexual suggestiveness of the product, which no doubt explains some of its popular appeal or at least the humour surrounding it.

Have A Break, Have A Kit-Kat
Rowntree's Kit-Kat; UK, from c. 1955.

Have A Capstan
See BETTER, OH, BETTER ...

Have A Coke And A Smile
See DRINK COCA-COLA

Have A Go
Police slogan encouraging public participation in the fight against crime; UK, 1964. Sir Ranulph Bacon, then Assistant Commissioner at Scotland Yard, caused a storm of protest when he urged members of the public to 'have a go' if, say, they saw an armed robbery taking place. His advice was labelled 'madness' and 'suicidal' by the British Safety Council. The phrase was presumably inspired by the title of a long-running BBC radio quiz, *Have A Go* (1946–67), though this had, in turn, taken its name from an old phrase known by the early nineteenth century.

Have You Ever Wished You Were Better Informed?
See TOP PEOPLE TAKE ...

Hayes, Hard Money And Hard Times
Presidential election slogan; US, 1876. This was a Democratic challenge to the Republican candidate Rutherford B. Hayes, who won after a disputed election.

Headache?
See NOTHING ACTS FASTER THAN ANADIN

He Ain't Heavy ... He's My Brother
Community Chest campaign ('35 appeals in 1'); US, 1936. Possible first use (by Jack Cornelius of the BBD&O agency), though it is

hard to tell what relationship this has, if any, with the similar line used to promote the Nebraska orphanage and poor boys' home known as 'Boys Town'. In the early 1920s, so the story goes, the Rev. Edward J. Flanagan – Spencer Tracy played him in the film *Boys Town* (1938) – admitted to this home a boy named Howard Loomis who could not walk without the aid of crutches. The larger boys often took turns carrying him about on their backs. One day, Father Flanagan is said to have seen a boy carrying Loomis and asked whether this wasn't a heavy load. The reply: 'He ain't heavy, Father ... he's m'brother.' In 1943, a 'two brothers' logo (similar to, though not the same as, the drawing used in the Community Chest campaign) was copyrighted for Boys Town's exclusive use. Today, the logo and the motto (in the 'Father/m'brother' form) are registered service marks of Father Flanagan's Boys' Home (Boys Town).

It seems likely that the saying probably predates both the above uses, though whether it goes back to Abraham Lincoln is anybody's guess. King George VI concluded his 1942 Christmas radio broadcast by reflecting on the European allies and the benefits of mutual cooperation, saying: 'A *former President of the United States of America* used to tell of a boy who was carrying an even smaller child up a hill. Asked whether the heavy burden was not too much for him, the boy answered: "It's not a burden, it's my brother!" So let us welcome the future in a spirit of brotherhood, and thus make a world in which, please God, all may dwell together in justice and peace.'

Benham's Book of Quotations (1948) suggests that the American President must have been Lincoln – though it has not been possible to trace a source for the story. In fact, the King's allusion could just have been a dignification of an advertising slogan and a charity's motto.

More recent applications have included the song with the title, written by Bob Russell and Bobby Scott, and popularized by The Hollies in 1969. Perhaps the brief Lennon and McCartney song 'Carry that Weight' (September 1969) alludes similarly – 'Boy – you're gonna carry that weight,/Carry that weight a long time'?

Hearts And Minds
Semi-official government slogan; US, during the Vietnam War

(c.1959–73). The war produced almost no patriotic American slogans – probably reflecting the mixed support for an unpopular and ultimately unsuccessful operation. 'Hearts And Minds', meaning what had to be won, was a slogan of sorts for the US government. John Pilger, writing on 23 August 1967, reported: 'When Sergeant Melvin Murrell and his company of United States Marines drop by helicopter into the village of Tuylon, west of Danang, with orders to sell "the basic liberties as outlined on page 233 of the Pacification Programme Handbook" and at the same time win the hearts and minds of the people (see same handbook, page 86 under WHAM) they see no one: not a child or a chicken' – quoted in *The Faber Book of Reportage* (1987).

The phrase's origins go back to Theodore Roosevelt's day when Douglas MacArthur, as a young aide, asked him in 1906 to what he attributed his popularity. The President replied: 'To put into words what is in their hearts and minds but not in their mouths.' (Safire)

Safire also points out that, in 1954, Earl Warren ruled in the case of Brown v. Board of Education of Topeka: 'To separate [Negro children] from others of similar age and qualifications solely because of their race generates a feeling of inferiority as to their status in the community that may affect their hearts and minds in a way unlikely ever to be undone.'

The Blessing in the Holy Communion service of the Prayer Book is: 'The peace of God, which passeth all understanding, keep your *hearts and minds* in the knowledge and love of God, and of his Son Jesus Christ Our Lord.' This is drawn from the Epistle of Paul the Apostle to the Philippians 4: 7.

A ribald Green Beret use of the phrase could be observed during the war above the bar in the den of Charles W. Colson (later indicted over the Watergate cover-up): **If You Got 'Em By The Balls, Their Hearts And Minds Will Follow**.

Heineken Refreshes The Parts Other Beers Cannot Reach

Heineken Lager; UK, from 1975 – still revived from time to time. 'I wrote the slogan,' said Terry Lovelock (1981), 'during December 1974 at 3 a.m. at the Hotel Marmounia in Marrakesh. After eight weeks of incubation with the agency (Collett, Dickenson, Pearce), it was really a brainstorm. No other lines were written. The trip was to refresh the brain. Expensive, but it worked.'

This slogan has always been linked to amusing visuals – the 'droop-snoot' of Concorde raised by an infusion of the brew; a piano tuner's ears sharpened; or a policeman's toes refreshed. There has also been a strong topical element: when Chia-Chia, a panda from the London Zoo, was sent off in 1981 to mate with Ling-Ling in Washington, a full-page press ad merely said 'Good Luck Chia-Chia from Heineken', the slogan being understood.

This kind of claim is allowed under the British Code of Advertising Practice, Section 4.2.3.: 'Obvious untruths or exaggerations, intended to catch the eye or amuse, are permissible provided that they are clearly to be seen as humorous or hyperbolic and are not likely to be understood as making literal claims for the advertised product.'

Much parodied – in graffiti: 'Courage reaches the parts other beers don't bother with'; 'Joe Jordan [Scottish footballer] kicks the parts other beers don't reach'; 'Hook Norton ale reaches the parts Heineken daren't mention'; 'Mavis Brown reaches parts most beers can't reach'; 'Vindaloo purges the parts other curries can't reach'; in political speeches: 'When I think of our much-travelled Foreign Secretary [Lord Carrington] I am reminded of … the peer that reaches those foreign parts other peers cannot reach' (Margaret Thatcher, Conservative Party Conference, 1980).

Compare the American proverb first recorded by Gelett Burgess in *Are You a Bromide?* (1907): 'The Salvation Army reaches a class of people that churches never do.'

Heinz 57 Varieties

Heinz canned foods; US, from 1896. In that year, Henry J. Heinz was travelling through New York City on the overhead railway. He saw a streetcar window advertising 21 styles of shoe. The idea appealed to him and, although he could list about 58 or so Heinz products, he settled on 57 because it sounded right. Heinz commented later: 'I myself did not realise how successful a slogan it was going to be.' Hence, a brand name which is also a slogan. (Source: Marjorie Stiling, *Famous Brand Names, Emblems and Trademarks*, 1980). In housey-housey or bingo, 'all the beans' is now the cry for '57'.

He Is Fresh When Everyone Is Tired

Mayoral re-election slogan; US, 1960s. Used by John Lindsay in his years as Mayor of New York City (1965–73), giving rise to the graffiti emendation: 'He is fresh when everyone is polite.' (Reisner).

He Kept Us Out Of War

Presidential election slogan: US, 1916. Also **Wilson's Wisdom Wins Without War.** Woodrow Wilson's slogans for re-election in 1916 were true at the time (although he had nothing to do with them) though he did take the US into the First World War the following year. 'He kept us out of war!' was said in a speech by Martin H. Glynn, Governor of New York State, when praising Wilson at the Democratic National Convention at St Louis (15 June 1916).

Compare the later jokey poster of Richard Nixon with the slogan **He Kept Our Boys Out Of Northern Ireland** (quoted in Barry Day, *'It Depends On How You Look At It ...'*, 1978).

Hell, No, We Won't Go

See ABOLISH THE DRAFT

Hello Boys

Wonderbra; UK, 1994. Posters featured the model Eva Herzigova glancing down at her impressive frontage. Other, less well-remembered captions, were 'Look me in the eyes and tell me that you love me' and 'Or are you just pleased to see me?' Also **The One And Only Wonderbra**.

Hello Tosh, Got A Toshiba?

See 'ELLO, TOSH, GOT A TOSHIBA?

Help Barnardo's Help A Child

See EVER-OPEN DOOR

Helps The Plain, Improves The Fair

Pomeroy Face Cream; UK, quoted 1925.

Helps You Break The Laxative Habit

Carter's Little Liver Pills; US, quoted 1958.

Her Cup Runneth Over
Joke corset slogan; US, undated. Suggested by Shirley Polykoff to a corset manufacturer – 'it took an hour to unsell him.' (Polykoff)

Her Honeymoon ...
See OFTEN A BRIDESMAID ...

He's A Big Shot In Steel ...
See HIS HANDS ARE INSURED ...

He's Got It And He's Happy Now
See HE WON'T BE HAPPY ...

He's Making Us Proud Again
Presidential election slogan; US, 1976. Gerald R. Ford needed to, having assumed the presidency in the wake of Watergate. At this election he was rejected in favour of the Democrat who used the catchphrase/slogan **My Name Is Jimmy Carter And I'm Running For President** and **The Grin Will Win**. The 'Man from Plains' also used the loftier cries, **Carter. A Leader, For A Change** and **Why Not The Best?** This last was Carter's official slogan, used as the title of a campaign book and song, which originated with an interview he had had with Admiral Hyman Rickover when applying to join the nuclear submarine programme in 1948. 'Did you do your best [at Naval Academy]?' Rickover asked him. 'No, sir, I didn't *always* do my best,' replied Carter. Rickover stared at him for a moment and then asked: 'Why not?'

He Treated Her Rough – And She Loved It!
Film, *Red Dust*; US, 1932. He was played by Clark Gable and she by Jean Harlow.

He Who Loves Me, Follows Me
Jesus Jeans; various countries, from 1970. In that year, Maglificio Calzificio Torinese, an Italian clothing manufacturer, launched an advertising campaign showing the rear view of a young girl in a tight-fitting pair of the company's new Jesus Jeans, cut very short. The slogan echoed the New Testament, as also did another one, **Thou Shalt Have No Other Jeans Before Me.**

Later, a company spokesman explained in the *International Herald Tribune* (12 January 1982): 'We were not looking for a scandal. It's just that it was the late 1960s and Jesus was emerging increasingly as a sort of cult figure. There was the Jesus generation and *Jesus Christ Superstar*. There was this enormous protest, in Italy and around the world, and Jesus looked to a lot of people like the biggest protester ever ... It's funny, we had no trouble in Mediterranean countries, but the biggest resistance came in the protestant countries, in North America and northern Europe.'

Jesus Jeans were eventually only sold in Italy, Greece and Spain. In Greece, there was a threat of prosecution for 'insulting religion and offending the Christian conscience of the public.' In France, complaints of blasphemy and sacrilege flooded in when the slogan *'Qui m'aime me suive'* was tried out in 1982, similarly located on a girl's behind.

He Who Runs May Read

The Golden Book; UK/US, 1920s. (Turner) An obscure allusion to a difficult biblical source – Habbakuk 2: 2: 'That he may run that readeth it'. The New English Bible translates this as 'ready for a herald to carry it with speed' and provides the alternative 'so that a man may read it easily'. Possibly the most famous use is in John Keble's hymn 'Septuagesima' from *The Christian Year* (1827):

> There is a book, who runs may read,
>   Which heavenly truth imparts,
> And all the lore its scholars need,
>   Pure eyes and Christian hearts.

He Won't Be Happy Till He Gets It

Pears' soap; UK, current 1880s; US, current 1888. Accompanying the picture of a baby stretching out of his bath to pick up a cake of Pears' soap (see p. 10). 'Cartoonists freely adapted this poster, converting the baby into the Czar or the Kaiser, and the cake of soap into the disputed territory of the day.' (Turner) There was also a companion picture with the slogan **He's Got It And He's Happy Now**. In early editions of *Scouting for Boys*, Robert Baden-Powell used the original slogan (with acknowledgement to Pears) to refer to the achievement of the scouts' first-class badge.

Hey, Hey, LBJ, How Many Kids Did You Kill Today?
Protesters' anti-Vietnam War slogan; US, c.1966. Richard Nixon
commented in his *Memoirs* (1978): 'The hatefulness of the attacks
on [President] Johnson's Vietnam policy was symbolized by that
awful mindless chant shouted by anti-war demonstrators ... First
it frustrated him, then it disillusioned him, and finally it
destroyed him.'

Nixon also puts in his *Memoirs* that on the day of his own inau-
guration as President in January 1969, he could hear the chant:
Ho, Ho, Ho Chi Minh/The NLF Is Going To Win. Ho Chi Minh
was President of North Vietnam.

High Speed Gas
The Gas Council; UK, 1960s. Term coined by William Camp, the
Council's PRO (according to Alexander & Watkins, *The Making of
the Prime Minister 1970*, 1970). Camp later went on to do PR work
in government.

**His Hands Are Insured For Thousands, But He Suffers From
Athlete's Foot**
Insurance company (name unknown); US, current 1934. Also **He's
A Big Shot In Steel, But He's A Dental Cripple**.

His Master's Voice
Brand name and trade mark with the strength of a slogan; UK and
everywhere, from 1899. In that year, the English painter Francis
Barraud approached the Gramophone Company in London to
borrow one of their machines so that he could paint his dog,
Nipper, listening to it. Nipper was accustomed, in fact, to a
phonograph but his master thought that the larger horn of the
gramophone would make a better picture. Subsequently, the
Gramophone Company bought the painting and adapted it as a
trade mark. In 1901, the Victor Talking Machine Company (slogan
Loud Enough For Dancing) acquired the American rights. The
company later became RCA Victor and took Nipper with them.
Eventually, Britain's EMI owned the trademark in most countries,
RCA owned it in North and South America, and JVC owned it in
Japan. It was used until 1991.

Occasionally the phrase is used to describe 'the voice of authority' or the practice of only carrying out what one is instructed to do – or of not revealing one's own thoughts, only those of one's superiors. From M.A. von Arnim, *Enchanted April* (1922): ' "Francesca!" shouted Briggs. She came running ... "Her Master's Voice," remarked Mr Wilkins.'

Ho, Ho, Ho Chi Minh ...
See HEY, HEY, LBJ ...

Hold It Up To The Light, Not A Stain And Shining Bright
Surf washing powder; UK, current late 1950s – a line from the 'Mrs Bradshaw' series of TV ads in which the eponymous lady never appeared but her male lodger did. From the BBC radio *Goon Show* of the same period: 'The BBC – hold it up to the light – not a brain in sight!'

Home, A Home, A Home!, (A)
If a slogan promotes a cause, then mottoes and war-cries can on occasion fulfil the same purpose. The word slogan or 'slug-horn' derives from the Gaelic *sluagh-ghairm*, meaning 'host-cry' or 'army-shout'. The Scottish Home family's famous cry not only identified them but spurred the soldiers on to action, despite the legend that on hearing it at the Battle of Flodden Field in 1513 they turned tail and headed for home.

Home Of Good Health
Wander Foods; UK, current 1982.

Home Rule (For Ever)
Political slogan; Ireland, from 1870 onwards. The phrase 'Home Rule' is said to have been coined by a Professor Galbraith, although it had been used incidentally in 1860. It was preferred to the official term of 'Home Government'. The Home Rule movement led by SINN FEIN wished to see the whole of Ireland become independent of British rule. The political battles which raged into the twentieth century ultimately led to the founding of the Irish Free State which eventually became the Republic of Ireland – but with Northern Ireland remaining part of the United Kingdom.

Hoover And Happiness, Or Smith And Soup Houses
Presidential election slogan; US, 1928. Herbert Hoover easily defeated the Democrat Alfred E. Smith in the prosperous calm before the economic storm. **Two Chickens For Every Pot** is said, erroneously, to have been used by Hoover in the campaign. The suggestion appears to have arisen because Smith mocked a Republican flysheet headed **A Chicken in Every Pot** – using the phrase coined by King Henry IV of France (1553–1610) who said: 'I wish that there would not be a peasant so poor in all my realm who would not have a chicken in his pot every Sunday.'

Hop Squash
See GUINNESS IS GOOD FOR YOU

Horlicks Guards Against Night Starvation
Horlicks (milk drink); UK, from 1930. The J. Walter Thompson agency evolved the concept of 'night starvation' (to add to the worries of the twentieth century – nobody had been aware of it before): 'Right through the night you've been burning up reserves of energy without food to replace it. Breathing alone takes twenty thousand muscular efforts every night.' Partridge/*Slang* records that the phrase became a popular term for sexual deprivation.

Before this, there had been the memorable picture ad of a man turning out his suitcase with the phrase **I Know I Packed It**. During the 1950s, JWT ran comic-strip sagas of the refreshing qualities of Horlicks for tired housewives, run-down executives, etc., which customarily ended with the slogan: **Thinks ... Thanks To Horlicks** or, simply, 'Thanks to Horlicks' in a speech bubble. This was not an original formula. 'Thinks. Thanks to *Radio Times*' had been used during the 1930s.

Hot Chocolate, Drinking Chocolate – The Late, Late Drink
Cadbury's Drinking Chocolate; UK, current 1960s.

Household Name, At Work (A)
Corporate slogan for Scott Paper; US, current 1980.

Howard Makes Clothes For Men Who Make Love/Babies
Howard menswear; US, undated. (Baker) It takes a dirty mind to

know one, but sex sells – or at least that is the conventional wisdom. No amount of protest from the women's movement can prevent some leggy model being stuck on the front of a combine harvester to advertise her charms, if not those of the product. Verbally, too, sex is thrown in to nudge you along – sometimes with quite shameless audacity.

How Do You Feel? I Feel Like A Toohey's
Toohey's beer; Australia, current 1980.

How Do You Spell Soap? Why P-E-A-R-S, Of Course
See GOOD MORNING ...

How'd You Like To Tussle ...
See MEAN! MOODY! ...

How To Win Friends And Influence People
Self-improvement courses; US, from c.1909. Dale Carnegie's courses incorporating the principle had been aimed at business people for a quarter of a century when, in 1936, an ad campaign launched the best-selling book on self-improvement. As a result, a million copies were sold between December 1936 and November 1939.

Human Hairpin, The
Bill-matter of the music-hall entertainer Carlton; UK, probably 1920s/30s. It clearly indicates that his was a contortionist's act.

I Am As Strong As A Bull Moose
Presidential election slogan; US, 1912. After two terms as President, Theodore Roosevelt had withdrawn from Republican politics but then, in 1912, unsuccessfully tried to make a comeback as a Progressive ('Bull Moose') candidate. The popular name stemmed from a remark Roosevelt had made when he was standing as Vice-President in 1900. Writing to Mark Hanna, he said, 'I am strong as a bull moose and you can use me to the limit.'

'I am not an animal! I am a human being! I ... am ... a man!'
Film, *The Elephant Man*; US, 1980. *Graffiti 3* (1981) contained a copy of this poster with the scribbled addition: ' ... I am Ronald Reagan!' The UK version of this promotion also used the P-word in another line: 'An incredible but true story ... *probably* this year's best film.' (Compare PROBABLY ...)

I Bet He Drinks Carling Black Label
Carling Black Label; UK, by 1990. This line was chiefly notable when uttered (in TV ads) about someone who had just accomplished some daring but frivolous exploit.

I Can Be Very Friendly
Sun Oil; US, from 1973. Jane Maas commented (1981): 'The chairman and founder of Wells, Rich, Greene, Mary Lawrence, is responsible for the line "I Can Be Very Friendly". During the gasoline crisis, when everyone (customers and dealers) were grouchy about no supplies and long waiting lines, this campaign showed the Sun Oil dealers declaring their intent to win customers over with extra care, concern and good will. It was summed up in the slogan which not only changed the image of Sun Oil in customers' eyes, but also motivated the Sun dealers to be, indeed, very friendly.'

I Can't Believe I Ate The Whole Thing
Alka-Seltzer (stomach powder); US, from 1972. Howie Cohen and Bob Pasqualine of Wells, Rich, Greene created two notable lines on the 'morning after' theme for Alka-Seltzer. 'I Can't Believe …' featured in a memorable TV ad delineating the agonies of over indulgence, as did **Try It, You'll Like It**. Jayne Maas commented (1981): 'Both these phrases entered the language, especially the latter, which was used by every comic, every mother, and certainly every waiter in the US for the entire year of the campaign [1971].'

Another Alka-Seltzer campaign **Plop, Plop, Fizz, Fizz** was created by Paul Margulies and Bob Wilvers. Jayne Maas explained: 'It described the incredible relief created by Alka-Seltzer, beginning with the wonderful sound of those two pills dropping into water, followed by the action.'

Ideas To Build On
Corporate slogan for Johns-Manville; US, current 1980.

Idle Gossip Sinks Ships
See WALLS HAVE EARS

I'd Like To Buy The World A Coke
See DRINK COCA-COLA

I'd Love A Babycham
Babycham (sparkling drink); UK, by 1955.

I'd Love A Beer
Generic slogan; New Zealand, current 1981. The aim of the campaign was to woo people away from wine-drinking.

I Dreamed I — In My Maidenform Bra
Maidenform brassières; US and elsewhere, from 1949 to c.1983. A classic ad from the days when bras were not for burning but for dreaming about – if, that is, women had ever fantasized about being out in their underwear. Evidently many had and the series, devised by the Norman Craig & Kummel agency, ran for twenty years. Maidenform offered prizes up to $10,000 for dream situations they could utilize in the advertising, in addition to: 'I

117

Dreamed I Took The Bull By The Horns/Went Walking/Stopped The Traffic/Went To Blazes/Was A Social Butterfly/Rode In A Gondola/Was Cleopatra ... In My Maidenform Bra.'

I'd Walk A Mile For A Camel

Camel cigarettes; US, current early 1900s. Discontinued in 1944. According to Watkins: 'A sign painter was painting a billboard one day and a man walked up and asked him if he could give him a cigarette. The painter said "yes" and offered him a Camel. The stranger thanked him with enthusiasm, and said "I'd walk a mile for a camel." The sign painter was smart enough to report the incident as a suggestion for a billboard and from this incident grew one of the best and most familiar slogans in advertising.'

In a very early Cole Porter song, 'It Pays to Advertise' (c.1912) is the allusion: 'I'd walk a mile for that schoolgirl complexion'. Then, '"I'd walk a mile for a Camel," murmured the hungry lion, as he watched a caravan crossing the Sahara' – is a Wellerism from California in *The Pelican*, Vol. 31, No. 1 (1925).

Also: **Camel – Where A Man Belongs**; US, current 1980.

If Clark Gable Offered You A Cigarette, It Would Be A De Reszke

De Reszke cigarettes; UK, 1940s. One of a series in which various movie stars were mentioned. Noël Coward is said to have remarked of the somewhat tight-fisted journalist Godfrey Winn: 'If Godfrey Winn offered you a cigarette ... it would be a bloody miracle!'

If It Isn't An Eastman ...

See YOU PRESS THE BUTTON ...

If It's Borden's, It's *Got* To Be Good

Borden's dairy products; US, current 1940s. Used in ads featuring 'Elsie the Cow.'

If It's Going On, It's Going In

Sunday Mail newspaper; Scotland, 1983. Ken Bruce commented (1985): 'Because the Scottish *Sunday Mail* was just about the only Sunday newspaper that was not imported from England, the Mirror Group's advertising agents came up with a slogan which, they felt, demonstrated the *Mail*'s ability to carry all the very latest news on its pages. The slogan was "If it's going on, it's going in".' This served well for some months, but was quietly withdrawn when it was discovered that some local wits had been going round public houses applying the promotional stickers to contraceptive vending machines … '

If It's Laughter You're After, Trinder's The Name
Bill-matter/slogan of the British comedian Tommy Trinder (1909–89); UK, 1930s. As an up-and-coming comedian, Trinder bought space on hoardings all over London to proclaim it. In 1939 he was also using the line 'Loads of Nonsense'.

If It Were A Lady …
See DESIGNED BY COMPUTER …

If There Were An 11th Commandment, They Would Have Broken That, Too
Film, *The Postman Always Rings Twice*; US, 1981 re-make.

If This One Doesn't Scare You, You're Already Dead
Film, *Phantasm*; US, 1979. The promotion of films takes slogan writing into realms of hyperbole seldom encountered in the marketing of political creeds or even consumer goods. The art of the come-on is at its peak in the tags applied to horror movies.

If Voting Changed Anything They'd Make It Illegal
Anarchist slogan; UK, by 1981. Has been dubiously ascribed to Tony Benn, the British Labour politician, but whatever else he may be, he is neither anti-democratic nor cynical. Fred Metcalf in *The Penguin Dictionary of Modern Humorous Quotations* (1987) merely places the slogan as on a 'badge, London, 1983'. In Rennie Ellis's *Australian Graffiti Revisited* (1979), there is a photograph of a wall slogan in Carlton, Victoria: 'IF VOTING COULD CHANGE THINGS, IT WOULD BE ILLEGAL.' This may well predate the original publication of the book in 1975.

If You Ain't Eatin' Wham, You Ain't Eatin' Ham
Fictional slogan; US, 1948. In the film *Mr Blandings Builds His Dream*

119

House, Cary Grant portrays an advertising man in search of a slogan which eludes him until his cook utters these immortal words.

If You Can Read This – Thank A Teacher
Bumper-sticker slogan; US, current 1981.

If You Can't Sleep At Night, It Isn't The Coffee – It's The Bunk
Fictional slogan; US, 1948. In the Preston Sturges film *Christmas in July*, Dick Powell quotes his winning coffee jingle.

If You Got 'Em By The Balls ...
See HEARTS AND MINDS

If You Keep Late Hours For Society's Sake, Bromo-Seltzer Will Cure That Headache
Bromo-Seltzer; US, by 1895. 'An early rhyming slogan, with snob appeal.' (Flexner, 1982)

If You See Sid, Tell Him
See TELL SID

If You Want A Nigger For A Neighbour – Vote Labour
Conservative general election slogan (one constituency only); UK, 1964. The Smethwick seat was won from Labour by Peter Griffiths, later described by the incoming Prime Minister, Harold Wilson, as 'a member who, until another election returns him to oblivion, will serve his time here as a parliamentary leper'.

If You Want To Get Ahead, Get A Hat
The Hat Council; UK, quoted 1965.

Ignorance Is Strength
See FREEDOM IS SLAVERY

I Hear They Want More
See ALAS! MY POOR BROTHER

'I' In Nixon Stands For Integrity, The
See NIXON'S THE ONE

I Know I Packed It
See HORLICKS GUARDS AGAINST ...

I Liked The Shaver So Much I Bought The Company
Remington electric razors; UK, current in 1985. The American businessman Victor Kiam (b. 1926) appeared in TV advertisements for the product and made much of this statement.

I Like Ike
Republican presidential slogan; US, 1952. In fact, this slogan had begun appearing on buttons as early as 1947 when the Second World War general, Dwight David Eisenhower, began to be spoken of as a possible presidential nominee (initially as a Democrat). By 1950 Irving Berlin was including one of his least notable songs, 'They Like Ike', in *Call Me Madam* and 15,000 people at a rally in Madison Square Gardens were urging Eisenhower to return from his military sojourn in Paris and run as a Republican in 1952, with the chant 'We Like Ike'. It worked. The three sharp monosyllables and the effectiveness of the repeated 'i' sound in 'I Like Ike' made it an enduring slogan throughout the fifties. Eventually, a sign observed during the 1960 Kennedy campaign, after Eisenhower retired, said 'We Like Ike But We Back Jack.'

K1C2 or **Korea, Communism And Corruption** was a harder-hitting slogan of the 1952 campaign, representing the three charges against the incumbent Democrats – that they were unable to end the war, were soft on Communism, and had created a mess in Washington. **I Shall Go To Korea** was an Eisenhower promise made in a campaign speech. **Had Enough?** pointed up the Republicans' long absence from power (although it had already been aimed at President Truman during the 1946 mid-term elections when things were going badly for him).

You Never Had It So Good was a Democratic slogan which failed to deliver for Adlai Stevenson. As early as 1946, *American Speech* (Vol. 21) was commenting on this phrase: 'A sardonic response to complaints about the Army; it is probably supposed to represent the attitude of a peculiarly offensive type of officer.' Stevenson also had **Madly For Adlai** – an unofficial slogan (on button). (Safire)

I'll Tell The World They Satisfy
See BLOW SOME MY WAY

I Love New York (especially in the form **I 💙 New York**)
New York State Department of Commerce; US, from 1977. Created
by Charlie Moss of the Wells, Rich, Greene agency – though
maybe he had heard the song 'How About You?' (lyrics by Ralph
Freed, music by Burton Lane) which includes the line 'I like New
York in June' and was written for the Garland/Rooney film *Babes
on Broadway* (1941). Earlier, Cole Porter had written 'I Happen to
Like New York' for his show *The New Yorkers* (1930).

The campaign began in June 1977 with a commercial which
showed various people enjoying themselves in outdoor activities
– fishing, horseback riding, camping, and so forth. Each one said
something like: 'I'm from New Hampshire, but I love New York,'
'I'm from Cape Cod, but I love New York,' and ended with a
funny little man, shown in a camping scene, saying: 'I'm from
Brooklyn, but I looooove New York.' Since when it has become
one of the best known advertising slogans in the world.

Jane Maas, who supervised the campaign from its inception,
pointed out (1981): 'In New York State, 91 per cent of the people
are aware of the phrase – that's more people than know
Christopher Columbus discovered America. "ILNY" is on T-shirts
in literally every country of the world. We hear that the "ILNY"
bumper sticker was seen on the Great Wall of China. The Japanese
version of our song is the number two on their Hit Parade.'

As familiar in its abbreviated form with 'love' replaced by a
heart-shape, 'I Love New York' has been widely copied. There is
'I Love Osaka', 'J'aime Paris', and almost every other place in the
world. The 'I Love —' formula on stickers and T-shirts has also
been used to promote hundreds of products, ranging from hotels
to hot dogs.

Ils Ne Passeront Pas [They shall not pass]
General military/political slogan. First said to have been uttered
(26 February 1916) by Marshal Pétain, the man who defended
Verdun with great tenacity. The official record appears in General
Nivelle's Order of the Day (23 June 1916) as: '*Vous ne les laisserez
pas passer!* [You will not let them pass].' Alternatively, Nivelle is

supposed to have said these words to General Castelnau on 23 January 1916. To add further to the mystery, the inscription on the Verdun medal was *'On ne passe pas'*. One suspects that the slogan was coined by Nivelle and used a number of times by him but came to be associated with Pétain, the more famous 'Hero of Verdun'.

Subsequently, as *'No pasarán'*, the phrase was used at the end of a radio speech by Dolores Ibarrurí (La Pasionaria), 18 July 1936, calling on the women of Spain to help defend the Republic: 'Fascism will not pass, the executioners of October will not pass.' It became a Republican watchword in the Spanish Civil War.

I'm As Mad As Hell And I'm Not Taking Any More!

Political slogan; US, 1978. It was adopted by Howard Jarvis, the California social activist (1902–86), when campaigning to have property taxes reduced. As a result, fifty-seven per cent voted to reduce their property taxes. Jarvis entitled a book *I'm Mad as Hell* but duly credited Paddy Chayevsky with the coinage. Chayevsky wrote the film *Network* (1976) in which Peter Finch played a TV pundit-cum-evangelist who exhorted his viewers to get mad: 'I want you to get up right now and go to the window, open it and stick your head out and yell: "I'm as mad as hell, and I'm not going to take this any more!" '

Jarvis added: 'For me, the words "I'm mad as hell" are more than a national saying, more than the title of this book; they express exactly how I feel and exactly how I felt about the ... countless other victims of exorbitant taxes.'

I'm Backing Britain

Political slogan; UK, 1968. The most curious revival of the BUY BRITISH theme was in January 1968 when, in the wake of the Labour Government's decision to devalue the pound sterling, all kinds of peculiar reactions were observed. In particular, Valerie, Brenda, Joan, Carol and Christine – typists at the Colt Heating and Ventilation offices at Surbiton – responded to a Christmas message from their boss to make some special work-effort. From 1 January they declared they would work half an hour extra each day for no extra pay. Was this spontaneous, or were they pushed? Whatever the case, the media leapt in. The slogan 'I'm Backing

Britain' appeared from somewhere and Prime Minister Harold Wilson added, 'What we want is "Back Britain", not back-biting.' The Industrial Society launched an official campaign on 24 January. Bruce Forsyth recorded a song 'I'm Backing Britain'. Two million badges and stickers were manufactured. A press ad listed 'three things retired folk could do' to help the economy or 'seven things a manufacturer could do'. People actually started sending money to the Chancellor of the Exchequer. It was as barmy as that. Then things turned sour. 'Back Britain' T-shirts were found to have been made in Portugal. Trade unions objected to the idea of anyone working extra hours for no more pay. A rival 'Help Britain' group led by Robert Maxwell MP conflicted with the Industrial Society's effort. The whole thing had fizzled out by August.

I'm Convinced The Goodyear Grand Prix-S Is A Major Contribution To Road Safety

Goodyear Grand Prix-S tyres; UK, 1978. A line oddly memorable because of the fact that it was intoned in TV ads over a period of about three years by Sir Robert Mark. He had retired as Commissioner of the Metropolitan Police in 1977. In those days it was still mildly surprising to see a public figure lend himself to a product endorsement of this type.

I'm —. Fly Me

National Airlines; US, current 1971. The campaign – air hostesses' names were inserted in the slogan – and also using **I'm Going To Fly You Like You've Never Been Flown Before**, aroused the ire of feminist groups. 'I'm Mandy, Fly Me' was the title of a song recorded by the group 10 C.C. (1976) and the British airline chief Freddie Laker was the subject of a book entitled *Fly Me, I'm Freddie!* by Roger Eglin and Berry Ritchie in 1981. Later, in the UK, Wall's Sausages sent up the slogan with **I'm Meaty, Fry Me** (1976).

Immediate Freedom For The Philippines
See FULL DINNER PAIL

I'm Only Here For The Beer
See DOUBLE DIAMOND WORKS WONDERS

Impeach Nixon
Unoffical political slogan; US, 1974. Reflecting the pressure on President Nixon to resign in the light of the Watergate scandal and cover-up.

I Must Have Left It Behind
See INNER CLEANLINESS

Independent. **It Is. Are You?,** (*The*)
The Independent newspaper; UK, 1986 – at its launch. Credited to Tim Mellors.

I Never Knew It Had So Much In It
See DON'T FORGET THE *TV TIMES*

In God We Trust
See *E PLURIBUS UNUM*

In Hoover We Trusted, Now We Are Busted
Democratic presidential slogan; US, 1932. After the stock-market and financial crash, President Herbert Hoover was roundly defeated by the Democratic challenger Franklin D. Roosevelt.

Inner Cleanliness, (Andrews For)
Andrews Liver Salts (laxative); UK, current from 1950s. 'To complete your inner cleanliness, Andrews cleans the bowels. It sweeps away troublemaking poisons, relieves constipation, and purifies the blood ...' An earlier generation of Andrews ads featured a man searching through his suitcase and saying **I Must Have Left It Behind**.

In Space, No One Can Hear You Scream!
Film, *Alien*; US, 1979.

Instrument Of The Immortals, The
Steinway pianos; US, from 1919. The slogan was coined 'in a flash' by Raymond Rubicam at the N.W. Ayer & Son agency: 'I learned that the piano had been used by practically all the greatest pianists and most of the great composers since Wagner ... without effort,

the phrase formed in my mind ... when the ad was finished I showed it to Jerry Lauck, the account executive, and by that time I was so enthusiastic about the idea that I urged him to persuade Steinway to use the phrase not just for one but for a whole series ... Lauck shared my enthusiasm for the idea, but said that Steinway did not believe in "slogans". I remember saying "all right, don't call it a slogan, call it an advertising phrase." ' (Watkins)

Inter-City Makes The Going Easy, And The Coming Back
British Rail; UK, from 1972 (London and South-East Region) and 1975 (Inter-City).

Internationally Acknowledged To Be The Finest Cigarette In The World
Dunhill cigarettes; UK, quoted 1981.

International Passport To Smoking Pleasure, The
Peter Stuyvesant cigarettes; UK, current 1960s. The preceding in line in cinema ads was: 'In city after city, country after country, more and more people are turning to Peter Stuyvesant ... ' Also **So Much More To Enjoy**.

Intern The Lot
Unofficial anti-alien slogan; UK, 1940. During the early stages of the Second World War. (Calder)

In Your Heart You Know He's Right
See ALL THE WAY WITH LBJ

— Is —
See SEAN CONNERY IS ...

I Shall Go To Korea
See I LIKE IKE

I Shall Return
Military/political slogan; US/The Philippines, 1942. During the Second World War, General Douglas MacArthur was forced by

the Japanese to pull out of the Philippines and left Corregidor on 11 March 1942. On 20 March he made his commitment to return when arriving by train at Adelaide. He had journeyed southwards across Australia and was just about to set off eastwards for Melbourne. So, although he had talked in these terms before leaving the Philippines, his main statement was delivered not there but on Australian soil. At the station, a crowd awaited him and he had scrawled a few words on the back of an envelope: 'The President of the United States ordered me to break through the Japanese lines and proceed from Corregidor to Australia for the purpose, as I understand it, of organizing the American offensive against Japan, a primary object of which is the relief of the Philippines. I came through and I shall return.'

MacArthur had intended his first words to have the most impact – as a way of getting the war in the Pacific a higher priority – but it was his last three words that caught on. The Office of War Information tried to get him to amend them to 'We shall return', foreseeing that there would be objections to a slogan which seemed to imply that he was all-important and that his men mattered little. MacArthur refused. In fact, the phrase had first been suggested to a MacArthur aide in the form 'We shall return' by a Filipino journalist, Carlos Romulo. 'America has let us down and won't be trusted,' Romulo had said. 'But the people still have confidence in MacArthur. If he says he is coming back, he will be believed.' The suggestion was passed to MacArthur who adopted it – but adapted it.

MacArthur later commented: ' "I shall return" seemed a promise of magic to the Filipinos. It lit a flame that became a symbol which focused the nation's indomitable will and at whose shrine it finally attained victory and, once again, found freedom. It was scraped in the sands of the beaches, it was daubed on the walls of the barrios, it was stamped on the mail, it was whispered in the cloisters of the church. It became the battle cry of a great underground swell that no Japanese bayonet could still.'

As William Manchester wrote in *American Caesar* (1978): 'That it had this great an impact is doubtful ... but unquestionably it appealed to an unsophisticated oriental people. Throughout the war American submarines provided Filipino guerillas with cartons of buttons, gum, playing cards, and matchboxes bearing the message.'

On 20 October 1944, MacArthur *did* return. Landing at Leyte, he said to a background of still continuing gunfire: 'People of the Philippines, I have returned ... By the grace of Almighty God, our forces stand again upon Philippine soil.'

Is It True ... Blondes Have More Fun?

Lady Clairol; US, from 1957. Devised by Shirley Polykoff and chosen from ten suggestions, including 'Is it true that blondes are never lonesome?' and 'Is it true blondes marry millionaires?' The phrase 'blondes have more fun' has entered the language and, apparently, has had great persuasive effect. The artist David Hockney once told on TV of how and why he decided to bleach his hair and become the blond bombshell he is today. It was in response to a television advertisement he saw late one evening in New York City. 'Blondes have more fun,' it said. 'You've only one life. Live it as a Blonde!' He immediately jumped up, left the apartment, found an all-night hairdresser and followed the advice of the advertiser.

The TV jingle managed to become a hit in the USSR c.1965. Also: **When Does A Blonde Give In?**

Is She ... Or Isn't She?

See DOES SHE ...

Is Your Journey Really Necessary?

Official anti-travel slogan; UK, 1939. First coined to discourage evacuated Civil Servants from going home for Christmas. 'From 1941, the question was constantly addressed to all civilians, for, after considering a scheme for rationing on the "points" principle, or to ban all travel without a permit over more than fifty miles, the government had finally decided to rely on voluntary appeals, and on making travel uncomfortable by reducing the number of trains.' (Source: Norman Longmate, *How We Lived Then*, 1973).

Is Your Man Getting Enough?

Milk Marketing Board; UK, undated.

Is Your Wife Cold?

National Oil Fuel Institute; US, undated. (Baker)

It Beats As It Sweeps As It Cleans
Hoover carpet sweepers; US, from 1919, still current 1981. Coined by Gerald Page-Wood of the Erwin Wasey agency in Cleveland, Ohio. 'The Hoover' began as an invention of James Murray Spangler in 1908. It was taken up by William H. Hoover whose company, until then, made high-grade leather goods, harnesses and horse collars. Spangler's idea was developed to include the principle of carpet vibration to remove dust. This gave 'Hoovers' their exclusive feature – a gentle beating or tapping of the carpet to loosen dirt and grit embedded in it. An agitator bar performed this function, together with strong suction and revolving brushes – giving the Hoover the 'triple action' enshrined in the slogan.

It Could Be YOU
National Lottery; UK, 1995. In the initial months of the lottery, ads featured a finger coming out of the sky, pointing at lucky winners.

It Crawls! It Creeps! It Eats You Alive! Run – Don't Walk From *The Blob*.
Film; US, 1958.

It Floats
See 99 $^{44}/_{100}$ PER CENT PURE

I Thought St Tropez Was A Spanish Monk Until I Discovered Smirnoff
Smirnoff vodka; UK, from c.1973. The common advertising technique of the 'before' and 'after' type was given memorable form in the series of Smirnoff slogans accompanying escapist visuals from 1970 to 1975. The variations included: **It Was The 8.29 Every Morning ... ; Accountancy Was My Life ... ; I Never Saw Further Than The Boy Next Door ... ; I Was The Mainstay Of The Public**

Library ... ; I'd Set My Sights On A Day Trip To Calais ... ; I Thought The Kama Sutra Was An Indian Restaurant ... Until I Discovered Smirnoff. The original copywriter at the Young & Rubicam agency was John Bacon and the art director David Tree. Tree recalled how they struggled for weeks to get the right idea. One day, after a fruitless session, he was leaving for lunch when he happened to glance at a pin-up adorning the wall of the office he shared with Bacon. 'If we really get stuck,' he said, 'we can always say, "I was a boring housewife in Southgate until ... " ' (Suburban Southgate was where he was living then.) (Kleinman)

There were, of course, objections to the 'leg-opener', inhibition-banishing promise implicit in all this. In 1975 the Advertising Standards Authority tightened up its rules on alcohol ads, laying down that 'advertisements should neither claim nor suggest that any drink can contribute towards sexual success' and that they 'should not contain any encouragement ... to over-indulgence'. The last requirement ruled out the tag-line **The Effect Is Shattering** because it might be taken as an inducement to 'get smashed'.

It Is Better To Have Lived One Day As A Tiger ...
See *MEGLIO VIVERE ...*

It Looks Good, Tastes Good And, By Golly, It Does You Good
Mackeson beer; UK, current 1950s. Memorably spoken in TV ads by the actor, Bernard Miles. The notion of beer being 'good for you' – a key element in Guinness advertising over the years – came to be frowned upon by consumer and advertising watchdogs. As if to avoid any conflict with the massed ranks of such people, Mackeson revived the slogan in 1981 but substituted a row of dots after 'By Golly ... '

It Makes You Feel Like The Man You Are
Buick automobiles; US, 1950s. Quoted in Peter Lewis, *The Fifties* (1978). Earlier: **When Better Automobiles Are Built, Buick Will Build Them**; US, current 1923.

It May Be December Outside, But It's Always August Under Your Armpits
Unidentified deodorant; US, 1940s/50s. Arriving in Los Angeles

after flying on an inaugural flight over the Pole, the Welsh broad-caster Wynford Vaughan-Thomas was – unusually for him – rendered speechless by an American colleague. V-T's description of the Greenland ice-cap apparently made the American broadcaster remember his sponsors who were makers of deodorants. And he came out with this slogan (as related in V-T's *Trust to Talk*, 1980.) However, *News Review* (13 November 1947) reproduced from the *Evening Standard*: 'He [John Snagge] had been against commercial broadcasting ever since he heard a Toscanini radio concert in New York interrupted by the sponsor's slogan "It may be December outside, ladies, but it is always August under your armpits".'

According to Miles Kington in *The Independent* (13 May 1994), when W.H. Auden was Professor of Poetry at Oxford (early 1960s), he said in a lecture: 'Never underestimate advertisers. One of the most impressive lines of poetry I have ever come across was contained in an ad for a deodorant. This was the line: "It's always August underneath your arms ... " '

It *Must* Be Bovril
See ALAS! MY POOR BROTHER

It Never Varies
Dewar's Scotch whisky; UK, from 1922. Variations on the slogan were still current in 1981.

I Told 'Em, Oldham
Oldham car batteries; UK, current late 1950s. Created by Joan Bakewell, then a copywriter. Later she became a successful broad-caster.

It Only Takes One Prick ...
See DON'T DIE OF IGNORANCE

It Pays To Advertise
The sloganeer's slogan. A proverbial saying which almost certain-ly originated in the US. Indeed, H.L. Mencken described it in 1942 as simply an 'American proverb'. *Bartlett's Dictionary of Familiar Quotations* (1980) quotes the following undated anonymous rhyme:

The codfish lays ten thousand eggs,
The homely hen lays one.
The codfish never cackles
To tell you what she's done.
And so we scorn the codfish,
While the humble hen we prize,
Which only goes to show you
That it pays to advertise.

There was a play co-written by Walter Hackett (1876–1944) called *It Pays To Advertise* in 1914, and this was turned into a film in 1931. Back even earlier, Cole Porter entitled one of his earliest songs 'It Pays to Advertise'. The song alluded to a number of advertising lines that were current when he was a student at Yale (c.1912):

I'd walk a mile for that schoolgirl complexion,
Palmolive soap will do it every time.
Oh cream, oh best cigar!
Maxwell Motor Car!
Do you have a baby vacuum in your home?
Gum is good for you,
Try our new shampoo,
Flit will always free your home of flies.
If you travel, travel, travel at all,
You know, it pays to advertise.

> *(included in* The Complete Lyrics of Cole Porter,
> *ed. Robert Kimball, 1983)*

This suggests that the phrase, though not Porter's own and though established – was not too much of cliché by 1912. Ezra Pound wrote in a letter to his father in 1908 about the launch of his poems: 'Sound trumpet. Let rip the drum & swatt the big bassoon. It pays to advertise.'

We are probably looking for an origin in the 1870s to 1890s when advertising took off in America (as in Britain). *Benham's Book of Quotations* (1960) lists an 'American saying c.1870' – 'The man who on his trade relies must either bust or advertise' – and notes 'Sir Thomas Lipton (d. 1931) is said to have derived inspiration and success through seeing this couplet in New York about 1875'.

It Takes Two Hands To ...
See BURGER KING ...

It's A Far, Far Butter Thing ...
Fictional slogan for margarine from the novel *Murder Must Advertise* (1933) by Dorothy L. Sayers. The whole of this novel is set in Pym's, an advertising agency modelled on the firm of S.H. Benson, where Sayers worked in the 1920s and 1930s. The book positively teems with suggested and (mostly) rejected advertising lines – some devised by Lord Peter Wimsey himself, disguised as Death Bredon, a trainee copywriter: **Bigger And Butter Value For Money ; You'd Be Ready To Bet It Was Butter; If You Kept A Cow In The Kitchen You Could Get No Better Bread-Spread Than G.P. Margarine; Don't Say Soap, Say Sopo!; Makes Monday, Fun-Day; Are You A Whiffler? If Not, Why Not?; It Isn't Dear, It's Darling; Everyone Everywhere Always Agrees/On The Flavour And Value Of Twentyman's Teas**.

It's A Lot Less Bovver Than A Hover
Qualcast Concorde lawnmowers; UK, current 1981. This knocking slogan was aimed at Flymo, the Swedish-owned company, whose hover mowers had taken a large slice of Qualcast's traditional market. In 1983, Flymo officially lodged an objection to the slogan with the ITCA which vetted advertising copy. Hoverspeed, the cross-Channel hovercraft company simply adapted the slogan and said **It's Much Less Bovver On A Hover**.

It's A Man's Life (possible continuation: **... In the Regular Army**)
Army recruitment slogan; UK, quoted 1963. Unverified. In a BBC TV *That Was The Week That Was* sketch (1963), a party political broadcast by an army candidate concludes: 'It's a Man's Life in the Bri'ish Government today; I thank you.'

It's Finger Lickin' Good
Kentucky Fried Chicken; US, from 1952. Registered in 1963. Sometimes written 'Fingerlickn'. Several songs/instrumental numbers with the title 'Fingerlic*kin*' Good' appear to have been inspired by this advertising use. In addition, Lonnie Smith had a record album called *Fingerlickin' Good Soul Organ* in 1968. In 1966,

'Finger Lickin' ', on its own, was the title of a (guitar) instrumental by Barbara Clark. But was the word 'fingerlickin' an established Southern US/possibly black/musicians' phrase before being made famous by the slogan? The *OED2* records the word 'finger-licking' in use by 1860. 'Licking good', on its own, was a phrase current by the 1890s, where 'licking' = 'very', when applied to piers, candy, etc.

Also **Real Goodness From Kentucky Fried Chicken** and **Corn And Cluck For A Buck**.

It's For Yoo-Hoo!
British Telecom (telephone system); UK, current c.1985. Obviously derived from the familiar phrase of someone telling another that they are wanted on the phone, 'It's for you'. But, in TV ads, it was pronounced in a distinctive way which no doubt led to it 'catching on'.

According to *The Guardian* (24 October 1985), detectives seeking a man on assault charges – a man known to be a keen Chelsea supporter – put an 'urgent message for Graham Montagu' sign on the electronic scoreboard at Stamford Bridge football ground. Thousands of fans spontaneously sang out, 'Montagu, it's for yoo-hoo!', the man fell for the ruse, and was arrested.

It's Good To Talk
British Telecom (telephone system); UK, 1994–6. In TV ads, featuring the actor Bob Hoskins.

It's Got To Be Gordon's
Gordon's gin; UK, current 1977. Tied to the famous green bottle, an inevitable line.

It's In The Public Eye
Squirt; US, quoted 1958. Well, it would be, from a product called Squirt. (Mayer)

It's Morning Again In America
Republican presidential re-election slogan for Ronald Reagan; US, 1984. Coinage ascribed to Hal Riney (b. 1932) in *Newsweek* Magazine (6 August 1984).

It's Not Fancy, But It's Good
Horn & Hardart (restaurants using vending machines); US, current 1966.

It Speaks For Itself
British Movietone News (cinema newsreel); UK, 1930s. As seen revived in the film *Gandhi* (UK, 1982).

It's Quicker By Rail
British Rail; UK, probably early 1960s. Unverified. Also **It's Quicker By Tube** – London Underground; UK, undated.

It's So Big, You've Gotta Grin To Get It In
Wagon Wheel biscuits; UK, probably 1950s.

It's So Bracing
Travel slogan for Skegness (seaside resort in Lincolnshire), promoted jointly with the London & North Eastern Railway company; UK, current 1909. The slogan is inseparable from the accompanying picture of a jolly fisherman drawn by John Hassall (1868–1948). Actually, Hassall did not visit Skegness until twenty-eight years after he painted the poster. His first visit was when he was made a freeman of the town.

It's Such A Comfort To Take The Bus And Leave The Driving To Us
Greyhound buses; US, 1956. (Ogilvy)

It's That Condor Moment
Condor pipe tobacco; UK, current 1970s.

It's That Little Daily Dose …
See THAT KRUSCHEN FEELING

It's The Real Thing
See DRINK COCA-COLA

It's The Refreshing Thing To Do
See DRINK COCA-COLA

It's The Tobacco That Counts
See PLAYER'S PLEASE

It's Tingling Fresh
Gibbs S.R. toothpaste; UK, current 1955. The phrase 'tingling fresh' was spoken in the first TV commercial ever shown in Britain. Of a tube embedded in a block of ice, it was stated: 'It's fresh as ice, it's Gibbs S.R. toothpaste, the tingling fresh toothpaste that does your gums good, too. The tingle you get when you brush with S.R. is much more than a nice taste. It's a tingle of health. It tells you something very important. That you're doing your gums good and toughening them to resist infection ... '

It's Toasted
Lucky Strike cigarettes; US, current from the late 1920s. Sometimes **They're Toasted** – as indeed are all cigarettes – but Lucky Strike seized the pitch and made a great deal of it. From the same period comes the line **Reach For A Lucky Instead Of A Sweet**. George Washington Hill of the American Tobacco Company was driving through New York City one day when he grabbed his colleague Vincent Riggio and cried, 'I've got it!' He had noticed a stout woman waiting to cross the street, eating a big piece of candy. Alongside, a taxi pulled up in which a 'nice-looking' woman was smoking a cigarette. The contrast precipitated this slogan. Understandably, the confectionery industry was not very pleased but it is said that this campaign created more women smokers than any other promotion. (Watkins)

Also **No Throat Irritation – No Cough; There's Never A Rough Puff In A Lucky; So Round, So Firm, So Fully Packed** (quoted 1958); and the 1940s radio ad catchphrase **LS/MFT** (Lucky Strike Means Finer Tobacco). A graffito collected in *Graffiti 4* (1982) translated the initials as 'Let's Screw, My Finger's Tired'.

It's What It's Not That Makes It What It Is
An all-purpose slogan, probably never used. Quoted by Keith Ravenscroft (1981). However, in 1997 the Guernsey Tourist Board was using it in advertisements in the form: 'It's what it isn't that makes it what it is.'

It's What Your Right Arm's For
Courage Tavern beer; UK, current 1972. Possibly of earlier origin.
Although this line became a popular catchphrase it risks being
applied to rival products, whereas the earlier **Take Courage** (current 1966) clearly did not.

It Takes All Kinds Of Critters To Make Farmer Vincent Fritters!
Film, *Motel Hell*; US, 1980. 'Benign motel owners are famous for
their spiced meat, which is in fact made from their human guests'
– *Halliwell's Film Guide* (1994).

It Takes A Tough Man To Make A Tender Chicken
Perdue Farms chicken; US, current 1976. The ads featured Mr
Perdue himself looking suitably tough.

It Takes Two Hands To Hold A Whopper
Whopper hamburgers; US, quoted 1981.

I've Got That Kruschen Feeling
See THAT KRUSCHEN FEELING

I've Never Tried It ...
See GUINNESS IS GOOD FOR YOU

I Want You For The US Army
See YOUR COUNTRY NEEDS YOU

I Was a Seven Stone Weakling
See YOU TOO CAN HAVE A BODY ...

J & B Rare Can Be Found
J & B Rare Whisky; UK, current 1980. Headline with the force of a slogan accompanying pictures of J & B bottles secreted in mazes, tulip fields, etc.

Jesus Saves
Widely used Christian slogan; UK and elsewhere, mostly twentieth century. ' ... (But) Moses invests' was one of several graffiti or lapel-button type jokes popular in the early 1980s. Known in the US and the UK, this particular example was known by 1979.

Jim Crow [clap, clap] Must Go!
Black activists' street cry; US, 1960s. The pejorative phrase 'Jim Crow' became common in the 1880s but goes back to the 1730s when blacks were first called 'crows'. By 1835 'Jim Crow' or 'Jim Crowism' meant segregation. (Flexner, 1976)

Jimmy Who?
See WHO'S POLK?

Join The Army/Navy And See The World
Forces recruitment slogan; UK (and probably US); current 1920s/1930s. Unverified. In the song 'Join the Navy' from the musical *Hit the Deck* (UK, 1927), there is the line 'Join the Navy and see the world'. In the film *Duck Soup* (US, 1933), Harpo Marx holds up a placard which says, 'Join the Army and See the Navy'. Irving Berlin's song 'We Saw the Sea' from *Follow the Fleet* (US, 1936) goes, 'I joined the Navy to see the world. And what did I see? I saw the sea.' 'I joined the Navy to see the world' is quoted ironically, by a sailor in the film *In Which We Serve* (UK, 1942). Partridge/*Catch Phrases* gives the response 'Join the Army and see the world – the next world!' as c.1948.

Join The Professionals
Regular army recruitment campaign; UK, current 1968. The phrase 'The Professionals' emerged from extensive research which showed that it 'encapsulated all that young men who were in the target range most admired' – Central Office of Information note (1981). Also **This Is The Army** (reminiscent of Irving Berlin's song and show title, *This Is the Army, Mr Jones*, 1942) and **Life In Today's Army** (both current 1963–4).

Join The Tea-Set
Typhoo tea; UK, current 1970s.

Jungle Fresh
Golden Wonder salted peanuts; UK, current late 1970s.

Just Add Milk
Pilsbury cake mixes; US, no date. (Ogilvy) Also used for Ovaltine in the UK – unverified.

Just A Part Of The Austin Reed Service
Austin Reed menswear stores; UK, from 1930. Devised by Donald McCullough, the firm's advertising manager, who subsequently found fame as the question-master in the popular BBC radio series, *The Brains Trust*. It was still in use on behalf of the stores in 1950. Presumably this was based on the catchphrase 'it's all (or just) part of the service!' – the response to an expression of gratitude from a customer or anyone for whom something has been done. Spoken by a tradesman, it suggests that thanks (or further payment) are not necessary as he has 'only been doing his job'.

Just Do It
Nike sportswear, especially running shoes; US, by August 1989. Hardly meaningful (though it has been glossed as 'If a thing's worth doing, it's worth doing well'), but a slogan that 'had become second nature to an entire generation', according to the *International Herald Tribune* (June 1994).

Just Like Mother Used To Make
General-use advertising line; US, since at least 1900. Meaning,

'like home cooking and very acceptable.' This expression seems to have acquired figurative quotation marks around it by the early years of the twentieth century. As such, it is of American origin and was soon used by advertisers as a form of slogan (compare the US song of the Second World War, 'Ma, I Miss Your Apple Pie'). **The Kind Mother Used To Make** was used as a slogan by New England Mincemeat around 1900. As such, it is one of numerous advertising lines playing on assumptions about the goodness of home produce and the good old days (reminding one of the small ad said to have made the pitch: 'Buckwheat cakes like mother used to make $1.25. Like mother thought she made $2.25.) Compare the line: 'The good old days – the home sweet home wine – **The Wine That Grandma Used To Make**' – Mogen David wine; US, undated. (Packard)

Just Say No

Anti-drug abuse campaign; US, from c.1984. Supported by Nancy Reagan when First Lady. From *The Washington Post* (22 February 1985): 'The 8-year-old [Soleil Moon Frye] is honorary national chairperson of the Just Say No Club movement organized by three elementary school youngsters in Oakland to encourage kids to say no to drugs instead of giving in to peer pressure. The program attracted the attention of Mrs Reagan last summer when she visited the participants.'

Just When You Thought It Was Safe To Go Back Into The Water

Film, *Jaws 2*; US, 1978. Following the immensely popular shark menace epic *Jaws* (1975), this was a natural slogan. Much imitated: 'Jaws 3 – just when you thought it was safe to go to the toilet' (graffito; UK, 1979); 'The return of Julian Bream – just when you thought it was safe to go to the lute' (graffito on poster, Amsterdam, 1983).

Kayser Is Marvelous In Bed
Kayser Hosiery; US, undated. (Baker)

Keep Britain Tidy
Anti-litter slogan; UK, from 1952. The simplest of messages and one of the most enduring. Promoted through the Central Office of Information, it first appears in their records as a sticker produced for the Ministry of Housing and Local Government in 1952. However, it was probably coined around 1949. Two years before that, the word 'litterbug' had been coined for use by the New York City Department of Sanitation.

Keep Britain White
Imperial Fascist League: UK, 1952. Still current at the time of the Notting Hill riots in London, 1958. Coinage has been ascribed to Arnold Leese, the League's president.

Keep Cool With Coolidge and **Coolidge Or Chaos**
Presidential re-election slogans for Calvin C. Coolidge; US, 1924. Coolidge had assumed the presidency in 1923 on the death of Warren Harding. He won this 1924 election by a wide margin. Comedian Will Rogers amended the first slogan to: 'Keep Cool With Coolidge – And Do Nothing'. (Safire)

Keep Death Off The Road (Carelessness Kills)
Road safety slogan; UK, by 1946. Sometimes, 'Keep death off the road, learn the Highway Code'. (Sunners) Nobody knows who created this message – the best known of any used in government-sponsored advertising campaigns through the Central Office of Information. It was used in the memorable poster by W. Little, featuring the so-called 'Black Widow', in 1946. George Orwell wrote in *Tribune* (8 November 1946): 'One interesting example of our

unwillingness to face facts and our consequent readiness to make gestures which are known in advance to be useless, is the present campaign to Keep Death off the Roads … We value speed more highly than we value human life. Then why not say so, instead of every few years having one of these hypocritical campaigns (at present it is "Keep Death off the Roads" – a few years back it was "Learn the Kerb Step"), in the full knowledge that while our roads remain as they are, and present speeds are kept up, the slaugher must continue?'

Keep 'Em Flying

Slogan in support of the US Air Force; US, during the Second World War. Accompanying a poster by Harold N. Gilbert.

Keep Going Well …

See GO WELL – GO SHELL

Keeping London's Traffic Moving

Traffic warden recruitment; UK, 1970s. According to Judith Hudson of Ayer Barker Recruitment (in 1981), this slogan was apparently based on a remark, justifying his/her job, made by an actual warden. A joke poster shown in *The Benny Hill Show* (ITV, January 1982) stated: 'Join The Traffic Wardens. Keep Britain Moving.'

Keep It Dark

Security slogan; UK, during the Second World War. The basic expression, meaning 'keep it secret', had been in use by 1681. As a war-time slogan, it appeared in more than one formulation, also in verse:

If you've news of our munitions
    KEEP IT DARK
Ships or planes or troop positions
    KEEP IT DARK
Lives are lost through conversation
Here's a tip for the duration
When you've private information
    KEEP IT DARK.

Shush, Keep It Dark was the title of a variety show running in London during September 1940, which suggests that the slogan must have been in use by that date. Later, the naval version of the BBC radio show *Merry Go Round* (1943–8) featured a character called Commander High-Price (Jon Pertwee) whose catchphrase was, 'Hush, keep it dark!'

None of this had been forgotten by 1983, apparently, when Anthony Beaumont-Dark, a Conservative candidate in the General Election, campaigned successfully for re-election with the slogan, 'Keep it Dark'.

Keep It Under Your Hat/Stetson
See WALLS HAVE EARS

Keep Mum, She's Not So Dumb
See BE LIKE DAD, KEEP MUM

Keep 'Regular' With Ex-Lax
Ex-Lax chocolate laxative; US, current 1934. Also **When Nature Forgets – Remember Ex-Lax**, current 1935.

Keep That Schoolgirl Complexion
Palmolive soap; US, from 1917. Coined by Charles S. Pearce, a Palmolive executive. Beverley Nichols wrote in *The Star-Spangled Manner* (1928) that, in his 'riotous youth', he was comforted through 'numberless orgies' only by the conviction that if he used a certain soap he would retain his schoolboy complexion: 'It did not matter how much I drank or smoked, how many nameless and exquisite sins I enjoyed – they would all be washed out in the morning by that magic soap ... I bought it merely because years ago a bright young American sat down in an office on the other side of the Atlantic and thought of a slogan to sell soap. And he certainly sold it.'

During the Second World War, Palmolive was still plugging the old line on ads in the UK: 'Driving through blitzes won't spoil that schoolgirl complexion'.

Keep The Peace Without Surrender
See LET'S GET AMERICA ...

Kills All Known Germs
See DOMESTOS ...

Kill The Kikes, Koons, And Katholics
Ku Klux Klan slogan; US, from the late nineteenth century. (Safire)
An all-embracing slogan of racial and religious prejudice. 'Kike' is
an offensive, mostly US term, and is thought to be a variant of *kiki*,
a duplication of the common *-ki* ending of the names of many
Jews from Slav countries. Leo Rosten in *The Joys of Yiddish* (1968)
suggests, however, that the word comes from Ellis Island immigration officers who, faced with Jewish immigrants unable to
write their names in the Roman alphabet, instructed them to sign
their names with a cross. Understandably, they chose to put
instead a circle as a means of identification. For the Jews, a circle
(Yiddish, *kikel*) is a symbol of unending life. To the immigration
officers, a person who asked to be allowed to make a *kikel* or a
kikeleh (a little circle) soon became a 'kikee' or simply a 'kike'.

Kinder, Kirche, Küche [Children, church, kitchen]
Nazi slogan; Germany, early 1930s. It was a Nazi doctrine that a
woman's place in the state should be confined to these so-called
womanly occupations. Noted by Dorothy L. Sayers in *Gaudy
Night*, Chap. 22 (1935). In fact, the idea is a good deal older than
this. In the 1890s, it also had a fourth 'K' at the end, for '*Kleider*'
[dress].

Kind Mother Used To Make, The
See JUST LIKE MOTHER ...

King Of Beers
See WHERE THERE'S LIFE ...

King Of The Road
Lucas cycle lamps and batteries; UK, current 1920s. In the song 'A
Transport of Delight' (1957), Flanders and Swann refer to a
London bus as a 'monarch of the road'. Also used as the title of a
song written and performed by Roger Miller (US, 1965), by way of
allusion to hoboes and tramps, who have more usually been

known as 'knights of the road'. In England, 'knight of the road' has also referred to a highwayman since 1665.

Korea, Communism And Corruption
See I LIKE IKE

Kraft durch Freude [Strength through joy]
German Labour Front; Germany, 1933. This Nazi organization provided regimented leisure. Coinage has been credited to its head, Robert Ley (1890–1945).

Labour Isn't Working
See LABOUR IS THE ANSWER

Labour Is The Answer
Labour general election slogan; UK, 1979. Labour lost to the Conservatives under Margaret Thatcher. Susbsequently, a graffito was added: 'If Labour is the answer, it's a bloody silly question'.

The Conservative slogan – **Labour Isn't Working – Britain's Better Off With The Conservatives** – first appeared in 1978 on posters showing a long queue outside an employment office. Created by the Saatchi & Saatchi agency, it was later widely used in the campaign that took Margaret Thatcher to Downing Street. When unemployment continued to rise under the Conservatives, the poster was recalled with irony. See also PUT A WOMAN ON TOP FOR A CHANGE.

Labour's Double Whammy
Conservative general election slogan; UK, 1992. During that year's campaign, the Conservative Party introduced a poster showing a boxer wearing two enormous boxing gloves. One was labelled '1. More tax' and the other '2. Higher prices'. The overall slogan was 'LABOUR'S DOUBLE WHAMMY'. This caused a good deal of puzzlement in Britain, though the concept of the 'double whammy' had been well known in the US since the 1950s. One source suggested that it had come from the Dick Tracy comic strip in which it referred to a death-ray glare emitted by one of the characters. Another stated that cartoonist Al Capp introduced the notion in his 'Li'l Abner' strip – the character Evil-Eye Fleegle boasted a 'double whammy ... which I hopes I never hafta use'. In other words, a double whammy was a powerful blow. Whatever the case, the Conservatives were returned to power.

Land Fit For Heroes, A (sometimes **A Country Fit For Heroes**)
Semi-official political slogan; UK, after the First World War. When
the war was over, Prime Minister David Lloyd George gave rise to
this slogan in a speech at Wolverhampton on 24 November 1918,
the exact words of which were: 'What is our task? To make Britain
a fit country for heroes to live in.' By 1921, with wages falling in
all industries, the sentiment was frequently recalled and mocked.

Land Landon With A Landslide and **Land A Job With Landon**
Presidential election slogans; US, 1936. President Roosevelt's NEW
DEAL policies were challenged in that year by the Republican
Governor, Alfred M. Landon. Telephone operators at the switch-
board of the Landon-supporting *Chicago Tribune* answered calls
with 'Only X more days to **Save The American Way Of Life**.'
(Safire) Democrats encouraged the incumbent to **Carry On,
Roosevelt**. He did.

Landlords Keep Away
See LOUSY BUT LOYAL

Last Of The Red-Hot Mamas, The
Bill-matter for the Russian-born American entertainer Sophie
Tucker (1884–1966). It was taken from the title of a song by Jack
Yellen, introduced by her in 1928.

Legal, Decent, Honest, Truthful
Advertising Standards Authority; UK, current 1981. That 'All
advertisements should be legal, decent, honest and truthful' is one
of the essences of good advertising, according to the British Code
of Advertising Practice. The ASA was founded in 1962 when, originally, the slogan was 'Legal, Clean, Honest, Truthful'. (Pearson)
Legal Decent Honest Truthful was, accordingly, the title of a BBC
Radio 4 comedy series about advertising (mid-1980s).

Lend A Hand On The Land
Volunteer recruitment; UK, during the Second World War. The
government sought volunteers to work in farming 'whatever your
front line job'.

Less Lust From Less Protein

One-man campaign by Stanley Green; UK, from 1969. Mr Green plodded up and down Oxford Street, London, until well into the 1980s, bearing a placard which called for 'less lust from less protein less fish meat bird cheese egg; peas beans, nuts and sitting'. His booklet entitled *Eight Passion Proteins With Care* (10p) had sold more than 30,000 copies by 1980.

Let's Get America Moving Again

Presidential election slogan; US, 1960. John F. Kennedy won with it but his slogan was virtually interchangeable with **Keep The Peace Without Surrender** which was his challenger, Richard M. Nixon's. As **Let's Get This Country Moving Again**, coinage of the Kennedy slogan is ascribed to Walt Rostow in David Halberstam, *The Best and the Brightest* (1972). A common theme of political sloganeering: compare **Get Our Country Moving Again** used by the Irish politician (and head of government), Jack Lynch, and quoted in 1980.

Let's Go With Labour, And We'll Get Things Done

Labour Party general election slogan; UK, 1964. At this election, the Labour Party overcame its earlier inhibitions about bringing in help from the advertising world, as the Conservatives had done for many years. As early as January 1963, Labour's advertising group agreed to use a thumbs-up sign derived from Norman Vaughan, host of the ITV show *Sunday Night at the London Palladium*. (They shrank, however, from incorporating his catchphrases 'swinging' and 'dodgy' in the slogan 'Tories Dodgy – Labour Swinging' for fear that not all the electorate would know what they were on about.) Anthony Howard and Richard West say in *The Making of the Prime Minister* (1965) that 'everybody agreed that the word "Go" was necessary to the slogan. It implied dynamism and action; it was short and pithy.' Suggestions included 'Labour's Got Go', 'Labour Goes Ahead', 'All Systems Go', 'Labour For Go', and 'Labour's On The Go'. Of this last one, Harold Wilson said that it sounded like 'Labour On The Po' and Percy Clark from Labour Party HQ said that it might sound as if the party had diarrhoea. The group finally hit on its successful slogan and 'Let's Go With Labour' was used for the eighteen months prior to the election. David Kingsley, one of the advertising people involved, said (1981) that the phrase was coined by Ros Allen. Labour won the election by a narrow margin.

Let's Make America Great Again
Ronald Reagan slogan during Republican primaries; US, 1980. American presidential elections have given rise to some of the quirkiest political slogans and, increasingly of late, to some of the dullest. This one, for example, has been used more than once and could apply to any candidate, Democratic or Republican, incumbent or challenger.

Let The Gold Dust Twins Do Your Work
Gold Dust Washing Powder; US, current in the 1880s. The Gold Dust Twins, as illustrated on the box, were two black moppets. (Flexner, 1982)

Let The Train Take The Strain
British Rail Awayday fares; UK, 1970. Copywriter: Rod Allen at the Allen Brady and Marsh agency.

Let Us Face The Future
Labour Party general election slogan; UK, 1945. In fact, this was initially a statement of policy by the party's National Executive as it prepared to withdraw from the war-time coalition and fight a general election. It then became the title of the party's manifesto for the May election, which it won. Nowadays, a politician's cliché.

'Let Us Go Forward Together'
Government morale-building slogan; UK, 1940. A direct quotation from Churchill's first speech on becoming Prime Minister (13 May 1940): 'I say, "Come then, let us go forward together with our united strength".' It was used to accompany his picture, in bulldog pose. His collected speeches show that he subsequently repeated the phrase some dozen times. But it was not new to him: 'I can only say to you let us go forward together and put these grave matters to the proof' (conclusion of a speech on Ulster, 14 March 1914); 'Let us go forward together in all parts of the

Empire, in all parts of the Island' (speaking on the war, 27 January 1940).

Accordingly, it became something of a political cliché. It occurs along with other rhetorical clichés during the 'Party Political Speech' (written by Max Schreiner) on the Peter Sellers comedy record album *The Best of Sellers* (1958): 'Let us assume a bold front and go forward together.'

Let Your Fingers Do The Walking
Yellow Pages (classified telephone directories) from American Telephone & Telegraph Co.; US, current 1960s. Used by Yellow Pages in the UK. Also **Want To Reach 8 Out Of 10 Adults? – Walk This Way**. A British graffito, quoted 1981: '8 out of 10 buying executives walk this way', to which was added: 'They should loosen their belts.'

Liberté, Égalité, Fraternité [Liberty, equality, fraternity]
Of earlier origin than the French Revolution, it was adopted by the revolutionary Club des Cordeliers as its offical motto on 30 June 1793. At first, the words '*Ou la mort*' [or death] were added but were dropped from 1795.

Liberty And Property, And No Stamps
Political slogan; British colonies in North America, from 1765. It was taken as the motto of various American newspapers following the Stamp Act of 1765, which was the first direct tax levied upon the American colonies by the British parliament.

Liberty Or Death
The New Yorker Magazine; US, 1920s. This somewhat unlikely (suggested?) motto for a witty goings-on-about-town sort of magazine was apparently chosen by the founding editor Harold Ross in 1925. He was undoubtedly thinking of Patrick Henry's famous speech in the Virginia Convention (23 March 1775) which helped carry the vote for independence: 'I know not what course others may take; but as for me, give me liberty or give me death!' Compare Joseph Addison, *Cato*, Act, Sc. 5 (1713): 'Chains or conquest, liberty or death.' Alexander Woollcott is supposed to have said to Harold Ross: 'I think your slogan "Liberty or Death" is

splendid and whichever one you decide on will be all right with me.'

Life. Be In It
Health campaign; Australia, from 1975. The Department of Youth, Sport and Recreation in the State of Victoria initiated a campaign to get people off their backsides and join in sports. Amid debate as to its worth, the slogan was taken up nationally and the Federal Government declared 2 December as 'Life. Be In It' day. Rejoinders include 'Life. Be Out Of It' and (from Barry Humphries) 'Life. Be Up It'. One of the healthy activities featured in the campaign was tennis. A TV commercial showed 'Norm', a fat armchair sportsman (or couch potato, as he would later have been described), watching national player John Newcombe and cheering him on with the phrase **Bewdy Newk!** ('Beauty, Newcombe!') This phrase caught on with something of the force of a slogan.

Life In Today's Army
See JOIN THE PROFESSIONALS

Life's A Beach
Unofficial slogan; Australia and elsewhere, late 1980s. Promoting the joys of surfing, etc., and punningly based on the expression 'Life's a bitch and then you die!', probably of North American origin and current by the early 1980s. *Campaign* (5 May 1989) quoted the view: 'Coke's image is like the kind of American musical which gets terrible reviews but pulls people in all the same. Life's a beach, basically.' During the summer of 1991, the Body Shop chain in the UK was promoting suntan products with a window display under the punning slogan, 'Life's a beach – and then you fry'.

Life's Better With The Conservatives – Don't Let Labour Ruin It
Conservative Party re-election slogan; UK, 1959. It helped bring the party a further period of office after an election in which many broadcasting and advertising techniques were applied to UK politics for the first time. There was much to justify the claim: material conditions had improved for most people; the balance of payments surplus, gold and dollar reserves were at a high level;

wages were up; and taxation had gone down. The slogan emerged from consultations between Central Office and the Colman, Prentis & Varley agency. In his book *Influencing Voters* (1967), Richard Rose said he knew of four people who claimed to have originated the slogan. Ronald Simms was the PR chief at Central Office from 1957 to 1967. He is said to have come up with 'Life Is Good With The Conservatives, Don't Let The Socialists Spoil It'. Lord Hailsham wanted 'better' instead of 'good' and CPV changed 'spoil' to 'ruin'. On the other hand, Maurice Smelt wrote (1981): 'The slogan was so successful that many people have claimed it (that always happens): but it was just a perfectly routine thing I did one afternoon in 1959, as the copywriter on the Conservative account at CPV. The brief from Oliver Poole was to say something like "You've Never Had It So Good", but with less cynicism and more bite. The first five words were the paraphrase: and the whole ten told what I still think was a truth for its time. It's the slogan I am proudest of.'

Inevitably, it leant itself to parody. When the Conservative minister John Profumo had to resign in 1963 because he had been sharing a call-girl with a Soviet diplomat, *Private Eye* Magazine carried a cartoon of Christine Keeler with the caption, 'Life's better under a Conservative'.

As is shown elsewhere, the phrase **You Never Had It So Good** was used by the Democrats in the 1952 US presidential election. Given the way Harold Macmillan's supposed view 'You've Never Had It So Good' (from a 1958 speech) came to dog him, it would be surprising if it had been used in any official campaign. The phrase was rejected by the Conservatives' publicity group, partly because it 'violated a basic advertising axiom that statements should be positive, not negative', but it hovered about unofficially, and there was an official poster which came very close with **You're Having It Good, Have It Better**.

Like Mother Used To Make
See JUST LIKE MOTHER ...

Like The Act Of Love, This Film Must Be Experienced From Beginning To End!
Film, *The Sailor who Fell from Grace with the Sea*; US, 1976.

Lion In Your Lap, A
Film, *Bwana Devil*; US, 1952. The first 3-D film.

Lipsmackin Thirstquenchin ...
See COME ALIVE ...

Liquid Engineering/Life
See CASTROL ...

Little Dab'll Do Ya, A
Brylcreem (hair cream); US, from 1949.

Loin King, The
Brass Monkeys men's underwear; UK, current 1996. This phrase accompanied the picture of a man in his underpants. When the company tried to convert ads that had run in men's magazines to poster use, it was told by the Committee of Advertising Practice that a 'smaller' model should be used. The caption **Full Metal Packet** was also deemed to be unacceptable.

Long And The Short Of It, The
Bill-matter for the British music-hall and radio entertainers (Ethel) Revnell and (Gracie) West, 1930s/40s: 'The long one's Ethel Revnell/And the short one's Gracie West!'

Long Live Death! Down With Intelligence! *[¡Viva la muerte! ¡Abajo la inteligencia!]*
Falangist Party slogan; Spain, late 1930s. This slogan of the Spanish Civil War has been ascribed to General Millán Astray of a right-wing faction.

Long Live The King. Down With The Landlord
See LOUSY BUT LOYAL

Look At All Three!
Chrysler Plymouth automobiles; US, from 1932. J.V. Tarleton, of J. Stirling Getchell Inc., recalled: 'The one big fact that gave rise to the whole "Look at all three" idea was that Henry Ford, whose plants had been out of production for almost a year while he

tooled up production of the new V-8, was planning to introduce this radically new model in the very same week when Mr Chrysler was planning to announce his new Plymouth ... Getchell and a writer proceeded to bat their brains out for a day or two looking for a unique and different way of announcing a new car – a way that would take advantage of the suspenseful situation created by Mr Ford and get Plymouth through the swinging door on his push ... One of their advertisements showed a large picture of Mr Chrysler in a very informal pose with his foot on the bumper of a new Plymouth. The headline on this ad had originally read "Look at all three low priced cars before you buy." In the process of making the layout, the writer had boiled this down to four big words, "Look At All Three" ... The day when [it] was published in newspapers all over the country, the reaction was unmistakable. Chrysler Corporation dealers reported that their doors started swinging early in the morning and didn't stop until late at night. Plymouth, over night, had become a real contender in the low-priced field.' (Watkins)

Looks Even Better On A Man
Tootal shirts; UK, from 1961. A Twiggy-like girl was featured wearing an oversize man's shirt. The slogan was revived in 1981.

Looks Like Fun, Cleans Like Crazy
Stripe toothpaste; US, quoted 1958. A man who had invented a tube nozzle which coloured the sides of the emerging ribbon of toothpaste was discovered by J. Walter Thompson in New York. Copywriters picked the name 'Stripe' and coined the slogan, then took the package to Lever Brothers, who found themselves with a ready-made product – the reverse of the usual process. (Mayer)

Loose Talk Costs Lives
See WALLS HAVE EARS

Loud Enough For Dancing
See HIS MASTER'S VOICE

Lousy But Loyal
Unofficial London East End slogan at King George V's Silver

Jubilee; UK, 1935. In 'The English People' (1947), George Orwell discussed this and other slogans at the time of the Jubilee (though he has it as **Poor But Loyal**): 'It was even possible to see in it the survival, or recrudescence, of an idea almost as old as history, the idea of the King and the common people being in a sort of alliance against the upper classes ... Other slogans, however, coupled loyalty to the King with hostility to the landlord, such as **Long Live The King. Down With The Landlord**, or more often, **No Landlords Wanted** or **Landlords Keep Away**.'

Love At First Flight
See WE'LL TAKE MORE CARE OF YOU

Loveliest Castle In The World, The
Tourist slogan for Leeds Castle, Kent; UK, by 1995. It is apparently a quotation from Lord Conway (unidentified): 'Wonderful in manifold glories are the great castle visions of Europe; Windsor from the Thames, Warwick or Ludlow from their riversides, Conway or Caernavon from the sea, Amboise from the Loire, Aigues Mortes from the lagoons, Carcassone, Coucy, Falaise and Château Gaillard – beautiful as they are and crowned with praise, are not comparable in beauty with Leeds, beheld among the waters on an autumnal evening when the bracken is golden and there is a faint blue mist among the trees – the loveliest castle, as thus beheld, in the whole world' – quoted in Lord Geoffrey-Lloyd, *Leeds Castle* (1976).

Love Means Never Having To Say You're Sorry
Film, *Love Story*; US, 1970. A line taken from the film – Ryan O'Neal says it to Ray Milland, playing his father-in-law. He is quoting his student wife (Ali MacGraw) who has just died. Segal, who wrote the script, also produced a novelization of the story in which the line appears as the penultimate sentence, in the form 'Love means *not ever* having to say you're sorry'. A graffito (quoted 1974) stated: 'A vasectomy means never having to say you're sorry'; the film *The Abominable Dr Phibes* (UK, 1971) was promoted with the slogan: **Love Means Not Having To Say You're Ugly**.

LS/MFT
See IT'S TOASTED

Lubitsch Touch That Means So Much, The
Promotional line used on posters for films directed by Ernst Lubitsch; US, from c.1925.

Lucozade Aids Recovery
Lucozade (health drink); UK, up to c.1986. The manufacturer, SmithKline Beecham, has stated that the line on bottle labels and poster ads was dropped long before AIDS became a major public health issue and the word 'aids' something of an embarrassment.

Macniven & Cameron's Pens
See THEY COME AS A BOON ...

Made By People Who Like Beer For People Who Like To Drink Beer – And Lots Of It
Blatz beer; US, undated. (Packard)

Made In England and British Made
General appeals to patriotism in purchasing; UK, since the early twentieth century. Such appeals have had a rough ride and met with limited response. Swan Vesta matches were using the slogan **Support Home Industries** as long ago as 1905. There was a campaign dedicated to the idea of buying British goods in preference to others in the wake of the First World War – part of an effort to revive British trade. But, as a commentator wrote in 1925: 'The slogan has never from its birth rung like true metal. There is nothing satisfying about it. It savours of a cry of distress – an S.O.S. – and does not begin to represent the spirit of a commerce that is reconstructing itself and paying its debts simultaneously.'

Somehow, patriotism (which can be appealed to legitimately in time of war) does not mix with commerce. Besides, there is a suspicion of boycott about such phrases. There is also the obstacle of identification – how does the consumer *know* what is British and what is not? How can he make the choice when he does not know what component parts are used in making a product?

All this has not prevented such slogans reappearing whenever things have looked bleak for the economy. **Buy British** was current in 1931 (when it appeared in a *Punch* cartoon) and was revived by BL for the Mini-Metro car in 1980. **British Is Best** has been used at regular chauvinistic intervals. See also I'M BACKING BRITAIN.

Madly For Adlai
See I LIKE IKE

Mail Must Get/Go Through, The
Semi-official slogan for the Pony Express mail service; US, 1860s. Unverified. Whatever the true facts, this is a slogan of probable North American origin – as indicated by use of the word 'mail' rather than 'post'. Though 'Royal Mail' is still very much used in the UK, the older term 'post' predominates. There is no citation of the precise slogan being used in Britain. The Longman *Chronicle of America* reports (as for 13 April 1860) the arrival in Sacramento, California, of the first Pony Express delivery – a satchel with 49 letters and three newspapers that had left St Joseph, Missouri, eleven days previously. 'The pace is an astounding improvement over the eight-week wagon convoys. But the brave riders, who vow "the mail must get through" despite all kinds of dangers ranging from hostile Indians on the prairie to storms in the mountains, may only be a temporary link [as the Iron Horse makes progress].'

The *Chronicle* does not provide a solid basis for invoking the slogan at this point but the connection with Pony Express seems very likely. There does not appear to an actual citation from the period. Raymond and Mary Settle in *The Story of the Pony Express* (1955) point out that the organization flourished only about 1860–1, soon being overtaken by telegraph and railroad, and add: 'A schedule, as exacting as that of a railroad timetable, was set up, and each rider was under rigid orders to keep it, day and night, fair weather or foul. Allowance was made for nothing, not even attack by Indians. Their motto was, "The mail must go through", and it did except in a very few, rare cases.'

Make Britain Great Again
See YOUR FUTURE IS IN YOUR HANDS

Make Do And Mend
Official morale-building slogan; UK, by 1943. A phrase which set the tone for British life during the Second World War and after. It was possibly derived from 'make and mend' which was a Royal Navy term for an afternoon free from work and often devoted to

mending clothes. In due course, there were Make-do-and-Mend departments in some stores. The phrase was designed to encourage thrift and the repairing of old garments, furniture, etc., rather than expenditure of scarce resources on making new.

Make It To Massachussetts
See I LOVE NEW YORK

Make Love, Not War
Informal 'peacenik' and 'flower power' slogan; US and elsewhere, from the mid-1960s. The war was undoubtedly that going on in Vietnam. The slogan was written up (in English) at the University of Nanterre during the French student revolution of May 1968. Coinage is attributed to the fictitious Sixties guru 'Terence Mann' in the film *Field of Dreams* (US, 1989) but has also been ascribed to the sexologist 'G. Legman' of the Kinsey Institute (*The Sunday Times*, 27 January 1991) – could this be the same G. Legman who edited the two volumes of *The Limerick*, 1964/9?

Make Someone Happy With A Phone Call
The Post Office, (afterwards British Telecom); UK, c.1975.

Makes Sensible Buying Simple
See ACCESS TAKES ...

Makes You Drunk
Fictional slogan for 'Bowen's Beer' from Kingsley Amis's novel *I Like It Here* (1958): 'He thought to himself now that if ever he went into the brewing business his posters would have written across the top "Bowen's Beer", and then underneath that in the middle a picture of Mrs Knowles drinking a lot of it and falling about, and then across the bottom in bold or salient lettering the words "Makes You Drunk".'

Makes You Feel Like A Queen
Summer County margarine; UK, current 1960s. Originally used in the US for Imperial Margarine (also a Unilever product). The idea of such elevation is not new. In November 1864, Tolstoy's wife Sonya wrote to him, 'Without you, I am nothing. With you, I feel

like a queen' – though this is from a translation for an American edition of a French biography (1967).

Make-Up To Make Love In
Mary Quant cosmetics; UK, early 1970s. (Nicholl)

Make Your Armpit Your Charm Pit
Stopette spray deodorant: US, current early 1950s. In about 1953, Lady Barnett, the British TV personality, visited the US and came across this ladylike advertising slogan, though she has it as 'Make the armpit the charm pit!' (related in her book *My Life Line*, 1956).

Making Machines Do More, So Men Can Do More
Corporate slogan for Sperry Rand; US, quoted 1976.

Maltesers – Chocolates With ...
See CHOCOLATES WITH ...

Man From Del Monte Says 'Yes', The
Del Monte canned fruit and fresh fruit; UK, from 1985. TV ads showed a representative of Del monte only purchasing the best possible produce from foreign markets. The graffito addition ' ... But ULSTER SAYS NO' was reported from Belfast in 1987.

Man From The Pru, The
Prudential Assurance Co. Ltd; UK, by the late 1940s. The firm was founded in 1848 and the phrase evolved from the name people gave to the person who called to collect their life insurance premiums. It had become a music-hall joke by the end of the century but there was no serious use of the term as a slogan, by the company, until after the Second World War, when it appeared in ads as **Ask The Man From The Pru**.

Man In The Hathaway Shirt, The
C.F. Hathaway shirts; US, from 1950. It was the eye-patch on the male model that made David Ogilvy's campaign famous, but people always refer to 'The Man in the Hathaway shirt' as such and the reason is plain – this was the bold headline to the advertisement. (Watkins)

Man's Cigarette That Women Like Too, A
See COME TO WHERE THE FLAVOR IS ...

Man-Sized Flavor
See COME TO WHERE THE FLAVOR IS ...

Man With The Golden Flute, The
Bill-matter for the Northern Ireland-born flautist, James Galway (b. 1939).

Man With The Golden Trumpet, The
Bill-matter for the British trumpet-player, Eddie Calvert (1922–78).

Man With The Orchid-Lined Voice, The
Bill-matter for the Italian tenor, Enrico Caruso (1873–1921). Said to have been coined by his publicist, Edward L. Bernays.

Man With The Plan, The
Labour Party general election slogan; UK, 1959. Posters carried the line under a picture of the party leader, Hugh Gaitskell, who did not win the election.

Man You Love To Hate, The
Film, *The Heart of Humanity*; US, 1918. Particularly referring to the Hollywood director Erich Von Stroheim (1885–1957) when he appeared as an actor in this First World War propaganda film. He played an obnoxious German officer who not only attempted to violate the leading lady but nonchalantly tossed a baby out of the window. At the film's premiere in Los Angeles, Von Stroheim was hooted and jeered at when he walked on stage. Now a phrase in general use to describe any somehow attractive or alluring villain or hate-figure.

Marine Corps Builds Men
See ARMY BUILDS MEN

Marlboro ...
See COME TO WHERE THE FLAVOR IS ...

Marples Must Go
Informal slogan aiming at the removal of the politician Ernest
Marples; UK, 1962–4. Marples (1907–78) was the hyperactive
Conservative Minister of Transport (1959–64). This slogan first
arose in October 1962 (and was quoted as such in a *Daily Herald*
headline) after he had intervened in the build-up to the publication of the Beeching Report, which recommended sweeping cuts
in rail services. 'Trades union leaders and Labour MPs have started a Marples Must Go campaign,' the *Herald* reported, 'convinced
that Marples must be sacked to save a head-on clash between railway unions and government.' When the report was finally published in March 1963, Marples was judged to have given a poor
defence of it in the House of Commons.

However, it was because of motoring matters that the slogan
was taken up at a more popular level. Marples had already introduced Britain to parking zones, car tests, and panda crossings. He
could claim that London's trafflc was moving 37.5 per cent faster
as a result of his draconian measures but many saw them as an
infringement of individual liberty. In May 1963, Marples introduced 'totting up' for motoring convictions and, shortly afterwards, a 50-miles-per-hour speed limit at peak summer weekends
in an effort to reduce the number of road accidents. It was this last
measure that produced a rash of car stickers bearing this cry. It
appeared daubed on a bridge over the M1 motorway in August.

When Barbara Castle became Labour Transport Minister in 1965
and introduced breath-tests to combat drunken driving, car stickers appeared saying 'Marples Come Back, All Is Forgiven.' A pre-
mier example of the — MUST GO slogan format.

Mars A Day Helps You Work, Rest And Play, (A)
Mars bar (confectionery); UK, from 1959. Dropped in 1995 and
replaced with **Now ... There Is Only One Mars**. Also **Mars Are
Marvellous**.

Martin, Barton And Fish
See WE WANT WILKIE

Martini Is ...
See RIGHT ONE

McKay: The Better Way
Fictional slogan from the political film *The Candidate*; US, 1972. Robert Redford plays a California lawyer who is persuaded to run for senator. When he wins, he has no idea what to do with the prize. This caught only too well the uninspired quality of most modern political slogans.

Mean! Moody! Magnificent!
Film, *The Outlaw*; US, 1943. The most notorious of all film promotional campaigns is the one for this Howard Hughes production which featured Jane Russell. **The Two Great Reasons For Jane Russell's Rise To Stardom** (skilfully supported by the Hughes-designed cantilever bra) were not enough in the various pictures of the skimpily clad new star (one version had her reclining with a long whip). Hughes also attached a smouldering succession of slogans: **Tall ... Terrific ... And Trouble!; Who Wouldn't Fight For A Woman Like This?; The Girl With The Summer-Hot Lips ... And The Winter-Cold Heart; How'd You Like To Tussle With Russell?**

Meet The Challenge, Make The Change
Labour Party Conference slogan; UK, 1989.

Meglio vivere un giorno di leone che cento anni di peccora [It is better to have lived one day as a tiger than a thousand years as a sheep]
Fascist slogan of Benito Mussolini; Italy, c.1930. Quoted in Denis Mack-Smith, *Mussolini's Roman Empire*, 1967). However, when the British climber Alison Hargreaves was killed on K2 in August 1995, her husband, Jim Ballard, quoted it as a 'Tibetan saying'. Another form: from the film *The King of Comedy* (US, 1983): 'Look, I figure it this way: better to be a king for a night than a schmuck for a lifetime.'

Melts In Your Mouth, Not In Your Hand
Treets (confectionery); UK, by 1967. Also adopted for Minstrels, current 1982. This idea would appear to have been borrowed from M & M candies in the US. Reisner reports a graffito c.1969: 'Melts in your mind not in your hand'.

Mennen For Men

The Mennen Company's talcum powder; US, current 1941. An obvious play on words designed to overcome male resistance to using the product. (Lambert)

Menthol Fresh ...

See COOL AS A MOUNTAIN STREAM

Men Who Make Opinion ...

See TOP PEOPLE TAKE THE TIMES

Merrill Lynch Is Bullish About America

Corporate slogan for the Merrill Lynch bank; US, current 1972. Also **A Breed Apart** (current 1980) – though not quite as apart as all that: the phrase has also been used by Triumph motorcycles in the UK. See also AMERICA'S STORYTELLER

Milk From Contented Cows

Carnation milk; US, from 1906. Elbridge A. Stuart was the man who gave rise to Carnation evaporated milk in 1899. Seven years later he went to Chicago to lay on an advertising campaign with the Mahin agency. John Lee Mahin and Stuart, having decided on the main lines of the campaign, called in a new young copywriter called Helen Mar.

'Mr Stuart gave me a description of the conditions under which Carnation was produced,' she recalled many years later. 'In his own sincere and quiet way he spoke of the ever-verdant pastures of Washington and Oregon, where grazed the carefully kept Holstein herds that supplied the raw milk. He described in a manner worthy of Burton Holmes the picturesque background of these pastures from which danced and dashed the pure, sparkling waters to quench the thirst of the herds and render more tender the juicy grasses they fed on. He spoke of the shade of luxuriant trees under which the herds might rest. Remembering my lectures in medical college and recalling that milk produced in mental and physical ease is more readily digested – I involuntarily exclaimed: "Ah! The milk of contented cows" Mr Mahin's pencil tapped on the table top and he and Mr Stuart spoke almost together: "That's our slogan." '

And so it has remained – or almost. The words on the can have usually been: '*From* Contented Cows'. In *The Cocoanuts* (US, 1929), Groucho Marx gets to say: 'There's more than two hundred dollars worth of milk in those cocoanuts – and *what* milk, milk from contented cow-co-nuts.' Later came the unofficial jingle:

> Carnation Milk is the best in the land,
> Here I sit with a can in my hand –
> No tits to pull, no hay to pitch,
> You just punch a hole in the son of a bitch.

(Ogilvy)

Milk's Gotta Lotta Bottle

Milk; UK, 1982. Milk comes in bottles, of course, but why was the word 'bottle' used to denote courage or guts in this major attempt to get rid of milk's wimpish image? Actually, the word 'bottle' has been used in this sense since at least the late 1940s. To 'bottle out' consequently means 'to shrink from', e.g. in *Private Eye* (17 December 1982): 'Cowed by the thought of six-figure legal bills and years in the courts, the Dirty Digger has "bottled out" of a confrontation with Sir Jams.'

One suggestion is that 'bottle' acquired the meaning through rhyming slang: either 'bottle and glass' = 'class' (said to date from the 1920s, this one); 'bottle and glass' = 'arse'; or, 'bottle of beer' = fear. But the reason for the leap from 'class/arse' to 'courage', and from 'fear' to 'guts', is not apparent, though it has been explained that 'arse' is what you would void your bowels through in an alarming situation. And 'class' is what a boxer has. If he loses it, he has 'lost his bottle'.

Other clues? Much earlier, in *Swell's Night Guide* (1846), there had occurred the line: 'She thought it would be no bottle 'cos her rival could go in a buster,' where 'no bottle' = 'no good'. In a 1958 play by Frank Norman, there occurs the line: 'What's the matter, Frank? Your bottle fallen out?' There is also an old-established brewers, Courage Ltd, whose products can, of course, be had in bottles.

The way forward for the 1982 advertising use was probably cleared by the ITV series *Minder* which introduced much south London slang to a more general audience.

Mint With The Hole, The
Life-Savers; US, current 1920. The full phrase is: **The Candy Mint With The Hole**. Also used for Rowntree's Polo mints; UK, from 1947.

Modess ... Because
Modess tampons; US, undated. These were the only words that appeared in advertisements showing portraits of beautiful women. How different from the more clinical approach of the 1980s and 90s. Hence, the suggested joke slogan for another brand: 'Tampax ... insofar as'.

Monarch Of The Dailies
San Francisco Examiner newspaper; US, since 1887. This was the year William Randolph Hearst took over the paper. Still in use a hundred years later.

More Dash Than Cash
General-use advertising – and journalistic – line; UK, from the 1950s. Especially in *Vogue*, for which the slogan appears to have been invented, and about clothing which, while stylish, is cheap or – given *Vogue*'s usual standards – cheaper than the norm. It was still being used over *Vogue* features in the 1990s. The phrase is also used in other contexts: 'The march of Waterstone's bookshops through the 1980s high streets owed more to dash than cash. With their bright staff and "reliable, wide-ranging stock", the stores showed that the marketing flummery of Thatcherism could serve both Mind and Mammon' *The Observer* (4 September 1994). Note, however, the possible demise of the slogan: 'If *Vogue* is a reliable financial sounding board we are in for prosperity and great good sense. In the October issue they have said farewell to the More Dash Than Cash section and welcomed back an old-timer called Great Good Buys' – *The Daily Telegraph* (19 September 1994).

More Stars Than There Are In Heaven
MGM studios; US, from 1929. Coinage ascribed to Howard Dietz in J.R. Colombo, *The Wit and Wisdom of the Movie Makers* (1979). The slogan appears on a poster for *Broadway Melody* (1929), the very first film musical.

More Than One Million Copies Sold
Book, *The Science of Life or Self-Preservation* by Dr W.H. Parker (US, 1882; pub. by the Peabody Medical Institute). 'This slogan, of course, has been used for many other books since then.' (Flexner, 1982)

More With Gore
Congressional election slogan; US, 1960. Used by Gore Vidal during his unsuccessful campaign as Democratic candidate for a New York district. Unhappily, his other slogan 'Vidal So Soon' appears to have been considered and rejected.

Most Talked About Film Of The Decade
See WHAT ONE LOVES ABOUT LIFE ...

Mother Wouldn't Like It
MG motor cars; UK, by April 1972. The phrase seems to have been very much around at the time. In his journals, Stephen Spender reports fellow poet W.H. Auden as saying, 'Naughty! Naughty! Mother wouldn't like it!' to Philip Larkin, also in 1972. The ironic warning, 'Your mother wouldn't like it' was used as the title of a rock music programme on London's Capital Radio, presented by Nicky Horne, from 1973. However, much earlier, Margaret Mitchell wrote in *Gone With the Wind* (1936): 'There, [Scarlett] thought, I've said "nigger" and Mother wouldn't like that at all.'

Motion Picture With Something To Offend Everyone, The
Film *The Loved One*; US, 1965. Based on Evelyn Waugh's novel about the American way of death, this film offended nobody at all – and hardly entertained them either.

Mounties Always Get Their Man, The
Unofficial motto/slogan of the Royal Canadian Mounted Police; Canada, since before 1900. John J. Healy, editor of the Fort Benton (Montana) *Record*, wrote on 13 April 1877 that the Mounties 'Fetch their man every time'. The official motto since 1873 has been 'Maintain the right *[Maintiens le droit]*'.

Mr Kipling Does Make Exceedingly Good Cakes
Mr Kipling Cakes; UK, current from the early 1970s.

Mrs Thatcher Helps Small Businesses (Get Smaller All The Time)
Informal slogan on window-sticker; UK, 1981.

Murraymints ...
See TOO-GOOD-TO-HURRY MINTS

Mussolini a sempre ragione [Mussolini is always right]
Fascist slogan; Italy, 1920s/30s. There is a poem with the title in *Punch* (28 February 1929). Compare NAPOLEON IS ALWAYS RIGHT.

— Must Go
Slogan format; UK, probably by 1900. A slogan incorporating the cry that he or she 'must go' is liable to pursue any prominent politician who falls seriously out of favour. To date, A.J. Balfour, Prime Minister 1902–6, is the first British example found. In his case, the cry was sometimes abbreviated to 'BMG.' After losing the 1906 election, Balfour lingered on as leader of his party. Leo Maxse, editor of the *National Review*, wrote an article in the September 1911 edition in the course of which, demonstrating that the Conservative Party needed a new leader, he invented the slogan, 'Balfour must go'. And he went in November. In the months preceding the Munich agreement, *Punch* (1 June 1938) showed a graffitist writing: 'CHAMBERLAIN MUST G ...' on a wall.

'Eden Must Go' arose during Sir Anthony Eden's inept premiership (1955–7) when he instigated the disastrous landings in Egypt to 'protect' the Suez canal. On the evening of 4 November 1956, while he met with his Cabinet ministers in 10 Downing Street, he could hear roars of 'Eden Must go!' from an angry mass meeting in Trafalgar Square. He went under the guise of illness early the following year.

See also MARPLES MUST GO and SALOON MUST GO.

My Bottoms Are Tops
Gloria Vanderbilt jeans by Murjani; US, current 1980.

My God Is Not Dead ... Sorry 'Bout Yours
Religious slogan on bumper-sticker; US, 1969. Probably a response

to the debate instigated by *Time* Magazine's famous cover story (c.1966), 'IS GOD DEAD?'

My Goodness, My Guinness
See GUINNESS IS GOOD FOR YOU

My Men Wear English Leather Or They Wear Nothing At All
English Leather after-shave/deodorant; US, quoted 1981.

My Name Is Jimmy Carter ...
See HE'S MAKING US PROUD AGAIN

My Word Is My Bond
Motto of the London Stock Exchange (with the force of a slogan); UK, since 1801. At the Stock Exchange bargains are made 'on the nod', with no written pledges being given and no documents being signed. The motto's Latin form is: *'Dictum meum pactum'*.

Napoleon Is Always Right

Fictional slogan from the novel *Animal Farm* (1945) by George Orwell. Compare MUSSOLINI A SEMPRE RAGIONE. Also **Vote For Napoleon And The Full Manger**. Napoleon is a pig – and something of a Stalin-like figure in this satire on Communist excesses.

Nation Shall Speak Peace Unto Nation

Motto of the British Broadcasting Corporation (with the force of a slogan); UK, from 1927. Suggested by Dr Montague Rendall, one of the first five governors, when the original company was incorporated and its coat of arms chosen. The motto echoes a passage in Micah 4: 3: 'Nation shall not lift up a sword against nation'. In 1932, however, it was decided that the BBC's mission was not, principally, to broadcast to other nations but to provide a service for home consumption – and for the Empire. *Quaecunque* ('Whatsoever') was introduced as an alternative, reflecting the Latin inscription, also composed by Dr Rendall, in the entrance hall of the then new Broadcasting House, London, and based on Philippians 4: 8: 'Whatsoever things are beautiful and honest and of good report'. In 1948 'Nation Shall Speak Peace Unto Nation' came back into use as the Corporation's main motto – appropriately, after the BBC's notable role promoting international understanding during the Second World War.

Naughty. But Nice

National Dairy Council fresh cream in cakes; UK, from 1977. In 1988, appearing on BBC Radio's *Desert Island Discs*, the novelist Salman Rushdie claimed to have originated this slogan for cream cakes. Indeed, before achieving fame and misfortune as a novelist, Rushdie had worked as a freelance advertising copywriter in London. But his claim was rejected by others who had worked on the account. Whatever his contribution, Rushdie certainly did not coin the phrase 'Naughty but nice'. A 1939 US film had the title. It was about a professor of classical music who accidentally wrote a popular song. Partridge/*Slang* glosses the phrase as a reference to copulation since c.1900, 'ex a song that Minnie Schult sang and popularized in the USA, 1890s'. Maybe, bu there have since been various songs with the title, notably one by Johnny Mercer and Harry Warren in *The Belle of New York* (film, 1952). Compare also the similarly alliterative, 'It's Foolish But It's Fun' (Gus Kahn/Robert Stolz) sung by Deanna Durbin in *Spring Parade* (1940).

Never Again

General-purpose anti-war slogan; UK, by 1915. Used specifically with regard to Germany in the First World War. T.F.A. Smith wrote in *Soul of Germany* (1915): 'The oft-quoted phrase is applicable to the case: Never again!' David Lloyd George said in a newspaper interview (*The Times*, 29 September 1916): ' "Never again" has become our battle cry.' Churchill in his *The Second World War* (Vol. 1, 1948) said of the French: 'With one passionate spasm [they cried] never again.'

Later, in the mid-1960s, 'Never again' became the slogan of the militant Jewish Defence League – in reference to the Holocaust. A stone monument erected near the birthplace of Adolf Hitler at Braunau, Austria, in 1989 (the centenary of his birth) bore the lines 'For Peace, Freedom and Democracy – Never Again Fascism *[Nie wieder Faschismus]* – Millions of Dead are a warning'.

The film *Never Say Never Again* (UK, 1983), which marked Sean Connery's return to the part of James Bond, was so called because he had declared 'never again' after playing Bond in *Diamonds Are Forever* in 1971.

Compare NO MORE WAR; NO WIDER WAR.

Never Knowingly Undersold

John Lewis stores; UK, since the 1930s. This line was formulated by the founder of the John Lewis Partnership, John Spedan Lewis, in about 1920 to express a pricing policy which originated with his father, John Lewis, who first opened a small shop in London's Oxford Street in 1864. The slogan is believed to have been used within the firm before it was given public expression in the 1930s in the form: 'If you can buy more cheaply elsewhere anything you have just bought from us we will refund the difference.' The firm does not regard 'Never Knowingly Undersold' as an advertising device in the generally accepted sense of the word, although it is displayed on the sides of its vehicles and, together with the undertaking 'If you can buy ... ', printed on the backs of sales bills. Its main purpose is 'as a discipline upon the Partnership's Central Buyers to insure that the best possible value is offered to customers'. The firm does not advertise its merchandise. Hence, the phrase has an almost mystical significance for the Partnership.

Never Underestimate The Power Of A Woman

Ladies' Home Journal; US, from c.1941. Gordon Page of the N.W. Ayer agency recalled: 'It came off the back burner of a creative range where ideas simmer while the front burners are preoccupied with meeting closing dates ... it was just a more direct way of stating the case for the leading woman's magazine of the day. But always believing that you can do things with a twinkle that you can't do with a straight face, it was trotted to Leo Lionni ... it's largely his fault that you can't say "never underestimate the power of *anything*", today, without echoing the line.' (Watkins) Even in 1981, the following ad was appearing in *The New York Times*: 'Ladies' Home Journalism – Never Underestimate Its Power'.

New Deal, (The)

Presidential election slogan; US, 1932. 'I pledge you, I pledge myself, to a New Deal for the American people,' declared Franklin D. Roosevelt in his acceptance speech to the Democratic Convention which had just nominated him. The phrase became the keynote of the ensuing election campaign but it was not new – in Britain, Lloyd George had talked of 'A New Deal For Everyone' in 1919. Woodrow Wilson had had a NEW FREEDOM slogan, and Teddy Roosevelt had talked of a SQUARE DEAL. Abraham Lincoln had used 'New deal' on occasions. The FDR use was engineered by either Samuel Rosenman or Raymond Moley. 'I had not the slightest idea that it would take hold the way it did,' Rosenman said later, 'nor did the Governor [Roosevelt] when he read and revised what I had written ... It was simply one of those phrases that catch public fancy and survive.' On the other hand, Moley claimed: 'The expression "new deal" was in the draft I left at Albany with Roosevelt ... I was not aware that this would be the slogan for the campaign. It was a phrase that would have occurred to almost anyone.' (Safire)

New Freedom, (The)
Presidential election slogan; US, 1912. Woodrow Wilson, campaigning successfully for the presidency, sought the New Freedom, safeguarding the democratic rights of small business against big business, 'a revival of the power of the people'.

New Frontier, (The)
Presidential election slogan; US, 1960. 'We stand today on the edge of a New Frontier – the frontier of the 1960s ... [it] is not a set of challenges. It sums up not what I intend to offer the American people, but what I intend to ask them' – John F. Kennedy, accepting the Democratic nomination in Los Angeles (15 July 1960). Theodore C. Sorensen in *Kennedy* (1965), suggests that Kennedy had a hand in coining the slogan for the forthcoming administraton: 'I know of no outsider who suggested the expression, although the theme of the Frontier was contained in more than one draft.' In 1964 Harold Wilson said in a speech in Birmingham: 'We want the youth of Britain to storm the new frontiers of knowledge.'

New Improved ...
All-purpose advertising phrase, as in 'new improved taste' etc. Undated.

New Labour, New Danger
Conservative Party pre-general election slogan; UK, 1996. In the run-up to the 1997 election, the Conservatives launched a scare campaign to try and convince voters that the newly reconstructed Labour Party was not a good thing. The phrase 'New Labour' had already become attached to the party following the use of **New Labour, New Britain** at its annual conference in October 1994. In August 1996, the Conservatives unveiled posters which showed the Labour leader, Tony Blair, with devil's eyes and accompanied

173

by the slogan 'New Labour, New Danger'. This was withdrawn after complaints but by then it had garnered considerable publicity.

Newport – Home Of The Mole Wrench
See SHIP THROUGH ...

New York's Finest
Unofficial slogan of the City of New York Police Department; US, since 1930. By that year,'the finest' was taken to refer either to the whole New York police force or to any individual policeman in it. By the 1960s, irony had crept in. A graffito read: 'New York's finest – the best that money can buy'. (Reisner)

Next To Myself I Like BVD's Best
BVD's (comfortable, loose-fitting underwear); US, from c.1920. (Lambert) (The name 'BVD' stands for Bradley, Voorhies and Day, the manufacturers.) In the UK, a girl in an underwear ad is remembered as having said: **Next To Myself I Like Vedonis**. Quoted 1982.

Next Year In Jerusalem [Le shanah ha ba'ah b'yerushalim!]
A familiar Jewish toast with the force of a slogan. In the centuries of the Diaspora, it was the eternal hope – expressed particularly at the Feast of the Passover – that all Jews be reunited, 'next year in Jerusalem', in the land of Israel. Passover originally celebrated the exodus of the Jews from Egypt and their deliverance from enslavement some 3200 years ago. In June 1967, following the Six Day War, when the modern state of Israel encompassed once more the old city of Jerusalem, all Jews could, if they were able, end their exile and make this dream a reality.

Nibble Nobby's Nuts
Nobby's Nuts (snack); Australia, quoted 1987. In no time, a T-shirt became available which proclaimed 'I'm Nobby'.

Nice 'Ere, Innit?
Campari; UK, 1976. A line from a TV ad which probably sold more of the product than many a conventional slogan. On a balcony in

174

Venice, an elegant-looking woman sips Campari and then shatters the atmosphere by saying in a rough Cockney voice, 'Nice 'ere, innit?' In the follow-up ad, a smooth type asks the same woman, 'Were you truly wafted here from Paradise?' She replies: '**Nah ... Luton Airport**.' Not exactly Shakespeare, but these nothing phrases were crafted by copywriter Terry Howard and let fall by Lorraine Chase. Campari sales rose by a record thirty-five per cent in a single year. Chase went on to record a song called 'It's Nice 'Ere, Innit?' (1979) and Cats UK recorded 'Luton Airport' the same year. Next step was for the Chase character to be written into a TV sitcom called *The Other 'Arf* (from 1980).

Nice One, Cyril!
Wonderloaf bread; UK, 1972. The story of this phrase is a classic instance of a line from an advertisement being taken up by the public, turned into a catchphrase, and then as suddenly discarded. Its origins were quite soon obscured, and then forgotten. The line, apparently written by Peter Mayle, caught the imagination of British TV viewers in a 1972 advertisement for Wonderloaf. Two bakers were shown wearing T-shirts labelled 'Nottingham' and 'Liverpool' respectively. 'All our local bakers reckon they can taste a Wonderloaf and tell you who baked it,' purred a voice-over commentary. 'It was oven-baked at one of our local bakeries.' The following exchange then took place between the bakers:

Liverpool: Leeds? High Wycombe? It's one of Cyril's. Mmm.
 Good texture, nice colour, very fresh ...
Nottingham: Cyril ... I think it's one of Frank's down at Luton
 ... it's definitely saying Newcastle to me ...

The voice-over then intervened: 'The truth is, they can't say for sure. But we can say ... ' : *Nottingham*: 'Nice one, Cyril!'
As a phrase, why did 'Nice one, Cyril!' catch on? It had a sibilant ease; it was fun to say. More importantly it could be used in any number of situations, not least sexual ones. In 1973, the phrase was taken up by Tottenham Hotspur football supporters who were fans of the player Cyril Knowles. They even recorded a song about him which went:

Nice one, Cyril
Nice one, son.
Nice one, Cyril,
Let's have another one.

Comedian Cyril Fletcher inevitably used it as the title of his 1978 autobiography. The following year the word 'Cyril' was observed scrawled on the first kilometre sign outside a certain seaside resort in the south of France. Shortly afterwards the phrase disappeared almost completely from use, although in February 1989 posters appeared for a credit card company which showed Sir Cyril Smith, the obese politician, attempting to touch his toes. The slogan was: 'Nice one, Sir Cyril ... but Access is more flexible.'

Nine Out Of Ten Screen Stars Use Lux Toilet Soap For Their Priceless Smooth Skins

Lux Toilet Soap; US, from 1927. The campaign ran for twenty years and among the stars who were listed as Lux users were Fay Wray, Mary Astor, Louise Brooks, Myrna Loy, Bebe Daniels, Clara Bow and Joan Crawford. This format presumably inspired all the statistical slogans that followed – see, for example, EIGHT OUT OF TEN CATS PREFER IT.

Ninepence For Fourpence

Semi-official political slogan for the Liberal Government's plans for the Welfare State; UK, 1908–9. The phrase indicated how people would stand to benefit from their contributions to the new National Health Insurance scheme. Associated with David Lloyd George and said by A.J.P. Taylor (in *Essays in English History*, 1976) to have been snapped up from an audience interruption and turned into a slogan by Lloyd George.

99 $^{44}/_{100}$ Per Cent Pure

Ivory Soap; US, from 1879. One of the clumsiest but most enduring slogans of all. Nobody remembers who first coined this bizarre line but it has stuck, along with the claim that **It Floats** (in use by 1898). A story has it that the floating character of the soap was not recognized until a dealer asked for another case of 'that soap that floats'. (Lambert)

In 1974, a US gangster film with Richard Harris was entitled *99 And ⁴⁴/₁₀₀ Per Cent Dead*. For the benefit of non-Americans who would not understand the allusion, the film was tardily retitled *Call Harry Crown*. *Variety* opined crisply that it was, 'As clumsy as its title'.

99% Is Shit
Anarchist slogan; UK, c.1979. When they got round to daubing this on the BBC at Broadcasting House in London, people began to wonder what the remaining 1% could possibly be?

Nixon's The One (or Nixon Is The One)
Presidential re-election slogan; US, 1968. So, indeed, Richard Nixon was, if his official slogan can be said to have any meaning at all. **Nixon's The One! – And Agnew Too** was also observed. Later in the campaign there appeared **This Time Vote Like Your Whole Life Depended On It**, not to mention **The 'I' In Nixon Stands For Integrity**, believe that if you will. Nelson Rockefeller had tried for the Republican nomination, but failed, with **Who Else But Nelse?** Nixon's Democratic opponent Hubert H. Humphrey countered in vain with **The Politics Of Joy**. 'Here we

are the way politics ought to be in America, the politics of happiness, the politics of purpose and the politics of joy' – speech in Washington (27 April 1968). Third-party candidate George C. Wallace sniped at the big boys with the charge that there was **Not A Dime's Worth Of Difference**. Nixon won.

Nobody Can Do It Like McDonald's Can
McDonald's hamburger restaurants; US, current 1970s. In this form it was a registered trade mark, but it is also remembered as **Nobody Does It Like McDonald's Can**. Also **We Do It All For You**. Undated. This probably pre-dated the Bryan Adams hit song 'Everything I Do, I Do It All For You' (1991).

Nobody Drowned At Watergate
Unofficial political slogan; US, 1974. In the early days of Watergate, supporters of President Nixon made this pointed reference to the stonewalling by Senator Edward Kennedy after the Chappaquiddick incident (1979). At the time, Kennedy seemed likely to be the most prominent Democratic challenger to Nixon at the next presidential election. (Safire) Compare BLONDE IN EVERY POND.

Nobody For President
Informal slogan, on buttons; US, 1980. This was during the presidential election year which saw Ronald Reagan beat Jimmy Carter.

No Destitute Child Ever Refused Admission
See EVER-OPEN DOOR

No F.T. ... No Comment
Financial Times newspaper; UK, by 1982.

No Jews – No Wooden Shoes
See NO POPERY

No Landlords Wanted
See LOUSY BUT LOYAL

No More War

A recurring slogan, mostly twentieth century. At the UN in 1965, Pope Paul VI quoted President Kennedy to the effect that 'mankind must put an end to war, or war will put an end to mankind ... No more war, NEVER AGAIN war.' (Said in Italian.)

Earlier, the phrase had been used by Winston Churchill at the end of a letter to Lord Beaverbrook in 1928 (quoted in Martin Gilbert's biography of Churchill, Vol. 5). A.J.P. Taylor in his *English History 1914–45* suggests that the slogan was 'irresistible' at the end of the First World War.

In *Goodbye to Berlin* (1939), Christopher Isherwood describes a Nazi book-burning. The books are from a 'small liberal pacifist publisher'. One Nazi holds up a book called *'Nie Wieder Krieg'* as though it were 'a nasty kind of reptile'. 'No More War!' a fat, well-dressed woman laughs scornfully and savagely, 'What an idea!'

No. 1 In Europe

British European Airways (later incorporated with BOAC in British Airways); UK, by 1969.

No Popery, No Tyranny, No Wooden Shoes

Anti-Roman Catholic slogan; England, after 1666. Daniel Defoe said that there were a hundred thousand fellows in his time ready to fight to the death against popery, without knowing whether popery was a man or a horse. After the initial impact of the Restoration had worn off, this was the cry that came to be heard. The wife of Charles II, Catherine of Braganza, was a Roman Catholic and so was Charles's brother (later James VII of Scotland and II of England). They were surrounded by priests, and the Fire of London (1666) was put down to papist action and foreign interference. Hence, the anti-Roman Catholicism of the slogan coupled with general English distrust of foreigners (wooden shoes = French sabots). The variation **No Jews – No Wooden Shoes** (obvious rhyming slang) occurred in 1753 when an anti-Jewish Bill was before Parliament.

The cry 'No Popery' is chiefly associated, however, with the Gordon Riots of 1780, when Lord George Gordon fomented a violent protest against legislation which had lightened penalties on Roman Catholics. The riots in London were put down by George III's troops (and form the background to Charles Dickens's novel *Barnaby Rudge*). The slogan was again used by supporters of the Duke of Portland's government opposed to Catholic Emancipation, in 1807.

No Smoking – Not Even Abdullahs
Abdullah cigarettes; UK, current 1930s. In dual-purpose notices, especially on the London Underground.

No Surrender
Protestant anti-Roman Catholic slogan; Ireland, from 1689. The year after the Catholic King James II was replaced with the Protestant William of Orange on the British throne, forces still loyal to James maintained a siege against the citizens of Derry in Ulster. The siege was raised after a month or two. 'No surrender!' was the Protestant slogan and 'Long Live Ulster. No surrender' has remained a Loyalist slogan in Ulster ever since. Another version is: 'NO POPERY, no surrender.' *No Surrender* was the title of a 1985 film written by Alan Bleasdale about warring Protestant and Roman Catholic factions in Liverpool.

Not A Cough In A Carload
Old Gold cigarettes; US, current 1928.

Not A Dime's Worth Of Difference
See NIXON'S THE ONE

Not A Penny Off The Pay, Not A Minute On The Day (and variants, with the phrases reversed; also ... Not A Second On The Day)
Miners' slogan; UK, 1926. Coined by A.J. Cook, Secretary of the Union of Mineworkers, and used in the run-up to the miners' strike of 1926 (which led to the General Strike). Compare:

> In his chamber, weak and dying
> While the Norman Baron lay,
> Loud, without, his men were crying
> 'Shorter hours and better pay' ...

Lives of great men all remind us
We can make as much as they,
Work no more, until they find us
Shorter hours and better pay.

From the anonymous 'A Strike Among the Poets' – included in *The Faber Book of Comic Verse* (1974 ed.) – and probably dating from the late nineteenth century.

No Taxation Without Representation
Colonists' anti-British slogan; North America, from the 1760s on. It was particularly current in the years before the War of Independence. In the form **Taxation Without Representation Is Tyranny**, coinage has been attributed to the lawyer and statesman James Otis. In 1763, he opposed British taxation on the grounds that the colonies were not represented in the House of Commons. (Echoed many years later by Arnold Toynbee: 'No annihilation without representation.')

Not Everything In Black And White Makes Sense
See GUINNESS IS GOOD FOR YOU

Nothing Acts Faster Than Anadin
Anadin analgesic tablets; UK, current from 1960s. This inspired the graffiti retort: 'Then why not use Nothing?' From earlier TV ads: **Headache? Tense, nervous headache? Take Anadin.** This formula seems also to have been used in the US. There was the graffito, 'Are you nervous, tense? Try my 8-inch relaxer'. (Reisner)

Nothing Over Sixpence
F.W. Woolworth & Co. stores; UK, from the 1910s. The first British Woolworth's opened in 1909 and was described as a 'threepence and sixpence' store, the equivalent of the 'five-and-ten' (cent) stores in the US. Hence, the phrase 'Nothing Over Sixpence' arose and endured until the Second World War, when prices could no longer be contained below this limit. A song dating from 1927 includes the lines:

> To Woolworth's, Hobbs and Sutcliffe [cricketers] always go to
>   get their bats,
> Stan Baldwin gets his pipes there, and Winston gets his hats;
> And the Prince [of Wales] would never think of going
>   elsewhere for his spats –
> And there's nothing over sixpence in the stores!

Aneurin Bevan said of speeches by Neville Chamberlain (late 1930s): 'Listening to Chamberlain is like paying a visit to Woolworth's – everything in its place and nothing above sixpence.'

Much later, from the Allen Brady and Marsh agency in c.1980 came **The Wonder Of Woolworths**, which was popularly reproduced as 'The Wonder Of Woollies'.

No Throat Irritation
See IT'S TOASTED

No Tits But A Lot Of Balls
News on Sunday newspaper; UK, 1987. Devised by the Bartle, Bogle & Hegarty agency for the Labour-supporting paper which opened and folded in the same year. Perhaps as well, it was never used.

Now And Forever
Stage musical *Cats*; UK and elsewhere, from c.1987. The longest-running musical ever in London's West End began to capitalize on its longevity with this promotional line about six years after its 1981 opening. But it was an old phrase – three films have been made with the title *Now and Forever*: 1934, with Gary Cooper; 1956, with Janette Scott; and 1983, with Cheryl Ladd. Presumably it is 'love' which is 'now and forever' in each case. Vera Lynn had a hit in 1954 with a song of this title, translated from the German. Indeed, the phrase enshrines an idea common to most languages. Basques demanding that Eta should not keep up its terror campaign (March 1989) bore a banner with the words; '*Paz ahora y para* [Peace now and forever]'.

Daniel Webster proclaimed: 'Liberty and union, now and forever, one and inseparable' (26 January 1830). '*Et nunc et semper*' at the end of the Gloria in religious services is sometimes translated as 'Now and forever [world without end. Amen]' but also (in the Anglican prayer book) as 'Now and ever shall be'.

Now Hands That Do Dishes
See FOR HANDS THAT DO DISHES

No Wider War
Political slogan; US, 1964. President Lyndon Johnson said in a broadcast address (4 August 1964), referring to the Vietnam War: 'We Americans know, although others appear to forget, the risks of spreading conflict. We still seek no wider war.'

'No wider war' is misleadingly reminiscent of the German phrase *Nie Wieder Krieg* [NEVER AGAIN war], a slogan of the 1920s and '30s.

Now ... There Is Only One Mars
See MARS A DAY HELPS ...

Nuclear Power? No Thanks
Friends of the Earth slogan; UK, 1981.

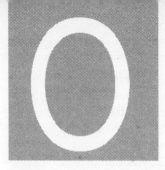

Obey That Impulse

Life (a humour magazine); US, undated. A call for subscriptions attributed to Thomas L. Masson (1866–1934) who was the magazine's editor (1893–1922). See also SAFE AND SANE FOURTH.

Often A Bridesmaid, But Never A Bride

Listerine mouthwash; US, from c.1923. One of the best known lines in advertising, by Milton Feasley of Lambert & Feasley, though there is an echo of the British music-hall song 'Why am I always a bridesmaid?', made famous by Lily Morris. A screen title in the newsreel sequence of *Citizen Kane* (1941) states (of Kane): 'In politics – always a bridesmaid, never a bride.' Also **Her Honeymoon – And It Should Have Been Mine!** and **The Taste You Love To Hate (Twice A Day)**, but especially **Even Your Best Friends Won't Tell You**: a line which originated in the 'Often A Bridesmaid' ad. Originally, it was **And Even Your Closest Friends Won't Tell You**. It also appeared as **And Your Best Friends Won't Tell You**. Partridge/*Catch Phrases* suggests that it became a catchphrase in the form 'your best friend(s) won't tell you' (= 'you stink!').

In the film *Dangerous Moonlight* (UK, 1941), the Anton Walbrook character says to a man putting on hair oil (in New York), 'Even your best friend won't *smell* you.'

O.K.

See TIPPECANOE ...

Omo Adds Brightness To Whiteness

Omo washing powder; UK, current late 1950s.

Once You've Driven One, You're Unlikely To Drive Another

Say that again? A UK ad for Mercedes-Benz cars, quoted in *The Times* (June 1980).

One And Only, The
Bill-matter for Phyllis Dixey, the noted British striptease artist of the 1940s. Also for comedians Dan Leno (1860–1904) and Max Miller (1895–1963) (see CHEEKY CHAPPIE). Might, indeed, be used as a promotional phrase about anything or anyone. The Gershwins wrote a song 'My One and Only' for *Funny Face* (1927). Dixey also used the line 'Peek-a-Boo'.

One And Only Wonderbra
See HELLO BOYS

One Crazy Calorie
Tab (soft drink); US, quoted 1980.

One Degree Under
Aspro headache pills; UK, current 1960s.

One Down, A Million To Go
Unofficial racist slogan (on the death of a black man): UK, probably 1950s. Ascribed to John Kingsley Read by Salman Rushdie in a talk on Channel 4 TV (1982).

One Film You Should Not See Alone. Where Your Nightmare Ends *Willard Begins!*, (The)
Film, *Willard*; US, 1971. The story of a man who bred rats to kill his enemies.

One Instinctively Knows When Something Is Right
Croft Original sherry; UK, by 1982.

One Man, One Vote
A slogan first coined in the nineteenth century for a campaign led by Major John Cartwright (1740–1824), a radical MP ('The Father of Reform'), in the fight against plural voting – 'One man shall have one vote' (*The People's Barrier Against Undue Influence*, 1780). It was possible in those days for a man to cast two votes, one on the basis of residence and the other by virtue of business or university qualifications. This right was not abolished until 1948. The phrase arose again during the period of the illegal Unilateral

Declaration of Independence in Rhodesia (1965–80) to indicate a basic condition required by the British government before the breakaway regime could be legitimized. The phrase has also been used in the US, in civil rights contexts.

In 1993, when the British Labour Party was trying to overthrow the 'block votes' that gave its trade union membership a disproportionate say in the formulation of policy, the phrase One Member One Vote was rendered by the acronym **OMOV**.

One More Heave
Liberal Party general election slogan; UK, October 1974. Perhaps distinctive of the party's then leader, Jeremy Thorpe.

On les aura [Let 'em have it]
From a French government poster of the First World War seeking war loans (revived in the Second World War).

Only Her Hairdresser Knows For Sure
See DOES SHE ...

Only 'Sauce' I Dare Give Father, The
Burma sauce; UK, current early twentieth century.

Only Thing Like Coca-Cola ...
See DRINK COCA-COLA

On To Berlin
See *AUF NACH BERLIN*

Opal Fruits – Made To Make Your Mouth Water
Opal Fruits (confectionery): UK, undated. Memorable especially because of the accompanying jingle in TV ads.

Orgasms For Women,
See VOTES FOR WOMEN

Our Bottles Are Washed ...
See BEER THAT MADE MILWAUKEE ...

Our Day Will Come [*Tiocfaidh Ar La*]
Slogan (in Gaelic) of the Provisional Irish Republican Army; Ireland, probably since the 1950s. Relatives of those accused of trying to blow up the British Prime Minister at Brighton in 1984 shouted it out as the defendants were being sentenced in court on 23 June 1986.

The phrase exists independently of this, of course. It is the title of a song performed by the American vocal group Ruby and the Romantics (1963). Compare 'Our day is come', as it appears in Lord Lytton's novel, *Leila* (1838).

Out Front. Pulling Away
Goodyear tyres; US, current 1980.

Out Of The Closets And Into The Streets
Gay Liberation Front; US, c.1969. The starting point was the term 'closet homosexual' or 'closet queen' for one who hid his inclinations away in a closet ('cupboard' in American usage rather than 'lavatory' or 'small room', as in British English).

Out Of The Strong Came Forth Sweetness
Lyle's Golden Syrup; UK, current 1930s onwards. A quotation from the Book of Judges 14: 14: 'Out of the eater came forth meat, and out of the strong came forth sweetness' – Samson's riddle. More recently the Tate & Lyle company has completely reversed the phrase by saying **Out Of Sweetness Came Forth Strength** as part of its occasionally necessary campaigns featuring 'Mr Cube' to ward off nationalisation of the British sugar industry.

Over The Hump With Humphrey
Unofficial election slogan; US, 1960. A sign on Hubert Humphrey's campaign bus when he sought the Democratic nomination, in vain, that year. (White, 1962)

Oxo Gives A Meal Man-Appeal
Oxo beef extract (for cooking and drinks); UK, from 1958. The Oxo cube first appeared in 1910 and has been supported by numerous slogans over the years. In the late 1950s, the Oxo company wanted

TV to 'take it off the streets and put it in the home'. Copywriter Joan Drummond was told to come up with a husband-and-wife domestic situation which would dramatize the youthful image the J. Walter Thompson agency wished to project. 'We want the idea that the chap is after the girl for her sexiness as well as her good cooking,' she was told, 'and we need a slogan to keep us on that line.' This slogan was what she came up with. (Pearson)

Hence, 'Emma Peel', the name of the character played by Diana Rigg in the British TV series *The Avengers* (from c.1965) who, the producers hoped, would have plenty of 'M appeal' – or 'Man appeal'.

Pack Your Trunks
See GIRLS, CAN WE INTEREST YOU ...

Palle, Palle! [Balls, Balls!]
Supporters of the Medicis in Florence during the Middle Ages are said to have adopted this as their cry – taking their cue from what they saw in the family coat of arms (five, or sometimes six, red balls, referring to the pharmacological associations of the name Medici).

Paris Is For Lovers
Unofficial tourist slogan promoting the French capital. Unverified. The phrase, spoken in Billy Wilder's film *Sabrina* (*Sabrina Fair* in the UK, 1954), almost has the ring of an official slogan, though this was long before the days of such lines as I LOVE NEW YORK (1977) and VIRGINIA IS FOR LOVERS (1981).
   Nor does there seem to be a song incorporating the phrase or using it as a title, though Cole Porter's Broadway musical *Silk Stockings* (US, 1955) has one called 'Paris Loves Lovers'.

Pathfinders, The Corporate slogan for ICI (Imperial Chemical Industries); UK, quoted 1981.

Pause That Refreshes, The
See DRINK COCA-COLA

Pay As You Ride
See GO NOW, PAY LATER

Peace At Any Price
See FREE SOIL, FREE MEN ...

Peace For Our Time
Unofficial political slogan; UK, 1938. In the run-up to the Second
World War, the hollowest slogan of all was Neville Chamberlain's
phrase. On 30 September 1938 he returned from signing the
Munich agreement with Hitler, hoping that his concessions
(including the virtual dismemberment of Czechoslovakia) would
pave the way for peace. If Hitler honoured the agreement, well
and good. If he did not, then at least the world would be able to
see that he was clearly guilty. And, to be fair to Chamberlain, such
was the desire for peace in Europe that, whatever personal mis-
givings he may have had – and there is evidence that he experienced great discomfort at the role he had to play – he was swept
along with the tide.

That night he spoke from a window at 10 Downing Street, 'not
of design but for the purpose of dispersing the huge multitude
'below' (according to Keith Feiling, *The Life of Neville Chamberlain*,
1946). He said: 'My good friends. This is the second time in our
history that there has come back from Germany to Downing Street
Peace With Honour. I believe it is peace for our time. Go home
and get a nice quiet sleep.' A week later, Chamberlain was asking
the House of Commons not to read too much into words 'used in a
moment of some emotion, after a long and exhausting day, after I
had driven through miles of excited, enthusiastic, cheering people'.

Interestingly, two days before Chamberlain made his remarks,
when someone had suggested that he use Benjamin Disraeli's
phrase 'peace with honour', Chamberlain had impatiently rejected
it (as Feiling records). Now, according to John Colville, *Footprints
in Time* (1976), Chamberlain used the phrase at the urging of his
wife. Disraeli had been talking about the Berlin Treaty of 1878
which forced the Russians to make a number of concessions but
created rather more problems than it solved. In an impromptu
speech from the steps of his railway carriage at Dover on 16 July,
Disraeli had said: 'Gentlemen, we bring you peace; and I think I
may say, peace with honour.' Later that day, in London, he had
repeated the claim: 'Lord Salisbury and myself have brought you
back peace – but a peace, I hope, with honour, which may satisfy
our sovereign and tend to the welfare of the country.'

Chamberlain's phrase is often misquoted as 'Peace *in* our time', as by Noël Coward in the title of a play set in England after the Germans have conquered it. Perhaps he, and others, were influenced by the phrase from the Book of Common Prayer: 'Give Peace in our time, O Lord.' Curiously, in the year before Munich, *Punch* (24 November 1937) had shown 'Peace in our time' as a wall slogan in a cartoon.

Peace Is Our Profession
Strategic Air Command; US, by 1962.

Peace Now
Unofficial anti-Vietnam War slogan; US, quoted 1968. It was on a poster and echoed the 'now' theme also used in civil rights slogans of that time (see FREEDOM NOW).

Peace With Honour
See PEACE FOR OUR TIME

Peanut Butter Is Love – Spread Some Around Today
Informal slogan on a placard supporting Jimmy Carter at the Democratic Convention; US, 1976. It helped Carter win the nomination and the presidency. The association with peanuts came through his family's farming interests.

Pearline Keeps White Things White And Bright Women Bright
Pearline washing powder; US, current 1896.

Penalty Of Leadership, The
See STANDARD OF THE WORLD

People Are Changing To Guards
Guards cigarettes; UK, current 1960s.

People Love Player's
See PLAYER'S PLEASE

People Who Like People Like Dial
Dial soap; US, quoted 1965. Also **Aren't You Glad *You* Use Dial Soap! Don't You Wish *Everybody* Did?** – quoted 1969.

Perfume Worth 9 Guineas An Ounce
See YOU'LL LOOK A LITTLE LOVELIER

Perhaps We Could, Paul. If ... You Owned A Chrysler
Chrysler motors; US, undated. (Baker)

Persil Washes Whiter
See SOMEONE'S MOTHER

Phyllosan Fortifies The Over-Forties
Phyllosan tonic; UK, probably from the late 1940s. Quoted 1974.
Echoed in the BBC saying: 'Radio 4 over-fortifies the over-forties'
(c.1978).

Pile It High, Sell It Cheap
Business motto (with the force of a slogan) of Sir John Cohen
(1898–1979), founder of Tesco Supermarkets. He built his fortune
on this golden rule. Hence, the title of Maurice Corina's book, *Pile
It High, Sell It Cheap: The Authorised Biography* ... (1971). Compare
the American maxim: **Stack It High, Watch 'Em Buy**. Tesco's actual slogan, c.1958, was **(The) Best For Less**. In 1963, Tesco was one
of the biggest traders to proclaim **We Give Green Shield Stamps**
– in a scheme run by the Green Shield Stamp Company.

Pin To An Elephant, A
See UNIVERSAL PROVIDER

Pint Sighs
See GUINNESS IS GOOD FOR YOU

Piss On Disco
Informal slogan on T-shirt; UK, 1980. The disco dancing craze was
at its height in the wake of the film *Saturday Night Fever* (1977).

Player's Please
John Player & Sons cigarettes; UK, from 1927. Three years earlier,
this enduring slogan appeared in the form 'Player's Will Please
You'. By 1925 this had become 'They're Player's And They Please'.
George Green, the firm's advertising manager entered a tobac-

conist's shop and overheard a customer asking for 'Player's, please'. He went back to his office, wrote the phrase out in his own immaculate hand (the one used in the ads) and the slogan took on its final form. **It's The Tobacco That Counts** was current in 1927, too. **People Love Player's** – 'a classic campaign revealing the romantic promise implicit in a puff of smoke' (Pearson) – was launched in 1960.

Plop, Plop, Fizz, Fizz
See I CAN'T BELIEVE I ATE ...

Politics Of Joy, The
See NIXON'S THE ONE

Poor But Loyal
See LOUSY BUT LOYAL

Poor Cold Fred
Electricity Council storage heaters; UK, from 1969. A briefly exposed but memorable line from copy written at the Hobson Bates agency by Roger Musgrave. A TV campaign featured a character called 'Fred' who thought that storage heaters would cost hundreds of pounds and thus remained cold until he was enlightened about them. Musgrave admitted (1981) that he was probably influenced by memories of the old epitaph 'Here lies Fred/Who was alive and is dead'.

Post Early For Christmas
Post Office; UK, probably from the 1920s. An enduring slogan of the British Post Office, intended to reduce the pressure on mail services caused by a sudden rush of Christmas cards and parcels. Date of inception unknown – though one unverified suggestion is that it was in 1882. The simple non-seasonal **Post Early** (i.e. 'in the day') was apparently new in June 1922. In the Second World War, there was the similar injunction **Post Early – Before Noon**, not to mention the very bald **Telegraph Less**.

Potatoes Are Fattening/Good For You
See BIG BROTHER IS WATCHING YOU

Pour Encourager Les Huîtres
See GUINNESS IS GOOD FOR YOU

Power To The People
Black Panther movement; US, from 1969. Shouted, with clenched fist raised, this slogan was publicized by the Black Panthers' leader, Bobby Seale, in Oakland, California, July 1969. Used by other dissident groups, as shown by Eldridge Cleaver: 'We say "All Power to the People" – Black Power for Black People, White Power for White People, Brown Power for Brown People, Red Power for Red People, and X Power for any group we've left out.' It was this somewhat generalised view of 'People Power' that John Lennon seemed to promote in the 1971 song 'Power to the People (Right on!)'.

Powerful Part Of Your Life, A
Corporate slogan for Westinghouse; US, current 1980.

P-P-P-Pick Up A Penguin
Penguin chocolate biscuits; UK, probably since the 1960s.

'P.P.' What About You?
Fictional slogan in *Keep The Aspidistra Flying* (1935), in which George Orwell describes an advertising campaign by the Queen of Sheba Toilet Requisites Co. for the deodorant, 'April Dew'. The firm is after a phrase like 'NIGHT STARVATION' that would 'rankle in the public consciousness like a poisoned arrow'. The problem of smelly feet becomes 'Pedic Perspiration' or 'P.P.'

Prepare To Meet Thy God
Religious slogan. Unlike the END IS NIGH, another favourite of placard-bearing religious fanatics, this one does actually come from the Bible: Amos 4: 12.

Preparing To Be A Beautiful Lady
Pears' Soap; UK, from 1932 – when young girls, some with their mothers, were featured using the product. In 1981, an announcement for the 'Miss Pears Contest' was still employing the phrase: 'We're looking for a radiant little girl who is preparing to be a beautiful lady by using pure transparent Pears' Soap every day.'

Priceless Ingredient Of Every Product Is The Honor And Integrity Of Its Maker, The

Squibb drug products; US, from 1921. 'Before that year, Squibb had never advertised to the public ... The problem given to Raymond Rubicam, then a writer at N.W. Ayer & Son, was to produce a series of advertisements which would sell Squibb to the public and not offend the publicity-sensitive medical profession '... One night at two in the morning he seemed as far away from the solution as ever. Wearily gathering up his yellow sheets before going to bed, he took one more look through the mass of headlines he had written. "Suddenly," he writes, "two separate word combinations popped out at me from two different headlines. One was 'The Priceless Ingredient' and the other 'Honor and Integrity'. Instantly, the two came together in my mind ... " The phrase became a permanent part of Squibb advertising.' (Watkins) 'Raymond Rubicam's famous slogan ... reminds me of my father's advice: when a company boasts about its integrity, or a woman about her virtue, avoid the former and cultivate the latter.' (Ogilvy)

A later Squibb slogan was: **For Years We've Been Making Our Products As If Lives Depend On Them**.

Prime Minister Of Mirth, The

Bill-matter of the British music-hall entertainer, Sir George Robey (1869–1954).

Probably The Best Lager In The World

Carlsberg; UK, from 1973. Even had it not been intoned by Orson Welles in the TV ads, the 'probably' inserted into this hyperbole would still have fascinated. In a 1982 ad, Kestrel lager (from Scottish & Newcastle Breweries) cheekily showed a beer bottle out of which was coming the words 'I only said we're *probably* the best lager in the world.'

Compare: **Probably The Finest Tobacco In The World** – Zephyr, imported by A. Gale & Co. Ltd of Glasgow; current 1961.

Product Of The Master Mind

See SENIOR SERVICE SATISFY

Prolongs Active Life
PAL dog food; UK, by 1967. Brand name acronym as slogan.

Prudential Has The Strength Of Gibraltar, The
Prudential Insurance Co. of America; US, from 1896. Mortimer Remington of the J. Walter Thompson agency was commuting to work in New York when, crossing the New Jersey meadows, he passed Snake Rock. This made him think of Gibraltar in answer to the Prudential president's demand for some 'symbol of lasting, enduring strength'. (Lambert)

Pure Genius
Guinness; UK, from 1985. Opined *Campaign* (10 January 1986): 'Like it or not, the campaign [from the Ogilvy and Mather agency] put the Guinness name back in the ad industry's consciousness.' A clever stroke by whoever saw the similarity between the words 'genius' and 'Guinness' and laid the foundation of numerous advertising campaigns upon it. But a very old phrase: Dryden wrote in 1695: 'Art being strengthened by the knowledge of things may be ... sublim'd into a pure Genius.'

Pure Gold
Benson & Hedges cigarettes; UK, current 1964. Originally this campaign used the phrase (to reflect the brand's gold packs) with lines like 'What's too precious to leave lying round?' Later the brand took to providing visual images that would inevitably recall the slogan, without actually using it.

Put A Smile On Your Face
See DRINK COCA-COLA

Put A Tiger In Your Tank
Esso motor fuel; US and elsewhere, from 1964. This was a slogan that really took off and gave rise to endless jokes and cartoons. I can remember taking part in a revue sketch about Noah's Ark at Oxford in 1965, the sole purpose of which seemed to be to lead up to the punch line, 'Put A Tiger In Your Tank'.

Esso's use of a tiger in its advertising (both in the US and the UK) pre-dated this particular campaign by a long while, however.

The tiger first appeared on a poster for Esso Extra in the UK in 1952 – realistic, fierce and far from friendly. In 1959, it reappeared in more human form in the US and the line 'Put A Tiger In Your Tank' was used, but in a throw-away fashion. In 1964, the slogan was revived to accompany a *cartoon* Esso tiger in the US – a year later in the UK – and the whole thing became a national craze, with countless tiger tails adorning the petrol caps of the nation's cars. Subsequently, the tiger went abroad: '*Mettez un tigre dans votre moteur*' appeared in France; in Germany, '*Pack den Tiger in den tank*'. In the US, particularly, it gave rise to numerous 'put a tiger' derivatives. A sample: 'If You Feel Like A Tiger Is In Your Throat Reach For Guardets Lozenges … ' A hamburger stand advertised: 'Put A Tiger In Your Tummy.' Tiger Beer in the Japanese *Times* sloganned: 'Put A Tiger In Your Tankard.' Standard Rochester Beer countered: 'Put A Tankard In Your Tiger.' The UK campaign ran for two years before it flagged, hence the need for SAVE THE ESSO TIGER.

Put A Woman On Top For A Change
Informal slogan of the Young Conservatives organization; UK, 1976 – promoting the idea of Margaret Thatcher as Prime Minister, following her election as party leader in 1975 and prior to her general election win in 1979. Rob Hayward MP said (in 1984) that the idea first came up when he was National Vice-Chairman of the Young Conservatives. Originally, 'Have a Woman on Top' (or 'Fuck Me, I'm a Tory'), it was devised by Young Conservatives in 1976 and distributed as a sticker at the Tory Party Conference. In 1979, it seems to have had some circulation as an official party slogan in the General Election that took Mrs Thatcher to Downing Street. A much later response was: 'Get her off, she's hurting.'

Putting People First
NALGO (local government union); UK, 1983. Used in an advertising campaign against public service cuts and privatization. Used shortly afterwards by British Airways. In the early 1990s, with the rise of political correctness, 'putting people first' became part of the creed. Hence, a PC phrase like 'person of colour' that, literally, puts the person before the fact that they have a distinctive colour.

Quaecunque
See NATION SHALL SPEAK ...

Quality Never Goes Out Of Style
Levi jeans; US, current 1980.

Queen Elizabeth Slept Here
Traditional tourist slogan promoting visits to stately homes, hotels and inns; UK, probably since such tourism began in the eighteenth century.

Often an unsubstantiated claim, though Queen Elizabeth I (1558–1603) was indeed an inveterate traveller and guest. By 1847, Thackeray was writing in *Vanity Fair*, Chap. 8: 'I think there are at least twenty bedrooms on the first floor; and one of them has the bed in which Queen Elizabeth slept.' By 1888, Jerome K. Jerome in *Three Men in a Boat* had: 'She was nuts on public houses, was England's Virgin Queen. There's scarcely a pub of any attractions within ten miles of London that she does not seem to have looked in at, stopped at, or slept at, some time or other.'

In the US, the equivalent slogan is **George Washington Slept Here**, as in the title of Kaufman and Hart's play (1940; film US, 1942), which, when adapted by Talbot Rothwell for the Strand Theatre, London, later in the 1940s, was called, naturally enough, *Queen Elizabeth Slept Here*.

Radio 1 Is Wonderful
BBC Radio 1 (national pop music station); UK, from 1967.

Radio's Bouncing Czech
Bill-matter for the Czech-born comedian Egon Regon who did indeed appear on British radio in the 1940s.

Rael-Brook Toplin, The Shirt(s) You Don't Iron
Rael-Brook shirts; UK, current mid-1960s. That rarity – a slogan created by the manufacturer. Johnny Johnson, who wrote the music for the jingle used in the TV ad, recalled: 'Harry Rael-Brook would not work through an agency. He came into my office and said, "I want a 30-second jingle." I said, "Oh yes, and what do you want to say?" And he said, "Rael-Brook Toplin, the shirt you don't iron." And that was that.' The jingle consisted of this phrase repeated over and over. (Source: Jo Gable, *The Tuppenny Punch and Judy Show*, 1980).

Reach For A Lucky Instead Of A Sweet
See IT'S TOASTED

Reach For A Murad
Murad cigarettes; US, 1920s/30s. Murads were 'All Turkish' factory-made cigarettes which 'had a higher-class appeal than those made from native American tobaccos.' (Flexner, 1982) The slogan makes an appearance in a New York settting in Noël Coward's play *Design for Living*, Act 3 (1933).

Read All About It
Traditional newspaper vendor's cry; UK, probably since 1900. The phrase follows the shouting of the main headline story: 'King to abdicate ... Bishop elopes with nun ... read all about it!' By exten-

sion applied to books and, hence, *Read All About It*, the title of a BBC TV review of new paperback books (1974–9).

Ready, Aye, Ready
Camp coffee; UK, from c.1883. This is almost a slogan in the old sense of a war-cry. In fact, it has been used as such by several Scots clans, including the Johnstons, Stewarts, Napiers and Scotts. Various institutions use it as a motto, too – Merchiston Castle School, Edinburgh, is one. But it has travelled farthest on the distinctive label for Camp coffee, manufactured by R. Paterson & Sons of Glasgow. The label remained virtually unchanged for nearly a hundred years. Today the basic elements are still in place: a Scots officer being served coffee by a turbanned attendant with the slogan up a flagpole. Additional phrases have adjured: **Drink Camp – It's The Best!** and **Don't Be Misled!!!**

Ready When You Are
See DELTA IS ...

Real Goodness From Kentucky ...
See IT'S FINGER LICKIN' GOOD

Real Thing, The
Marconi radios; UK, undated. (Sunners) See also DRINK COCA-COLA.

Reclaim The Night
See WOMEN RECLAIM THE NIGHT

Register Communists Not Guns
John Birch Society; US, 1970.

Remember —!
Slogan format, particularly enabling wars and revolutions to begin or continue by keeping alive a cause of anger. From Robert Kee, *Ireland: A History* (1982): 'The village of Ballingarry in County Tipperary ... the history books will tell you, was the scene of that 1848 Rising to assert Irish national sovereignty and freedom ... [And in it] you recognize at once the building which can be found in an *Illustrated London News* engraving of August 1848. A plaque

above the door enjoins: "**Remember 1848**".' Consider also: **Remember The River Raisin!** – a war-cry of Kentucky soldiers dating from the war of 1812. In the Raisin River massacre, 700 Kentuckians, badly wounded trying to capture Detroit, were scalped and butchered by Indians who were allies of the British. **Remember The Alamo!** The Alamo Mission in San Antonio, Texas, was used as a fort during the rebellion against Mexican rule in 1836. On 6 March, five days after Texas declared her independence, President Antonio Lopez de Santa Anna with more than 3000 men attacked the Alamo. In it were a hundred or so Texans, including Davy Crockett. After a thirteen-day siege, every Texan had been killed or wounded, and even the wounded were put to death. Lopez was defeated and captured at the Battle of San Jacinto (21 April 1836) by a Texan army under Commander-in-Chief Sam Houston. Sidney Sherman, a colonel in this army, is credited with devising the battle-cry. **Remember Goliad!** from the same conflict refers to Santa Anna's shooting of 330 Texans who had retreated from Goliad. **Remember the *Maine*!** The US battleship Maine exploded and sank in Havana harbour on 15 February 1898, taking 258 American lives with it. The vessel had been sent to protect US residents and their property during the Cuban revolution. The cause of the explosion was never established, but the Spanish-American War started ten weeks later. (Graffito reported shortly after: 'Remember the Maine,/ To hell with Spain,/Don't forget to pull the chain'.) **Remember the *Lusitania*!** The *Lusitania* was a British liner carrying many American passengers which was sunk off the Irish coast on 7 May 1915 by a German submarine. The sinking helped bring the US into the First World War. **Remember Belgium!** Originally a recruiting slogan referring to the invasion of Belgium by the Germans at the start of the First World War. It eventually emerged with ironic emphasis amid the mud of Ypres, encouraging the rejoinder: 'As if I'm ever likely to forget the bloody place!' (Partridge/*Catch Phrases*). **Remember Pearl Harbor!** The initial war-slogan and battle-cry of the US after the bombing of Pearl Harbor by the Japanese in December 1941. **Remember the *Pueblo*!** A bumper sticker with one of the rare battle-cries of the Vietnam War. Coined by Young Americans For Freedom following the capture of the USS *Pueblo* by North Korea in 1968.

Return To Normalcy With Harding
See BACK TO NORMALCY

Right One, The
Martini; UK, from 1970. In a conscious attempt to switch Martini from being a 'woman's drink' to a 'his and hers' drink, the McCann-Erickson agency created a romantic, high-life world full of young, beautiful people engaged in skiing, speedboating, even ballooning. Not the least ingredient was the song composed by Chris Gunning:

> Try a taste of Martini
> The most beautiful drink in the world,
> It's the bright one, the right one.
> There's much more to the world than you guess,
> And you taste it the day you say yes
> To the bright taste, the right taste
> Of Martini ...

In 1981, Barry Day admitted responsibility for the phrase 'The Right One'. When it comes to the other major Martini slogan, **Any Time, Any Place, Any Where**, Day agreed there was more than a hint of Bogart in the line: 'As a Bogart fan of some standing, with my union dues all paid up, I think I would have known if I had lifted it from one of his utterances, but I honestly can't place it.' This has been a line from Martini ads since the early 1970s. Possibly there is a hint of Harry Lime, too. In the film *The Third Man* (1949), Lime says (in the run-up to the famous cuckoo-clock speech): 'When you make up your mind, send me a message – I'll meet you any place, any time ... ' Two popular songs of the 1920s were 'Anytime, Any Day, Anywhere' and 'Anytime, Anywhere, Any Place – I Don't Care'. The exact phrase 'any time, any place, anywhere' had occurred earlier, however, in the song 'I Love To Cry at Weddings' from the musical *Sweet Charity* (1966) and in the film script of Tennessee Williams's *Cat on a Hot Tin Roof* (US, 1958). In 1950, and precisely as 'Anytime, Anyplace, Anywhere', it was the title of an R&B hit for Joe Morris – sung by (the female) Little Laurie Tate. Even earlier it was spoken in the film *The Strawberry Blonde* (US, 1941) of which the last lines are: 'When I want to kiss my wife, I'll kiss her anytime, anyplace, anywhere. That's the kind of hairpin I am' – this was written by the Epstein brothers who co-wrote *Casablanca*, so perhaps *that* is the Bogart connection?

In April 1987, a woman called Marion Joannou was jailed at the Old Bailey in London for protecting the man who had strangled her husband. She was nicknamed 'Martini Marion' because, apparently, she would have sex 'any time, any place, anywhere'.

Also, **Martini is ...**

Road Of Anthracite, The

The Delaware Lackawanna & Western railroad; US, from 1900. The character of 'Phoebe Snow' was created to promote the idea of cleanliness in travelling on a railroad which used sootless anthracite coal as locomotive fuel. She appeared for half a century and the railroad came to call itself **The Route Of Phoebe Snow.** Her adventures were described in short verses, such as:

Yes, Phoebe,
I can now see why
The praises of
This road you cry.
My gloves are white
As when last night
We took the Road
Of Anthracite.

(Watkins)

Room With A Bath For A Dollar And A Half, A

Statler hotels; US, c.1900. Created by the hotelier Ellsworth M. Statler himself.

Roses Grow On You

Cadbury's Roses chocolates; UK, current mid-1960s. Norman Vaughan, who presented the TV ads, recalled (1979): 'This was shouted at me wherever I went from about 1965. The campaign only ran for two years but on personal appearances even now people still ask me, "Where are your roses?" ' Maurice Drake, who was with the Young & Rubicam agency at the time, added (1981): 'This was a famous line that originally went into the waste-paper basket, but was rescued a couple of hours later, just before the cleaners came in.'

Route Of Phoebe Snow, The
See ROAD OF ANTHRACITE

Rum, Romanism, Rebellion
Republican presidential election slogan; US, 1884. Samuel Dickinson Burchard, speaking on behalf of clergymen who supported the Republican candidate, James G. Blaine, said: 'We are Republicans, and don't propose to leave our party and identify ourselves with the party whose antecedents have been rum, Romanism, and rebellion.' His Irish-Catholic audience in New York took none too kindly to this. Blaine lost the state's vote, and the presidency, to Grover Cleveland.

Safe And Sane Fourth, A

Occasional slogan from *Life* (humour magazine); US, probably from the 1890s. It was devised by Thomas Masson, editor from 1893 to 1922. Referring to the Fourth of July celebrations which sometimes got out of hand. (Flexner, 1976)

Safe And Sure

Nation Life Assurance company; UK, early 1970s. In 1974, it became the first such company to collapse in a hundred years. It was presided over by William Stern who was later found bankrupt, some £104 millions in debt.

Safe Place, With The Nice Face

See WE'RE WITH THE WOOLWICH

Safety Fast

MG Motors; UK, current before the Second World War.

Safety First

Conservative Party general election slogan; UK, 1929. Stanley Baldwin fought for re-election with it. Posters showed the 'wise and honest' face of the Prime Minister, who, inevitably, was smoking a pipe, and the further words: 'Stanley Baldwin, The Man You Can Trust.' He was even shown as a sea-captain, wearing a sou-wester, accompanied by the slogan **Trust Baldwin, He Will Steer You To Safety**. Conservative Central Office had thought that the General Strike of not so long before (1926) called for this reassuring approach but, with growing unemployment and the depression on the way, the slogan proved a loser. The party chairman, J.C.C. Davidson, who had accepted the idea from Benson's agency, took the blame for the Tories' defeat at the hands of Ramsay MacDonald and the Labour Party.

The phrase 'Safety First' had first come into use in the 1890s when railway companies maintained that 'the Safety of the Passenger is our First Concern'. In 1916, the London General Bus Company formed a London Safety First Council. The 1922 general election first saw the phrase in use as a political slogan for the Conservatives. They subsequently won with it in 1931. In 1934 the National Safety First Association was formed, concerned with road and industrial safety.

Salada Is Delicious Tea
Salada tea; US, from c.1890.

Saloon Must Go, The
Slogan of the Anti-Saloon League; US, from 1895. When saloons were a proliferating, noisy, smelly nuisance, the League used political pressure to bring the temperance movement to a successful climax in Prohibition.

Savage Story Of Lust And Ambition, A
Film, *Room at the Top*; UK, 1958.

Save It
Energy conservation slogan; UK, April 1975 to May 1979 – on behalf of the government's Department of Energy. Specifically, during the long, dry summer of 1976, it was applied to conservation of water supplies. Variations have included **Turn It Off** and the informal **Save Water – Bath With A Friend** (Reisner, 1974, had already recorded the graffito, 'Save water, bathe with friends'). In the UK, the South Eastern Gas Board (Segas) had also already run an advertisement in January 1974 showing a couple sharing a bath, with the line: 'Put a bit of romance into your bath by sharing the water.'

Save The American Way Of Life
See LAND LANDON ...

Save The Esso Tiger
Esso; UK, from 1967. In *Campaign* (7 November 1980), Dennis Page recalled how he was hired to revive the tiger (see PUT A TIGER

IN YOUR TANK): 'I had the ad manager on television advertising the end of the Esso tiger and the tiger saying he was not going to go. Far from saving the tiger, it actually hastened his demise [in 1968].'

Save Ulster From Sodomy
Anti-homosexual slogan; Northern Ireland, 1982. 'When the British government four years ago sought to relax Northern Ireland's stern laws against homosexuality, the most fiery religious leader in Ulster mounted a successful campaign to thwart the move. Trumpeting the slogan "Save Ulster from Sodomy", Fundamentalist Presbyterian minister Ian Paisley ... persuaded London not to change [the] law' (*Time* Magazine, 8 March 1982).

Save Water – Bath With A Friend
See SAVE IT

Say Hello To A Brand New World
See WE FLY THE WORLD ...

Say It Loud, We're Gay And We're Proud
Gay Liberation Front; US, c.1970. Clearly derived from the James Brown song 'Say it loud, I'm *black* and I'm proud' with which he had had a hit in 1968. Compare the New York City graffito 'Say it loud, I'm yellow and I'm mellow.' (Reisner)
 Also **2-4-6-8/Gay Is Just As Good As Straight/3-5-7-9/Lesbians Are Mighty Fine**; US, 1970s.

Say It With Flowers
Society of American florists; US, 1917. Henry Penn of Boston, Mass., originated the phrase as chairman of the society's national publicity committee. He was discussing the need for such a slogan with Major Patrick K. O'Keefe, head of an agency. The Major suggested: 'Flowers are words that even a babe can understand' – a line he had found in a poetry book. Mr Penn considered this too long. The Major, agreeing, rejoined: 'Why, you can say it with flowers in so many words.' Mr Penn's hand went bang! on the table. They had found their slogan. (Lambert) Later came several songs with the title. (See over.)

Say it with Flowers

**FLOWERS BY WIRE ANYWHERE IN THE WORLD
PROMPT DELIVERY AND QUALITY GUARANTEED**

Schweppervesence Lasts …
See WHAT IS THE SECRET OF SCHHH?

Sean Connery *Is* James Bond
Film, *You Only Live Twice*; UK, 1967 – a debatable proposition at
the best of times and only likely to encourage a regrettable ten-
dency, particularly among journalists, to confuse actors with their
roles. The slogan format '— *is* —' has accordingly become a cliché
of sloganeering. Other examples: 'Michael Caine is Alfie is wicked!'
(1966); 'Paul Hogan *is* Crocodile Dundee' (1987); 'Phil Collins *is*
Buster' (title of a video about the making of the film *Buster*, 1988);
'Domingo *is* Otello' [*sic*], ad in *Los Angeles* Magazine, March 1989;
'Jessye Norman *is* Carmen', ad on LBC radio, August 1989.

Second Front Now
Unofficial political slogan; UK, 1942–3. This was a demand
chalked on walls (and supported by the Beaverbrook press) for an
invasion of the European mainland, particularly one in collabora-
tion with the Soviet Union. The Allied military command dis-
agreed and preferred to drive Axis troops out of North Africa and
the Mediterranean first. Churchill's argument against a second
front was that Britain's resources were fully stretched already.

See America First
Great Northern Railway Co.; US, from c.1914. Variously credited
to G. Herb Palin, a leading American slogan writer, and Louis W.
Hill Senior, president of the company. The slogan was splashed all
over the US and helped turn the tide of travel from the east coast
to the west. Hill said he picked up the phrase from an ad and adopted it as his company's slogan. Perhaps Palin wrote the original?

By 1916, Cole Porter was using the phrase as the title of a show and a song.

'See Britain First' which may never actually have been used in UK advertising appears, nevertheless, in a Ghilchick cartoon in *Punch* (7 October 1931).

See How It Runs!
Cerebos salt; UK, from 1919. Cerebos salt was invented in 1894 by George Weddell, who discovered that his compound flowed much better than ordinary table salt. This property was emphasized when in 1906 the Cerebos company bought up a rival, Birdcatcher salt, whose trademark was a little boy pouring salt on a chicken's tail. This character first appeared on the Cerebos packs after the First World War.

See That Hump?
The Long Patented Hook & Eye Company; US, from 1891.

Send Him Back To Finish The Job
Conservative Party general election slogan; UK, 1945. Referring to Winston Churchill who was seeking to be re-elected as the Prime Minister of a Conservative government after his leadership of an all-party War Cabinet since 1940. The slogan backfired when it was seen to be supported by those who had tried to keep Churchill out of power in 1940. A Labour victory brought in Clement Attlee as Prime Minister.

Send Them A Message
Presidential election slogan of George C. Wallace; US, 1972. Third-party candidate Wallace sought to attract votes away from the incumbent President, Richard Nixon, and the Democrat George McGovern by pointing up the gulf between the 'little people' in the electorate and the aloof politicians in power. But he failed. (Safire)

Senior Service Satisfy
Senior service cigarettes; UK, current 1981. Before 1950, there had been the bizarre line **A Product Of The Master Mind**.

209

Set The People Free

Conservative Party general election slogan; UK, 1951. Taken from the lyrics of a patriotic song of the Second World War. In 'Song of Liberty' (1940), A.P. Herbert put words to the *nobilmente* theme from Edward Elgar's 'Pomp and Cicumstance March No. 4':

> All men must be free
> March for liberty with me
> Brutes and braggarts may have their little day,
> We shall never bow the knee.
>
> God his drawing His sword
> We are marching with the Lord
> Sing, then, brother, sing, giving ev'ry thing,
> All you are and hope to be,
> To set the peoples free.

The Conservatives won the election and in a radio broadcast (3 May 1952), Winston Churchill, as Prime Minister, returned to the theme: 'We think it is a good idea to set the people free as much as it is possible in our complicated modern society, from the trammels of state control and bureaucratic management.' Many years later, in a House of Commons debate on the Rates Bill (17 January 1984), Edward Heath recalled how he had entered the House having fought an election on Mr Churchill's theme that Conservatives were to set the people free. 'It was not a theme,' he said, 'that we were to set the people free to do what we tell them'.

Seven Million Every Day And Still Going Down

See GUINNESS IS GOOD FOR YOU

Shaped To Be Raped

Karl Lagerfeld fashion show; Italy, October 1984. Designer Lagerfeld chose this controversial slogan to launch a number of his latest creations at the Milan Fashion Show though, when a furore was created, he claimed that this was a mistranslation of the original and he had merely been indulging in a little word play. Nevertheless, the slogan occurred over Lagerfeld's signature in an English publicity handout. The phrase was omitted from the

Italian copy. The French translation was the more acceptable '*Une forme pour être désirée* [shaped to be desired].'

Share The Wealth
Political slogan of Huey P. Long; US, from 1928 to his assassination in 1935. Also **Everyman A King (But No Man Wears A Crown)**. The thrust of Long's campaigning was that 10 per cent of the people owned 70 per cent of the wealth and that this should be shared. (Safire) The Louisiana Governor (and demagogue) found this slogan for his Share-the-Wealth platform – in William Jennings Bryan's 'Cross of Gold' speech at the 1896 Democratic convention. The slogan used 'everyman' as one word.

Sharp's The Word For Toffee
Sharp's toffee; UK, from 1927. Sir Edward Sharp first manufactured toffee in 1880. The old firm became Trebor Sharps Ltd during the 1960s (Trebor is 'Robert' backwards).

Shave Yourself
Gillette Safety Razor; US, current in the early 1900s.

She's No Lady!
Bill-matter for the British music-hall entertainer, George Lacy. He was a female impersonator and made himself famous as a pantomime 'dame' (from 1924). Also sometimes billed as 'The Ace of Jokers'.

Ship Through Newport, Home Of The Mole Wrench
Postal franking slogan for Newport and the Mole Wrench (a type of tool); UK, 1960s. From *The Independent* (21 March 1989): 'In the Sixties the town of Newport had somehow managed to achieve the status of a music-hall joke. For a while all letters were franked with [this] message. With a national Inland Revenue office in the town, tax demands went out all over the country broadcasting Newport's Mole Wrench. Newport had played a glorious role in the birth of the trade union movement when the Chartists' uprising was bloodily put down outside the Westgate Hotel. But now Newport was famous for its Mole Wrench and a perpetually incompetent football team.'

Shoot To Live!
The Weathermen (militant revolutionary group); US, c.1969.

Shopping Days To Christmas
See CUSTOMER IS ALWAYS RIGHT

Simply Years Ahead
Corporate slogan for Philips electronics; UK, c.1973.

Since When I Have Used No Other ...
Pears' Soap; UK, 1880s/90s. At one time, Pears' advertised through a signed testimonial (with picture) from Lillie Langtry, the actress and mistress of King Edward VII (when he was Prince of Wales): 'Since using Pears' Soap for the hands and complexion *I have discarded all others.*' This ad is undated and may have come before the cartoon parody of such testimonials drawn by Harry Furniss and which appeared in *Punch* (26 April 1884). This showed a grubby tramp penning his own testimonial with the caption: 'GOOD ADVERTISEMENT. I used your soap two years ago; since then I have used no other.' Not missing a trick, Pears, with permission from Punch, rearranged the words, added the firm's name to the cartoon and issued it as one of thousands of handbills distributed in the last two decades of the nineteenth century. The slogan was changed slightly to: 'Two years ago I used your soap *since when* I have used no other!'

Singer With The Smile In His Voice, The
Bill-matter of the singer Jack Smith. If this is the same as the American 'Whispering' Jack Smith (1899–1951), he was also known as **The Whispering Baritone**.

Sinn Fein [Ourselves Alone/We Alone/We Ourselves]
Motto/slogan of the Irish Nationalist Movement, which was also called Sinn Fein; Ireland, since 1905. Also adopted by Breton separatists.

Sixpence Worth Of Heaven
Cadbury's Flake (confectionery); UK, current 1965.

Skin You Love To Touch, The
Woodbury's Facial Soap; US, from 1910. The records of the
Andrew Jergens Company show that 'The Skin You Love To
Touch' was originally the title of a booklet about the skin and how
to care for it. The *Ladies' Home Journal* for May 1911 carried it first.
Carl Naether commented in *Advertising To Women* (1928): 'It is a
lure to make women believe that, by using the soap in question,
she will be able to cultivate a skin sufficiently beautiful to consti-
tute an infallible safeguard against the waning of male affection.
In other words, the promise was that the soap would do more for
her than just cleanse her skin.'

'Before this romantic slogan was used, the soap was less ele-
gantly advertised as a remedy for "conspicuous nose pores".'
(Flexner, 1982)

Sleep Like A Kitten
Chesapeake & Ohio Lines (railroad); US, from 1933. This slogan
appeared with the logo of a kitten tucked up in bed. The company's
vice-president came across a picture entitled 'The Sleepy Cat' in a
New York newspaper and asked around the office what phrase
best signified sound sleep. Among the suggestions were 'like a
top' and 'like a kitten'. The latter was voted the winner. (Lambert)

Sleep Sweeter, Bournvita
Bournvita (night drink): UK, current 1960s. Featured memorably
in a TV commercial which simply consisted of a smiling mug and
the slogan followed by a yawn and 'Goodnight'.

Slip Of A Lip May Sink A Ship, The
See WALLS HAVE EARS

Small Is Beautiful
Economics slogan; UK, 1973. The German-born British economist,
Professor E.F. Schumacher (1911–77) entitled a book (1973) *Small
Is Beautiful. A Study of Economics As If People Mattered*. The first
phrase provided a catchphrase and a slogan for those who were
opposed to the expansionist trend in business and organizations
(very apparent in the 1960s and 1970s) and who wanted 'economics

on a human scale'. However, it appears that Schumacher nearly did not bother with the phrase. According to his daughter and another correspondent (*The Observer*, 29 April and 6 June 1984), the book was to be called 'The Homecomers'. His publisher, Anthony Blond, suggested 'Small*ness* is Beautiful', and then Desmond Briggs, the co-publisher, came up with the eventual wording.

Smirnoff
See I THOUGHT ...

Smoke Craven 'A'
See FOR YOUR THROAT'S SAKE ...

Smokers Are Requested To Use Swan Vestas
Swan Vesta matches; UK, current 1920s and 1930s. The captions on the matchboxes have changed to reflect current conditions: **The Smoker's Match** (1905); **Use Matches Sparingly** (1941).

Smoking Allowed – Abdullah's Preferred
Abdullah cigarettes; UK, current 1930s – especially on advertisements in the London Underground.

Snap! Crackle! Pop!
Kellogg's Rice Krispies; US, from c.1928, later in the UK. A version early in the century went 'It Pops! It Snaps! It Crackles!' Something of a red herring has been raised by H.R.F. Keating, the crime writer, who in an introduction to a reprint of *Epitaph for a Spy* by Eric Ambler, wrote that the immortal phrase had been coined by Ambler when working in advertising before becoming a thriller writer (in the great tradition of copywriters-turned-novelists). But no, Ambler said it was someone else at the agency he worked for. As Ambler worked in advertising from 1929–35, it seems pretty apparent that the slogan had been coined before he started anyway. It is nearly certain, too, that the slogan was coined in the US rather than in the UK.

Softness Is A Thing Called Comfort
Comfort fabric conditioner; UK, late 1960s. Coined by Barry Day. Ran till the 1980s.

Soft, Strong And Very Long
Andrex toilet tissue; UK, current 1981. Did Andrex also proclaim
Stays Stiff Even When Wet?

Someone Isn't Using Amplex
Amplex (breath purifier); UK, 1950s. Ads showed two people
reacting to a smelly colleague with this slogan – as parodied in a
Private Eye cartoon (1964/5) showing Soviet leaders watching a
May Day parade. Or perhaps it was 'somebody's not using
Amplex', as reported in *The Lyttelton Hart-Davis Letters*, Vol. 2
(1979) – for 5 January 1957.

Someone's Mother
Persil washing powder; UK, current 1940 – a theme carried from
posters and press ads on to TV.

> What someone's mum really ought to know,
> So someone's mum better get to know,
> That Persil washes whiter, whiter –
> **Persil washes whiter**.

Also the phrase **What Is A Mum?** featured in a series of TV ads
from 1961.

Someone, Somewhere, Wants A Letter From You
Post Office; UK, by 1964.

Somewhere West of Laramie
Jordan 'Playboy' motor car; US, 1923. Ads showed a 'spirited cowboy next to a beautiful girl at the wheel.' (Flexner, 1982)

So Much More To Enjoy
See INTERNATIONAL PASSPORT ...

Song, A Smile, And A Piano, (A)
Bill-matter for the British comedian Norman Long, particularly on
the radio, 1920s/30s. The BBC apparently changed his billing to **A
Song, A Joke And A Piano** on the basis that you could not broadcast a smile on radio. Often alluded to: in BBC Radio *The Last Goon*

215

Show of All (1972), 'That demonstration of Mr Secombe's senility – "A smile, a song, a wheelchair" ... ' *Punch* (13 July 1977) referred to a BBC breakfast-time radio programme, *Up To the Hour* as, 'A prayer, a joke, a song, a chat, a cup of tea and a quick cigarette ... '

So Round, So Firm, So Fully Packed
See IT'S TOASTED

Sounds Better Than it Looks
Unnamed television set manufacturer; India, quoted 1981. Perhaps it is as well that we do not know the name of the set which was advertised all over India thus.

South Will Rise Again, The
Political slogan; US, probably from the late nineteenth century. Referring to the aftermath of the American Civil War and presumably coming out of the period that followed it, known as Reconstruction. Meaning, 'the (American) South is not finished yet and has a future'. Somewhat tainted in that it has also been used as a rallying cry of segregationists. But did any particular person say it originally? Was it an actual slogan? Curiously little information is to hand on these points.

Modern allusions: from *The Washington Post* (11 November 1984): 'President Reagan himself took some giant steps backward in race relations during the campaign ... telling an audience in Macon, Ga., that "the South will rise again!", a rallying cry of segregationists in an earlier era.' From the *Financial Times* (7 June 1985): 'Along the 100-mile highway that now links the two old civil war capitals – Washington (The Union) and Richmond (The Confederacy) – you can stop and buy a tee-shirt that bears the proud slogan "Save your Confederate money, the South will rise again".' From the London *Times* (18 February 1988): 'Jubilant [George Bush, seeking re-election], told cheering supporters on Tuesday night: "I feel I have a lot in common with Mark Twain: reports of my death were greatly exaggerated." He said he was now going on to the South, "where we will rise again".'

Speak Softly And Carry A Big Stick
Political slogan; US, 1901. Speaking at the Minnesota State Fair in

September of that year, President Theodore Roosevelt gave strength to the idea of backing negotiations with threats of military force when he said: 'There is a homely adage which runs, "Speak softly and carry a big stick; you will go far." If the American nation will speak softly and yet build and keep at a pitch of the highest training a thoroughly efficient navy, the Monroe Doctrine will go far.' The homely adage is said to have started life as a West African proverb.

Spend Wisely – Save Wisely
Brooke Bond Dividend tea; UK, current 1930s.

Splash It All Over
Brut after-shave; UK, c.1974. TV ads featured the popular ex-boxer Henry Cooper – to show that using the product was somehow not an unmanly thing to do.

Spotless Town
See USE SAPOLIO!

Spreads Straight From The Fridge
Blue Band margarine; UK, current late 1960s.

Square Deal, The
Political slogan; US, 1901. Theodore Roosevelt succeeded to the presidency on the assassination of President McKinley. For some US presidents it is not enough to attain the White House, they have to dignify their policies with a resounding label, so Roosevelt declared: 'We demand that big business give people a Square Deal' and 'If elected I shall see to it that every man has a Square Deal, no more and no less.' He was still using the slogan in 1913, with specific reference to its original use regarding big business.

Squeeze A Fruit For Anita
Informal pro-homosexual slogan; US, late 1970s. Anita Bryant – who had once appeared in an orange juice commercial – mounted a ferocious anti-gays campaign and inspired much mockery, of which this slogan is an example.

Stack It High, Watch 'Em Buy
See PILE IT HIGH ...

Standard of the World
Cadillac Motor Co.; US, current 1912. Created by the MacManus, John & Adams agency of Detroit, the copy ran: 'You know it to be true – you know that the Cadillac is a criterion wherever motor cars are discussed ... all the Cadillac arguments we could advance in a score of announcements would not be one-hundredth part as impressive as the positive knowledge you hold in your mind at this moment. You know that the Cadillac is in very fact the standard of the world. What more is there to be said?' The phrase was incorporated in the Cadillac logo in 1915. Also: **The Penalty Of Leadership** – headline over a famous piece of advertising copy which appeared once only – in *The Saturday Evening Post* (2 January 1915) – discussing Cadillac's claim to be the best in the field: 'If the leader truly leads, he remains – the leader ... That which deserves to live – lives.'

Stand Pat With McKinley
See AMERICA CANNOT STAND PAT

Station Of The Stars, The
Radio Luxembourg; UK, from the 1950s onwards. 'Radio Lux' beamed pop radio to the UK when commercial broadcasting was not permitted in the country. Compare **The Station Of The Nation** – Radio Caroline, the pirate radio ship; off-shore UK, current 1966.

Stays Stiff Even When Wet
See SOFT, STRONG AND VERY LONG

Step Out With A Stetson
Hats manufactured by John B. Stetson Co.; US, current 1930s.

Stop Me And Buy One
Wall's ice cream; UK, from 1923. The phrase is believed to have been invented by Lionel and Charles Rodd, who were on the board of T. Wall & Sons. With the slogan on their tricycles, 8,500 salesmen then pedalled round Britain out of a national network of 136 depots. One salesman whose brakes failed as he descended a very steep hill introduced a slight variation as he hurtled to destruction: 'If you can stop me, you can have the lot.'

Stops Body Odour (or B.O.)
Lifebuoy soap; US, current by 1933. 'B.O.' was a notable phrase given to the language by advertising. On US radio in the 1930s, there used to be the jingle:

> Singing in the bathtub, singing for joy,
> Living a life of Lifebuoy –
> Can't help singing, 'cos I know
> That Lifebuoy really stops B.O.

'B.O.' was sung *basso profundo*, emphasizing the horror of the offence. In the UK, TV ads showed pairs of male or female friends out on a spree, intending to attract partners. When one of the pair was seen to have a problem, the other whispered helpfully, 'B.O.'

Stops Halitosis!
Listerine mouthwash; US, from 1921. At first, Listerine was promoted as a 'safe antiseptic' with countless hygienic uses. Then, in

1921, the Lambert Company decided to use a clinical term for the ordinary unpleasantness known as 'bad breath' – halitosis. An anxiety was not only stimulated, it was labelled. Listerine sales climbed from 115,000 a year in 1921 to four million a year in 1927. (Atwan) From Rosser Reeves, *Reality in Advertising* (1960): 'Who can steal "Stops Halitosis" from Listerine? Dozens of other mouthwashes stop halitosis. Many tried to move in on this great classic UNIQUE SELLING PROPOSITION, until it became almost a source of embarrassment to them, seeking ways to phrase their imitation, so that they did not advertise the leader. This U.S.P., in the public's mind, belongs to Listerine.' Also **For Halitosis, Use Listerine**.

Strength Through Joy
See *KRAFT DURCH FREUDE*

Stronger Than Dirt
Ajax laundry detergent; US, 1960s.

Sunday Dispatch, Best Of The Batch
See *DAILY MAIL* ...

Sunday Isn't Sunday Without *The Sunday Times*
The Sunday Times (newspaper); UK, from 1968. Peter Phillips recalled (letter to *Campaign*, 17 April 1981): 'In 1968 I asked the whole creative department at Thomson Group Marketing to come up with a slogan for *The Sunday Times* and the person who presented me with this deathless slogan was Frank Page, later motoring correspondent of *The Observer*. I was not aware that the *Empire News* had already used it (as **Sunday Isn't Sunday Without The Empire News**) – nor were the countless people who have claimed authorship since then.' By 1993, the slogan **The Sunday Times *Is* The Sunday Papers** was in regular use.

Sunny Jim
Force (breakfast cereal); US, from c.1903. Few people who use the nickname 'Sunny Jim' know that it originated in ads for Force. The Force Food Company was formed in 1901. A London office was established the following year. By 1903, advertising on both

sides of the Atlantic was featuring the character called 'Sunny Jim'. He was the invention of two young American women, a Miss Ficken and Minnie Maud Hanff (usually credited with the phrase), who had submitted a jingle and rough sketch to the company. One of the first jingles was:

Vigor, Vim, Perfect Trim;
Force made him, Sunny Jim.

In the 1920s came:

High o'er the fence leaps Sunny Jim,
Force is the food that raises him.

In the 1930s, Force was advertised on commercial radio broadcasts to the UK from Radios Luxembourg, Lyons and Normandy. In the US, the product has now disappeared from sale, but in 1970 the A.C. Fincken Company relaunched it in the UK. The name of the cereal was long a gift to jokesters:

A: I can't coax my husband to eat any breakfast.
B: Have you tried Force?
A: You don't know my husband.

Hence, however, the term 'Sunny Jim' applied in various ways as an appellation. One might say, 'Ah, there you are ... I've been looking for you, Sunny Jim' – even if the person isn't called Jim. It is a name applied to a cheerful person. From *Lady Cynthia Asquith's Diary* (for 13 July 1918): 'I like McKenna. He is such a "Sunny Jim" and ripples on so easily.' When James Callaghan became British Prime Minister in 1976, the phrase inevitably became much used. Headline from *The Observer* (18 March 1979): 'Sunny Jim tires of wheeler-dealing'.

Sun, Sea, Sand (And Sex)
Travel journalistic and promotional line (with the force of a slogan); UK, probably since the 1960s. The origin of this slogan is not known, though in the 1939 film version of *The Four Feathers*, the Sudan is referred to, with similar alliteration, as 'sun, sweat and

sunstroke'. In 1972, I interviewed a group of children born in London of West Indian parents, who were about to pay their first visit to Barbados. When I asked one of them what he expected to find there, he quite spontaneously said: 'All I know is, it's sun, sand and sea.' This line was used as the title of a BBC Radio programme which reported their reactions before and after the visit. Clearly, the child had absorbed the phrase at an early age. It is never very far away. Several songs have the title. Listed as part of the 'travel scribes' armoury' of clichés in *The Guardian* (10 April 1993). 'Sun, sand and sea are no longer enough for the Yuppie generation of fun-seekers' – photo caption in *The Observer* (26 June 1988); 'We bought the beachfront land [in Barbados] a couple of years ago. Sunshine, sand and sea, it's the stuff that dreams and travel brochures are made of' – Bob Monkhouse, *Crying With Laughter* (1993); 'Sea, sand and celebration: a guide to the Brighton Festival' – *Big Issue Weekly* (17 May 1995).

Support Home Industries
See MADE IN ENGLAND

Support Your Local Police, Keep Them Independent
Police bumper-sticker; US, 1969. The film *Support Your Local Sheriff* appeared in 1968 and was followed three years later by *Support Your Local Gunfighter*, but the idea of supporting or consulting your local or neighbourhood whatever was already well established. 'Support Your Local —' was thus a slogan format, almost certainly of US origin. Compare YOUR FRIENDLY NEIGHBOURHOOD ...

Swedish Nightingale, The
See WIGAN NIGHTINGALE

Sweet As The Moment When The Pod Went 'Pop'
Birds Eye peas; UK, from c.1956. Written by Len Heath at the Lintas agency.

Sweet You Can Eat Between Meals (Without Ruining Your Appetite), The
Milky Way (confectionery); UK, from 1960.

Take Back The Night
See WOMEN RECLAIM THE NIGHT

Take Courage
See IT'S WHAT YOUR RIGHT ARM'S FOR

Takes The 'Ouch' Out Of Grouch
See FRESHEN UP ...

Take Stock In America
US Savings Bonds; US, quoted 1976.

Tall, Dark And Have Some
See GUINNESS IS GOOD FOR YOU

Tall ... Terrific ... And Trouble!
See MEAN! MOODY! ...

Tan – Don't Burn
Coppertone sun lotion; US, from 1953. Together with the cry **Don't Be A Paleface** these words supported a famous picture of a little girl having her bathing suit pulled down by a playful puppy. In 1991, the slogans came under threat because of the political incorrectness of the use of the word 'paleface'.

Taste As Good As It Smells
See GOOD TO THE LAST DROP

Taste Of Home, A
Suggested all-purpose food slogan, noted by Barry Day (1981) – but has it ever been used?

Taste Of Paradise
See BOUNTY ...

Taste The Difference
See COME ALIVE ...

Taste You Love To Hate, The
See OFTEN A BRIDESMAID ...

Taxation Without Representation ...
See NO TAXATION ...

Tea You Can Really Taste, The
Brooke Bond P.G. Tips; UK, current 1960s. Also **Tea You Can Taste To The Last Delicious Drop**.

Telegraph Less
See POST EARLY FOR CHRISTMAS

Tell Sid
Privatisation of British Gas (stock market launch); UK, 1986. 'Sid' characterised the small, private investor being encouraged to take part in this share issue. The actual slogan was **If You See Sid, Tell Him**. 'Sid' became journalistic shorthand for the archetypal small-scale 'democratic' share-buyer/holder, as in *The Guardian* (18 January 1989): 'Among the workforce [of the National Freight Consortium], the concept of share-ownership has won over "Sids" that multi-million pound Government marketing schemes have failed to reach. Nearly 26,000 of the 32,000 workforce have bought shares.' And from *The Sunday Telegraph* (30 January 1994): 'House of Fraser stores group will be embarking on a "Sid-style" marketing campaign to woo private investors and shoppers.'
   The slogan was found to be irritating by many. A graffito seen scribbled in the dirt on the side of a lorry in South London at the height of the original campaign and advertising frenzy: 'Sid's dead. He's gassed himself.' (Source: Paul Beale, 1994)

Ten Acres And A Mule
Political slogan; US, from 1862 onwards. Sought by slaves who

thought that their masters' plantations would be divided up to their benefit after the Civil War. However, this escalated to **Forty Acres And A Mule** when, in January 1865, General Sherman stated, 'Every family shall have a plot of not more than forty acres of tillable ground' – a promise which had nothing to do with the Federal government. Consequently, this Reconstruction slogan dwindled to **Three Acres And A Cow**.

That cry had originated in John Stuart Mill's *Principles of Political Economy* (1848): 'When the land is cultivated entirely by the spade and no horses are kept, a cow is kept for every three acres of land.' In the UK, Jesse Collings (1831–1920), a henchman in the 1880s of Joseph Chamberlain, proposed that every smallholder should have three acres. He was an advocate of radical agrarian policies and the smallholding movement. Hence, he became known as 'Three Acres And A Cow Collings'. (Noël Coward once described Edith, Osbert and Sacheverell Sitwell as 'two wiseacres and a cow'.)

Tense, Nervous Headache?
See NOTHING ACTS FASTER THAN ANADIN

Tetley Make Tea-Bags Make Tea
Tetley's tea; UK, current 1970s.

That Gleam Is Back In George's Eye Again
Serta Perfect Sleeper mattress; US, undated. 'The photo showed a leering George in bed, tousling his wife's red hair. Why the imminent attack? He switched to Serta Perfect Sleeper mattress, offered as the modern man's aphrodisiac.' (Baker)

That 'Good-Morning' Feeling
Welgar Shredded Wheat; UK, current mid-1940s.

That Kruschen Feeling, I've Got
Kruschen salts; UK, current 1920s and 1930s. The ads featured an athletic man who attributed his powers to Kruschen salts. Also **It's The Little Daily Dose That Does It** (*Time* Magazine, 3 May 1928).

That'll Do Nicely, (Sir)!
See DON'T LEAVE HOME WITH IT

That's A H**l Of A Way To Run A Railroad!

Boston & Maine railroad; US, probably 1930s. The inspiration for this slogan may have been the caption to a cartoon said to have appeared in the American *Collier's* magazine (though *Ballyhoo* in 1932 has also been suggested) which shows two trains about to collide. A signalman is looking out of his box and the caption is: 'Tch-tch- what a way to run a railroad!'

The Boston & Maine railroad picked up this line when it sought, 'a statement which would explain some of the problems of the railroad in times of inclement weather'. It took the 'stock railroad phrase', derived from the cartoon, and put it between each paragraph of the advertisement in the above form. Added at the foot of the ad was the line, 'But the railroad always runs.' Thus was reinforced (rather than coined) the popular expression 'What a way [*or* hell of a way] to run a railroad/railway!' – used as an exclamation concerning mismanagement or chaos of any kind,

Echoes or developments of this construction occur (in the UK) in the title of G.F. Fiennes's *I Tried to Run a Railway* (1967) – he had worked for British Rail – and the Conservative Party 1968 poster: 'Higher unemployment ... Higher unemployment ... Higher taxation ... Higher prices ... What a way to run a country!' And from *The Independent* Magazine (4 February 1989): 'The shop told me that it only had demonstration [satellite TV] dishes and suggested I call back in a fortnight. This is, surely, no way to run a revolution!'

That's Shell – That Was!

Shell motor fuel; UK, current from late 1930s. A picture of a one-headed man swivelling it round with the slogan 'That's Shell – That Is', current in 1929, was developed into that of a two-headed man with this more widely known slogan. A possibly apocryphal story is that the two-headed man was devised by a member of the public called Horsfield, who received £100 for his trouble.

There Is A Lion On My Egg

See GO TO WORK ON AN EGG

There Is No Substitute

Dr Collis Browne's Compound (stomach medicine); UK, probably since 1900, quoted 1978.

There Is Nothing Worth Dying For
Informal anti-draft registration slogan on placard; US, 1980.

There's A Ford In Your Future
Ford Motor Co.; US, 1944. Ford's original 1904 slogan had been **A Good Name Is Better Than Promises**.

There's A Reason
Postum and Post (breakfast cereals); US, from 1899 to 1924. Charles William Post invented the beverage known as Postum, but the slogan was also applied to other products. A 1908 ad for Postum Grape-Nuts used it thus: 'One of Uncle Sam's Navy boys was given up by the doctor. His stomach would not retain food or medicine until a mess-mate suggested Grape-Nuts. On this world-famed food and milk he gained about 40 lb. in four months and got well. It requires no "Expert Chemist" to prove that "THERE'S A REASON" for Grape-Nuts.'

'One could interpret the "reason" as being good nutrition and good health or the mildly laxative effect of the products.' (Flexner, 1982)

There's Never A Rough Puff In A Lucky
See IT'S TOASTED

They Come As A Boon And A Blessing To Men, / The Pickwick, The Owl, And The Waverley Pen
Macniven & Cameron Ltd's pens, made in Edinburgh and Birmingham; UK, current c.1920. Apparently derived from J.C. Prince, 'The Pen and the Press', in *The Thousand Best Poems in the World*, ed. E.W. Cole (1891): 'It came as a boon and a blessing to men, / The peaceful, the pure, the victorious PEN!' Also: **Macniven & Cameron's Pens Are Recommended By 3,050 Newspapers**.

They Had A Date With Fate In ... Casablanca
Film, *Casablanca*; US, 1941.

They Laughed When I Sat Down At The Piano ... But When I Started To Play ...
US School of Music piano tutor; US, from 1925. John Caples, the

copywriter, also came up with, 'They grinned when the waiter spoke to me in French – but their laughter changed to amazement at my reply' (presumably for another client). The slogan gave rise to various jokes: 'They laughed when I sat down to play – someone had taken away the stool / how did I know the bathroom door was open/etc.' In *Lyrics On Several Occasions ...* (1959), Ira Gershwin declared that the song 'They All Laughed' (' ... at Christopher Columbus / When he said the world was round; / They all laughed when Edison recorded sound)' (1937) was inspired by the ad: 'Along this line, I recall writing a postcard from Paris to Gilbert Gabriel, the drama critic, saying: "They all laughed at the Tour d'Argent last night when I said I would order in French." So the phrase "they all laughed" hibernated and estivated in the back of my mind for a dozen years until the right climate and tune popped it out as a title.'

In the film *Much Too Shy* (UK, 1942) there is actually a song with the title, 'They Laughed When I Sat Down at the Piano'.

They're G-R-Reat!
Kellogg's Sugar Frosted Flakes; US, from c.1951.

They Respect Your Throat
Alligator cigarettes; UK, undated. (Sunners)

They're Toasted
See IT'S TOASTED

They're Young ... They're In Love ... And They Kill People!
Film, *Bonnie and Clyde*; US, 1967.

They Shall Not Pass
See *ILS NE PASSERONT PAS*

They Were Going To Rape Her One By One. She Was Going To Kill Them ... One By One
Film, *Death Weekend*; Canada, 1976.

Things Go Better With Coke
See DRINK COCA-COLA

Things Happen After A Badedas Bath
Badedas (bath additive); UK, from 1966. Helicopters land on your lawn, dashing men lurk beneath your window. But it is an old fantasy: two hundred years ago a bath additive claimed to be: 'Admirable for those who have been almost worn out by women and wine ... it will render their intercourse prolific.' (Nicholl)

Think First – Most Doctors Don't Smoke
See DANGER: H. M. GOVERNMENT ...

Think Globally, Act Locally
Friends of the Earth (environment lobby); UK, by 1985. Meaning, 'Do your bit where you can; personal action counts. Test ideas on your own doorstep.' Adopted as a maxim in business and other areas.

Think Pink
Fictitious fashion slogan, from the film *Funny Face*; US, 1957. Kay Thompson plays a fashion editor (based on Diana Vreeland) at a fake *Harper's Bazaar*. 'Take a letter to the women of America,' she says at one point, 'Think pink.'

Think Small
Volkswagen automobiles; US, from c.1959. Created at the Doyle, Dane, Bernbach agency, this slogan led to the connection between DDB and the Democratic Party. It is said that John F. Kennedy had enjoyed the 'Think Small' campaign so much – it appealed to his sense of humour – that he suggested the link-up.

Thinks ... Thanks To Horlicks
See HORLICKS GUARDS AGAINST ...

Think What We Can Do For You
Corporate slogan for Bank of America; US, current 1980.

Thirst Knows No Season
See DRINK COCA-COLA

Thirteen Years Of Tory Misrule
Unofficial Labour Party catchphrase (with the force of a slogan)

prior to a general election; UK, 1964. Labour won the election over the Conservatives (who had been in power since 1951), so it may have had some effect. In his maiden speech to the House of Lords as the Earl of Stockton, Harold Macmillan recalled his days as (Conservative) Prime Minister (for six of the years in question): 'Of course, politics being politics, the Socialist party naturally called those years the "thirteen years of Tory misrule". But nobody seemed to mind very much.' Also in the form **Thirteen Wasted Years**. From the 1964 Labour Party election manifesto: 'A New Britain ... reversing the decline of thirteen wasted years.'

Compare Winston Churchill's earlier use of 'four wasted years of Labour Government' (to Denis Kelly, in private conversation, 1949 – quoted in Martin Gilbert, *Never Despair*, 1988).

This Ad Insults Women
Feminist anti-sexist-advertising slogan; UK, current 1970s. Usually attached to the offending ad with a sticker. In 1979, there was an Elliott shoe shop ad showing a couple of female models wearing woollen thigh boots upon which a graffitist had written 'This insults and degrades sheep'.

This Famous Store Needs ...
See CUSTOMER IS ALWAYS RIGHT

This Is Luxury You Can Afford By Cyril Lord
Cyril Lord carpets; UK, current early 1960s.

This Is The Age Of The Train
British Rail; UK, from 1980 – somewhat wishful thinking on the part of the Allen Brady and Marsh agency. The public countered with graffiti: 'Yes, it takes an age to catch one' and 'Ours was 104'. British Airways immediately countered with **This Is The Time Of The Plane**.

This Is The Army
See JOIN THE PROFESSIONALS

This Time Vote Like Your Whole Life ...
See NIXON'S THE ONE

Thousands Who Have Read The Book Will Know Why We Will Not Sell Any Children Tickets To See This Picture!, The
Film, *The Grapes of Wrath*; US, 1940.

Thousand Thrills … And Hayley Mills, A
Film, *In Search of the Castaways*; UK, 1961.

Thou Shalt Have No …
See HE WHO LOVES ME, FOLLOWS ME

Three Acres And A Cow/Mule
See TEN ACRES AND A MULE

301 Miles An Hour On Special Esso Ethyl!
See FLAT OUT ON ETHYL

Tide's In, Dirt's Out
Tide washing powder; UK, current 1950s. Also 'Get your clothes clean. Not only clean but **Deep Down Clean**, Tide clean.'

Time By My H. Samuel Ever-Rite …, The
H. Samuel watchmaker; UK, probably from the 1950s. Used on Radio Luxembourg.

Time For A Change
Presidential election slogan; US, 1944. Twelve years of Franklin D. Roosevelt as president led his Republican challenger, Thomas E. Dewey, to say, 'That's why it's time for a change.' But the call was ignored, as it was when he repeated it four years later (challenging Harry S. Truman). It was finally effective for the party, but not for Dewey, when Dwight D. Eisenhower used it to win in 1952.

Time Is Now, The
Presidential election slogan; US, 1980. Another incontestable statement but one that helped bring Ronald Reagan to power. But it was an old phrase. In a speech at Wheeling, West Virginia (20 February 1950), Senator Joseph McCarthy began his career as America's leading Red hunter by asking: 'Can there be anyone who fails to realize that the Communist world has said, "The time

is now" – that this is the time for the show-down between a democratic Christian world and the Communist atheistic world?'

In the 1980 race, Reagan and his supporters continued to use **Win This One For The Gipper** – a reference to Reagan's earlier existence as a film actor. In *Knute Rockne – All-American* (1940), he had played George Gipp, a real-life football star who died young. At half-time in a 1928 army game, Rockne, the team coach, had recalled something Gipp had said to him: 'Rock, someday when things look real tough for Notre Dame, ask the boys to go out there and win one for me.' Reagan subsequently used the slogan countless times throughout his political career. One of the last was at a campaign rally for Vice-President George Bush in San Diego, California, on 7 November 1988. Reagan's peroration included these words: 'So, now we come to the end of this last campaign ... And I hope that someday your children and grandchildren will tell of the time that a certain President came to town at the end of a long journey and asked their parents and grandparents to join him in setting America on the course to the new millenium ... So, if I could ask you just one last time. Tomorrow, when mountains greet the dawn, would you go out there and win one for the Gipper? Thank you, and God bless you all.'

In 1980, the incumbent President, Jimmy Carter, who was ousted by Reagan, had to put up with detractors within and without his own party. They came up with the unofficial slogan **A.B.C. – Anyone But Carter**.

Time ... Marches On!
Stock phrase (with the force of a slogan) from the 'March of Time' news-documentary-dramas on radio; US, 1931–45. The programmes were sponsored by *Time* Magazine. It is not clear whether this was the coinage of the expression meaning, 'It's getting on, time is moving forward, time flies ... ' The phrase 'the march of time' had been known since the 1830s.

Time To Re-Tire
Fisk Rubber Co. tyres; US, from 1907. Burr Griffin did the original sketch for the long-running pun of an ad which showed a yawning child with candle, night-shirt, and a huge tyre over his shoulder. The original slogan was **When It's Time To Re-Tire, Buy A Fisk**.

Let your
next tire be

Trade Mark Reg U.S Pat Off.
Time to Re-tire?
(Buy Fisk)

*Y*OUR *second Fisk tire will
mean a repetition of the
big and satisfying mileage of
your first one.*

Sold only by dealers

Tippecanoe And Tyler Too
Presidential election slogan; US, 1840. 'Tippecanoe' referred to
General William Henry Harrison, the Whig candidate, who had
defeated Indians at Tippecanoe Creek in 1811. John Tyler stood as
Vice-President. The Democrats renominated President Van Buren
and characterized Harrison as the 'Log Cabin And Hard Cider'
candidate – a challenge the Whigs turned to their advantage by
forming log cabin clubs and serving hard cider at rallies. Van
Buren, in turn, was portrayed as an effete New Yorker drinking

wine from 'coolers of silver', and acquired the nickname 'Old Kinderhook' from the name of his birthplace in New York State. **O.K.** became a slogan in the 1840 campaign, too, adding to the colourful etymology of that phrase. It was not O.K. for Van Buren, however – he was unseated.

Tittle Tattle Lost The Battle
See WALLS HAVE EARS

Today Germany, Tomorrow The World! *[Heute gehört uns Deutschland – morgen die ganze Welt]* – literally, 'Today Germany belongs to us – tomorrow the whole world'
Nazi political slogan; Germany, by the mid-1930s. Although John Colville, *The Fringes of Power* (Vol. 1, 1985) states that by 3 September 1939, Hitler 'had already ... proclaimed that "Today Germany is ours; tomorrow the whole world"',' an example of Hitler actually saying this has yet to be found. However, in *Mein Kampf* (1925), Hilter had written: 'If the German people, in their historic development, had possessed tribal unity like other nations, the German Reich today would be the master of the entire world.'

An example of the 'today —, tomorrow —' slogan format had already been used in Germany by the National Socialist Press in the early 1930s, *'Heute Presse der Nationalsozialisten, Morgen Presse der Nation* [Today the press of the Nazis, tomorrow the nation's press]'. As also in the chorus of a song in the Hitler Youth 'song-book':

> *Wir werden weiter marschieren*
> *Wenn alles in Scherben fällt*
> *Denn heute gehört uns Deutschland*
> *Und morgen die ganze Welt*

which may be roughly translated as:

> We shall keep marching on
> Even if everything breaks into fragments,
> For today Germany belongs to us
> And tomorrow the whole world.

Another version replaces the second line with '*Wenn Scheiße vom Himmel fällt* [When shit from Heaven falls]' Sir David Hunt recalls hearing the song in 1933 or possibly 1934.

By the outbreak of the Second World War, the format was sufficiently well known, as John Osborne recalled in *A Better Class of Person* (1981), for an English school magazine to be declaring: 'Now soon it will be our turn to take a hand in the destinies of Empire. Today, scholars; tomorrow, the Empire.' In the 1941 British film *Forty-Ninth Parallel*, Eric Portman as a German U-boat commander gets to say, 'Today, Europe ... tomorrow the whole world!' Interestingly, the format does seem to have existed outside Germany in the 1930s. In 1932, William B. Pitkin (1878–1953), Professor of Journalism at Columbia University, New York, published a book called *Life Begins at Forty* in which he dealt with 'adult reorientation' at a time when the problems of extended life and leisure were beginning to be recognized: 'Life begins at forty. This is the revolutionary outcome of our new era ... TODAY it is half a truth. TOMORROW it will be an axiom.'

So common is the construction now that a New York graffito stated: 'Today Hollywood, tomorrow the world' (Reisner), and one from El Salvador (March 1982) ran: '*Ayer Nicaragua, hoy El Salvador, mañana Guatemala!* [Yesterday Nicaragua, today El Salvador, tomorrow Guatemala!]' *The Guardian* (6 July 1982) carried an advertisement with the unwieldy headline: 'Self-managing Socialism: Today, France – Tomorrow, the World?'

A variation: from the British MP Paul Boateng's victory speech in the Brent South constituency (June 1987): 'Brent South today – Soweto tomorrow!'

Today Is The First Day Of The Rest Of Your Life
Synanon anti-drug and alcohol centres; US, from c.1969. Said to have been coined by Charles Dederich, the addiction specialist and founder of the centres. Also known in the form 'Tomorrow is ... ' and as a graffito. 'Today Is the First Day of the Rest of *My* Life' was apparently sung in a late 1960s musical *The Love Match* (by Maltby & Shire).

Today's Delivery Problems Solved Tomorrow
See COURIER EXPRESS ...

Today Something We Do Will Touch Your Life
Corporate slogan for Union Carbide; US, quoted 1976.

Together We Make A Great Team
See COME AND TALK TO ...

Toilers in Agriculture! Strengthen The Fodder Basis Of Animal Husbandry! Raise The Production And Sale To The State Of Meat, Milk, Eggs, Wool And Other Products!
Communist Party Central Committee; Soviet Union, 1980. One of seventy-five slogans prepared for the May Day parade and reported in *The Times* (15 April 1980). Hardly one to trip off the tongue, even in Russian.

Tomorrow Belongs To Me/Us
Fictional Nazi slogan from the musical *Cabaret*; US, 1966; film US, 1972. The song 'Tomorrow Belongs to Me' has lyrics by Fred Ebb and music by John Kander, and goes, in part:

> The babe in his cradle is closing his eyes, the blossom
> embraces the bee,
> But soon says a whisper, 'Arise, arise', Tomorrow belongs
> to me.
> O Fatherland, Fatherland, show us the sign your children
> have waited to see,
> The morning will come when the world is mine, Tomorrow
> belongs to me.

Clearly this lyric may have been inspired by the actual German song quoted under TODAY GERMANY, TOMORROW THE WORLD. But has 'Tomorrow belongs to me' or 'to us' ever been used as an actual political slogan? Harold Wilson in his final broadcast before the 1964 British General Election said, 'If the past belongs to the Tories, the future belongs to us – all of us'. At a Young Conservative rally before the 1983 General Election, Margaret Thatcher asked: 'Could Labour have organized a rally like this? In the old days perhaps, but not now. For they are the Party of Yesterday. Tomorrow is ours.' What one *can* say is that, in *Cabaret*, Ebb wrote a convincing pastiche of a Hitler Youth song, so much so that the song was denounced as a real Nazi anthem. Ebb told *The Independent* (30 November 1993): 'The accusations against "Tomorrow Belongs to Me" made me very angry ... "I knew that song as a child," one man had the audacity to tell me. A rabbinical person wrote me saying he had absolute proof it was a Nazi song.' The *idea*, rather, seems likely to have been current in Nazi Germany. Apart from the song already cited, one called *'Jawohl, mein Herr'*, featured in the 1943 episode of the German film chronicle *Heimat* (1984), included the line, 'For from today, the world belongs to us'.

The nearest the slogan appears to have been actually used by any (admittedly right-wing) youth organization is referred to in this report from *The Guardian* (30 October 1987): 'Contra leader Adolfo Calero ... was entertained to dinner on Wednesday by Oxford University's Freedom Society, a clutch of hoorays ... [who] got "hog-whimpering" drunk ... and songs like "Tomorrow Belongs To Us" [*sic*] and "Miner, Cross that Picket Line" were sung on the return coach trip.' The same paper, reporting a meeting addressed by the SDP leader, Dr David Owen (1 February 1988) noted: 'Down, sit down, he eventually gestured; his eyes saying Up, stay up. It reminded you of nothing so much as a Conservative Party conference in one of its most Tomorrow-belongs-to-us moods.' In each of these last two examples, it is the song from the musical that is being evoked, of course, rather than any Nazi original.

Tonic Water By You-Know-Who
See WHAT IS THE SECRET OF SCHHH?

Too-Good-To-Hurry-Mints
Murray Mints; UK, from late 1950s. Howard 'Boogie' Barnes wrote the lyric for one of the most catchy early British TV jingles. A typical situation in which it was sung was on an army parade ground (in cartoon):

> *Sergeant:* Hey, that man there!
> *Soldier* (rifle leaning against the wall): Sorry, you'll just have to wait – I'm finishing my Murray Mint, the too-good-to-hurry-mint.

Chorus of soldiers: Murray Mints, Murray Mints,
Too-good-to-hurry-mints.
Why make haste
When you can taste
The hint of mint
In Murray Mints.

Too Mean To Tell You What They Do
Bill-matter for the British music-hall contortionists, The Three
Aberdonians, 1930s–50s.

Toothpaste For Thinking People, The
Pebeco; US, current 1931.

*The tooth paste
for thinking people*

To Our Members We're The Fourth Emergency Service
Automobile Association (motoring breakdown service); UK, from
1993. Evoked some criticism for appearing to rank the organization with the fire, police and ambulance services. *Campaign* reported (23 July 1993) that John Asbury, H.M. Coastguard's chief oper-
ations officer, had criticized the slogan, adding that the AA, 'was
in the same category as the gas board or the plumber.'

Top Breeders Recommend It
Pedigree Chum dog food; UK, 1964.

Top People Take *The Times*
The Times newspaper; UK, from 1957. In the mid-1950s, the

London *Times* was shedding circulation, the end of post-war newsprint rationing was in sight, and an era of renewed competition in Fleet Street was about to begin. So, in 1954, the paper's agency, the London Press Exchange, commissioned a survey to discover people's attitudes towards 'The Thunderer'. They chiefly found it dull, but the management of *The Times* was not going to change anything, least of all allow contributors to be identified by name. *The Times* would have to be promoted for what it was. A pilot campaign in provincial newspapers included one ad showing a top hat and a pair of gloves with the slogan **Men Who Make Opinion Read *The Times***.

It was not the London Press Exchange but an outsider who finally encapsulated that idea in a more memorable slogan. G.H. Saxon Mills was one of the old school of advertising copywriters and had been copy director at Crawford's agency. But he was out of a job when he bumped into Stanley Morison of *The Times*. As a favour, Mills was asked to produce a brochure for visitors to the newspaper. When finished, it contained a series of pictures of the sort of people who were supposed to read the paper – a barrister, a trade-union official, and so on. Each was supported by the phrase: 'Top People Take *The Times*'. (Nicholl)

This idea was adopted for the more public promotional campaign that first appeared in poster form during 1957, running into immediate criticism for its snobbery. But sales went up and, however toe-curling it may have been, the slogan got the paper noticed and ran on into the early 1960s. Sometimes the statement was followed by the query – 'Do *You*?'

Another slogan from the pompous years (undated): **When *The Times* Speaks, The World Listens**. (Nicholl) In 1979–81, when the survival of the title was in doubt and at the time of a close down of the presses, the paper's slogan was **Have You Ever Wished You Were Better Informed?**

Toshiba
See 'ELLO, TOSH ...

Tranquillity
Conservative Party general election slogan; UK, 1922. It won the prime ministership for Andrew Bonar Law, though he died the

following year. It is said to have emerged from an exchange between Bonar Law and the future Lord Swinton, then a party official. Law: 'They tell me that we have to have what is called a slogan. What shall we have for this election?' Swinton: 'Well, I know what the country is feeling, they don't want to be buggered about.' Law: 'The sentiment is sound ... let us call it "Tranquility".' Another version of this story is given by Swinton in *I Remember* (1948).

Travail, Famille, Patrie [Work, family, fatherland]
Political slogan of the Vichy government; France, 1940–4.

Triumph Has The Bra For The Way You Are
Triumph foundation garments, swimwear and lingerie; UK, from c.1977.

Trust Baldwin
See SAFETY FIRST

Try A Little VC10derness
See WE'LL TAKE MORE CARE OF YOU

Try It, You'll Like It
See I CAN'T BELIEVE I ATE ...

Try Our Rivals, Too
Van Camp's pork and beans; US, current in the late nineteenth century. Claude C. Hopkins (d. 1932) said: 'I urged people to buy the brands suggested and compare them with Van Camp's ... if we were certain enough of our advantage to invite such comparisons, people were certain enough to buy.' He had found that the executives of the company could not tell their own product and its competitors apart. (Mayer)

Turn It Off
See SAVE IT

Turn On, Tune In, Drop Out
Hippie slogan; US, from c.1967. Meaning, 'Tune in to my values,

reject those of your parents, turn on [drug] yourself; deal with your problems and those of society by running away from them' – this was the meaning of the hippie philosophy as encapsulated in a slogan by one of the movement's gurus, Dr Timothy Leary (1920–96). It was used as the title of a lecture by him in 1967, and the theme was explored further in his book *The Politics of Ecstasy*. Towards the end of his life, Leary took to attributing the origin of the phrase to Marshall McLuhan.

A joke variant of what was also known as 'the LSD motto', was: 'Turn on, tune in, drop dead'.

Twice As Much For A Nickel, Too
See COME ALIVE ...

Two Chickens For Every Pot
See HOOVER AND HAPPINESS

2/4/6/8 ...
See SAY IT LOUD ...

Two Great Reasons For Jane Russell's
See MEAN! MOODY! ...

Two Infallible Powers ...
See ALAS! MY POOR BROTHER

Two's Company
See GENTLE GIANT

Two Ton Tessie
Bill-matter for the impressively bodied British entertainer, Tessie O'Shea (1913–95). In 1937, she was billed as 'The Girl with the Irresistible Humour' and, two years later, she was 'Still Bubbling Over'.

Typhoo Puts The 'T' In Britain
Typhoo tea; UK, by 1969.

Ulster Says 'No'

Political slogan; Northern Ireland, from 1985. The agreement signed on 15 November at Hillsborough between the British and Irish governments – and henceforth known as the Hillsborough Agreement – set out to encourage a greater degree of 'cross-border' co-operation on the problems of Northern Ireland. It was rejected by Loyalist politicians who saw it as the first step on the road to Irish re-unification. This simple slogan of rejection gained a curious hold. See also MAN FROM DEL MONTE ...

Ulster Will Fight, And Ulster Will Be Right

Ulster Volunteers; Britain and Ireland, 1913–14. In an open letter to a Liberal-Unionist in May 1886, Lord Randolph Churchill had written about the opposition of elements within the six northern counties of Ireland to any possibility of the granting of HOME RULE to the whole of the country: 'Ulster will not be a consenting party; Ulster at the proper moment will resort to a supreme arbitrament of force; Ulster will fight and Ulster will be right.' This was taken up by Ulster Volunteers, loyal to the British Crown, who opposed Irish Home Rule in 1913–14. From Randolph Churchill, *Youth: Winston Churchill* (1966): 'This famous slogan became the watchword of Ulster; it pithily explains why Ulster is still a part of the United Kingdom of Great Britain and Northern Ireland.'

Ultimate Driving Machine, The

BMW automobiles; US/UK, current 1981.

Un-Cola, The

See FRESHEN UP WITH 7-UP

United Colors Of Benetton

Benetton clothing; UK, from the late 1980s onwards. This (fairly meaningless) slogan attempted to sell the Italian knitwear brand in conjunction with purposely shocking photographs on controversial topics – HIV, Bosnia, oil spills, race, etc.

United We Stand, Divided We Fall
Political slogan; US, from the late eighteenth century. Jonathan Dickinson wrote 'The Patriot's Appeal' (sometimes called 'The Liberty Song') in 1768:

> Then join hand in hand, brave Americans all!
> By uniting we stand, by dividing we fall.

The State of Kentucky gave it the precise form in its 1792 motto. The idea can, however, be traced back to 550 BC and Aesop's Fable of the Four Oxen and the Lion. Compare the idea as expressed in biblical form: 'If a house be divided against itself, that house cannot stand' (Mark 3: 5). Compare also **Unity Is Strength** – motto of the National Union of General & Municipal Workers; UK, by 1980.

Universal Provider, The
Whiteley's store, London; UK, since 1860s. First in Westbourne Grove and later in Queensway, Whiteley's introduced department store shopping to London in 1863. William Whiteley (1831–1907), the self-styled 'Universal Provider', claimed to supply anything from **A Pin To An Elephant**. One morning, as Whiteley described it: 'An eminent pillar of the Church called upon me and said, "Mr Whiteley, I want an elephant." "Certainly, sir. When would you like it?" "Oh, today!" "And where?" "I should like it placed in my stable." "It shall be done!" In four hours a tuskiana was placed in the reverend gentleman's coach-house. Of course, this was a try-on designed to test our resources, and it originated in a bet. The Vicar confessed himself greatly disconcerted because, as he frankly avowed, he did not think we would execute the order. He displayed the utmost anxiety lest I should hold him to the transaction. But I let him down with a small charge for pilotage and food only, at which he confessed himself deeply grateful.' (Source: R.S. Lambert, *The Universal Provider*, 1937).

Unzipp A Banana (also, **Unzipp Ya Banana**)
Banana importers; UK, 1959. Somewhat nudging slogan run by the Mather & Crowther agency a joint promotion on behalf of the three main British banana importers.

Up, Up And Away With TWA
See YOU'RE GOING TO LIKE US

USA For LBJ
See ALL THE WAY ...

Use Matches Sparingly
See SMOKERS ARE REQUESTED ...

Use Sapolio
Sapolio soap; US and elsewhere, quoted 1952 – as 'once ubiquitous in the USA' and probably dating from the 1880s. The words **Spotless Town** were also synonymous with Sapolio. They came from rhymes devised by J.K. Fraser, like this one:

> This is the maid of fair renown
> Who scrubs the floors of Spotless Town
> To find a speck when she is through
> Would take a pair of specs or two,
> And her employment isn't slow.
> For she employs SAPOLIO.

' "Spotless Town" (while selling Sapolio by the ton) was parodied in many papers and a syndicated political series ran all over the country. At one time four theatrical companies booked shows called *Spotless Town* ... and one community changed its name permanently thereto.' (Watkins)
From Gerald Frow, '*Oh, Yes It Is!*' – *A History of Pantomime* (1985): 'In an 1892 *Little Bo-Peep*, for example, Prince Poppetty challenges Squire Oofless ... to a duel, with the cry: "Draw, sir! This can only be washed out by blood!" To which the Squire coolly replies: "I wouldn't use that. Try Sapolio!" '

Velvet Fog, The

Sobriquet but also unofficial bill-matter for the American singer, Mel Tormé (b. 1925). He was noted for his ultra-smooth crooning style. In 1983, he commented: 'By the age of 18, I'd been labelled "the Singer's Singer" and, although I agree it's a lovely label, I'm anti-labels ... I was known as The Velvet Fog. I was a little churlish about it at first but later I realised it was an affectionate thing.'

¡*Venceremos!*

See WE SHALL OVERCOME

Very —, Very Sanderson

Sanderson furnishing fabrics and wall-coverings; UK, by 1973. Various celebrities were photographed amid what purported to be their natural, furnished, surroundings. Among them: Joan Bakewell, Petula Clark, Jilly Cooper, Britt Ekland and Kingsley Amis. I happened to be visiting Mr Amis in his home the day after the first advertisement featuring him had appeared in the colour magazines (May 1974). I took the opportunity to exclaim 'Very Kingsley Amis, Very Sanderson' as we stepped into his sitting-room. The novelist seemed perturbed at my reaction and was at pains to point out that, although he and the other celebrities had had a room decorated by Sanderson in addition to their fees, the photograph in the ad bore little resemblance to the conditions under which he actually lived (I saw that it did not). He described the wallpaper chosen to reflect his refined tastes as 'superior Indian restaurant'. Alan Coren, writing in *Punch*, warned Alexander Solzhenitsyn, just arrived in the West, that he might find the role of the writer a bit different this side of the Iron Curtain. He would know that he had finally settled in when he heard people declaring 'Very Solzhenitsyn, Very Sanderson'.

Virginia Is For Lovers
See I LOVE NEW YORK

Virginian Rolls OK
Virginian pipe tobacco; UK, 1981. Alluding to the curious affirmative construction 'so-and-so rules OK' which was all the rage at that time. This was said to have begun in gang-speak of the late 1960s in Scotland and Northern Ireland, though some would say it dates back to the 1930s. Either a gang or a football team or the Provisional IRA would be said to 'rule OK'. Later, around 1976, this was turned into a joke with numerous variations – 'Queen Elizabeth rules UK', 'Rodgers and Hammerstein rule OK, lahoma' and so on. It soon became an all but unstoppable cliché and, naturally, ended up in advertising. The French cigarettes Gauloises were even promoted in the UK with *Gauloises à rouler, OK*.

¡Viva la Muerte!
See LONG LIVE DEATH

Vive le Québec libre! [Long live free Quebec!]
Political slogan; Canada, 1967. 'Extempore remark' – in full, '*Vive le Québec! Vive le Québec libre! Vive le Canada français! Vive la France!*' – made by French President Charles de Gaulle to the crowd outside Montreal City Hall (25 July 1967). It led to his rapid departure for home, having incurred the displeasure of the Federal Government for interfering in Canada's internal affairs. '*Québec libre*' was a separatist slogan.

Vladivar From Warrington
See WODKA FROM VARRINGTON

Vorsprung durch Technik [Advancement through technology]
Audi motor cars; UK, from 1982. Use of a German phrase (which few would understand) was apparently designed to bring home to British buyers that the Audi was a German car and, hence, a reliable, quality product. The phrase was the company's own exhortation to its workers, written up over the factory gates in Germany. In no sense can it be described as a catchphrase, as it did not catch on, but it certainly intrigued and tantalized and was noticed.

Vote As You Shot
Unofficial political slogan; US, from c.1865. Used by veterans' groups for many years after the American Civil War. (Safire)

Vote Early And Vote Often
Unofficial political slogan; US, from the mid-nineteenth century. In *Josh Billings' Wit and Humour* (1874), there is ' "Vote early and vote often" is the Politishun's golden rule' – which seems to be recalling an adage. Indeed, earlier, William Porcher Miles had said in a speech to the House of Representatives (31 March 1858): ' "Vote early and vote often", the advice openly displayed on the election banners in one of our northern cities.' Safire ignores both these sources but mentions that historian James Morgan found 'in his 1926 book of biographies' that the original jokester was John Van Buren (d. 1866), a New York lawyer and son of President Martin Van Buren.

Vote For Any Candidate, But If You Want Well-Being And Hygiene, Vote For Pulvapies
Advertising slogan at time of mayoral election; Ecuador, 1967. The town of Picoaza in Ecuador was treated to this advertising slogan during a local campaign for mayor in 1967. Pulvapies was not the name of a candidate but of a locally produced foot-powder. And, when it came to the ballot, 'vote for Pulvapies' was exactly what the Picoazans did. (Safire)

Vote For Hogg Is A Vote For Hitler, A
Anti-Conservative political slogan; UK, 1938. A famous by-election took place at Oxford in the month after the Munich agreement was signed. Quintin Hogg (later Lord Hailsham) stood as the champion of Munich and the Prime Minister, Chamberlain; A.D. Lindsay, Master of Balliol and a member of the Labour Party, stood as a representative of the anti-fascist Popular Front. Hogg won.

Vote For Snowball And The Three Day Week
Fictional slogan from George Orwell's novel *Animal Farm* (1945).

Vote For The Liberals ... , A
See YOUR FUTURE IS ...

Votes for Women

Women's suffrage slogan; UK, 1906–14. If a slogan is judged purely by its effectiveness, 'Votes For Women' is a very good one. The words may not sparkle, but they achieved their end. Emmeline and Christabel Pankhurst, founders of the Women's Social and Political Union, both described how this particular battle-cry emerged. In October 1905, a large meeting at the Free Trade Hall, Manchester, was due to be addressed by Sir Edward Grey, who was likely to attain ministerial office if the Liberals won the forthcoming general election. The WSPU was keen to challenge him in public on his party's attitude to women's suffrage in Britain.

'Good seats were secured for the Free Trade Hall meeting. The question was painted on a banner in large letters, in case it should not be made clear enough by vocal utterance. How should we word it? "Will you give women suffrage?" – we rejected that form, for the word "suffrage" suggested to some unlettered or jesting folk the idea of suffering. "Let them suffer away!" – we had heard the taunt. We must find another wording and we did! It was so obvious and yet, strange to say, quite new. Our banners bore this terse device: "WILL YOU GIVE VOTES FOR WOMEN?" '

The plan had been to let down a banner from the gallery as soon as Sir Edward Grey stood up to speak. Unfortunately, the WSPU failed to obtain the requisite tickets. It had to abandon the large banner and cut out the three words which would fit on a small placard. 'Thus quite accidentally came into existence the slogan of the suffrage movement around the world.'

Alas, Sir Edward Grey did not answer the question, and it took rather more than this slogan – hunger-strikes, suicide, the First World War – before women got the vote in 1918. The slogan was put to other uses: a newspaper with the title *Votes for Women* was launched in October 1907. At a meeting in the Royal Albert Hall, someone boomed 'Votes for Women' down an organ pipe. The International Labour Party used to refer to it as 'Votes for Ladies'. Other slogans used were **Deeds, Not Words**; **Arise! Go Forth And Conquer**; and **The Bill, The Whole Bill, And Nothing But The Bill**.

In the US, the Nineteenth Amendment, extending female franchise on a national scale, was ratified in time for the 1920 elections.

In due course, some feminists were to campaign with the slogan **Orgasms For Women**.

Walk The Barratt Way
Barratt shoes; UK, current early 1940s.

Walk This Way
See LET YOUR FINGERS ...

Walls Have Ears
Government security slogan; UK, during the Second World War.
The idea of inanimate objects being able to hear is, however, a
very old one. In Vitzentzos Kornaros's epic poem *Erotokritos*
(c.1645) there is the following couplet (here translated from the
Greek):

> For the halls of our masters have ears and hear,
> And the walls of the palace have eyes and watch.

Jonathan Swift wrote in 1727, 'Walls have tongues, and hedges
ears'). From W.S. Gilbert's *Rozenkrantz and Guildenstern* (1891): 'We
know that walls have ears. I gave them tongues – / And they were
eloquent with promises.'
    Also, from the Second World War: **Tittle Tattle Lost The Battle**
and **Keep It Under Your Hat** (US: **Keep It Under Your Stetson**).
Loose Talk Costs Lives and **Idle Gossip Sinks Ships** were additional US versions of the same theme, together with **The Slip Of
A Lip May Sink A Ship** and **Enemy Ears Are Listening**. The only
drawback to these generally clever slogans was that they tended
to reinforce the notion that there *were* spies and fifth columnists
under every bed even if there were not.

Want To Reach 8 Out Of 10 Adults?
See LET YOUR FINGERS ...

War Is Peace
See FREEDOM IS SLAVERY

WARNING: THE SURGEON GENERAL HAS DETERMINED THAT CIGARETTE SMOKING IS DANGEROUS TO YOUR HEALTH
Government health wearning; US, from 1970. On all cigarette advertising and packs. In 1964, Congress passed the Federal Cigarette Labeling and Advertising Act following a Surgeon General's report on smoking. The first pack label was: CAUTION: CIGARETTE SMOKING MAY BE HAZARDOUS TO YOUR HEALTH.

War to End Wars, The
Unofficial slogan referring to the Great War; UK, from 1914. H.G. Wells confessed long after the war was over, 'I launched the phrase The War To End Wars and that was not the least of my crimes'. (*The War That Will End War* was a book he had written in 1914.) Lord Ponsonby commented in *Falsehood In War-Time* (1928): 'This was hardly an original cry. It had been uttered in previous wars.'

Was There A Lion On Your Egg This Morning?
See GO TO WORK ON AN EGG

Watch Of Railroad Accuracy, The
Hamilton Watch Co.; US, from 1908. The phrase first arose from a testimonial sent to the company by a railroad worker.

Watch Out There's A Humphrey About
Milk; UK, current 1974. The Humphreys were members of a mythical race supposed to steal milk when nobody was looking. They were not actually seen in TV ads – only the red-striped straws through which they sipped the milk.

Watch Out, There's A Thief About
Crime prevention slogan; UK, from c.1966. Home Office campaigns run by the Central Office of Information.

Watch That Made The Dollar Famous, The
Ingersoll dollar watches; US, from c.1892. Soon after the first dollar

watch appeared, Mr R.H. Ingersoll was being introduced at some ceremony by a flushed hostess who forgot his name. So she said: 'Oh, the man that made the dollar famous.' Next day, Mr Ingersoll presented the company with its long-lasting slogan. (Lambert)

Watch The Fords Go By
Ford Motor Co.; US, from 1908. Started off as a baseball cry in support of the team at the company's Highland Park factory. Applied to ads upon the introduction of the Model T. (Lambert)

We Are Not Alone
Film, *Close Encounters of the Third Kind*; US, 1977. Also **Watch The Skies** which was the film's original title. This was taken from the last words of the film *The Thing* (US, 1951): 'Watch everywhere, keep looking, watch the skies!'

We Are The Ovaltineys/Happy Girls And Boys
Ovaltine (milk drink); UK, from 1935. Lines from one of the most happily remembered jingles of all. The Ovaltiney Club was launched over Radio Luxembourg. Children were given badges, rule books, secret codes and comics, and by 1939 there were five million active members. In 1946 the show was revived to run for several more years.

Watch This Space
Semi-slogan; UK, by 1917. A light-hearted way of indicating that further details will follow. Possibly of American origin. Perhaps it would be put on advertisement hoardings to await the arrival of a new poster? From there transferred to newspaper, even broadcasting, use – meaning 'pay attention to this slot'. The *OED2*'s earliest example is, however, taken from an advertisement in the *B.E.F. Times* [British Expeditionary Force newspaper] in 1917.

Wear Your Poppy With Pride
British Legion annual 'poppy' fund-raising appeal; UK, since the 1970s.

We Bring Good Things To Life
Corporate slogan for General Electric; US, current 1980.

We Build Your Kind Of Truck
Corporate slogan for International Harvester; US, quoted 1980.

We Carry Everything
Pickford's removals; UK, quoted 1982. See also GENTLE GIANT.

We Do It All For You
See NOBODY CAN DO IT ...

We Circle The World
Master Charge (credit card); US, current 1980.

We Don't Like Anyone Very Much
Informal political slogan; US, 1964. Placard observed in Illinois during the presidential election. (White, 1965)

Weekend Starts Here, The
TV pop show *Ready, Steady, Go*; UK, current 1964. The programme was transmitted live by Associated-Rediffusion early on Friday evenings.

We Fly The World The Way The World Wants To Fly
Pan Am; US, current 1980. Also: **Say Hello To A Brand New World** – though putting this on the emergency exit of a Pan Am jet was hardly reassuring for the passengers.

We Give Green Shield Stamps
See PILE IT HIGH ...

We Guarantee Tomorrow Today
New York Life; US, quoted 1976.

We Have Seen The Lions At Longleat
Longleat Wildlife Park; UK, from late 1960s. On window-sticker. The 6th Marquess of Bath (1905–92), owner of Longleat House, Wiltshire, was a pioneer of the stately homes business. He opened a drive-in lion park – really the first such park of any size outside Kenya – in 1966. This set a trend for other safari parks in Britain.

We Have To Earn Our Wings Every Day
Eastern Airlines; US, current 1980.

We Lead – Others Follow
Dodds Transport of Acton, London; UK, probably since the 1920s. Still current in the 1980s. Just the sort of slogan you want to see on the back of a truck when you are stuck behind it … From J.B. Priestley, *The Good Companions*, Chap. 4 (1929): 'Joby completed his preparations for the day by tacking a number of little placards to the posts of the stall [selling rubber dolls at a market]: "Don't forget the Little Ones," they screamed at the passer-by. "Shops Can't Compete"; "We lead. Others follow"; "British Workmanship Can't Be Beat" – which was probably true enough and worth saying, even though all Mr Jackson's stock seemed to come out of boxes bearing foreign labels.'

We'll Take *More* Care Of You
British Airways; UK, current 1976. Originally **BOAC Takes Good Care Of You (All Over The World)** and adapted when the airline changed its name. The 'taking care' theme was part of the airlines' advertising from 1948 to 1982. Japan Airlines began to say they would **Take Good Care Of You, Too** but were persuaded to drop the line, although they had used **Love At First Flight** a dozen years before BOAC took up the slogan. (Nicholl) In its time, BA has ranged from the patriotic **Fly The Flag** to **Try A Little VClOderness.** See also PUTTING PEOPLE FIRST and WORLD'S FAVOURITE AIRLINE.

We Love Him For The Enemies He Has Made
Presidential election slogan; US, 1884. Grover Cleveland was the Democratic 22nd and 24th President. This slogan when running for the first of his two separate terms derives from a speech made by Governor Edward Stuyvesant Bragg, seconding Cleveland's nomination (9 July 1884): 'They love him most for the enemies he has made.'

We Make Things That Bring People Closer
Corporate slogan for Western Electrics; US, quoted 1976.

We Must Export Or Die
See EXPORT OR DIE

We Never Closed
Windmill Theatre, London; UK, from Second World War. Vivien Van Damm, the proprietor, coined this slogan for the venerable comedy and strip venue which was the only West End showplace to remain open during the blitz. An obvious variant: 'We Never Clothed.'

We Never Forget You Have A Choice
British Caledonian airline; UK, current 1981.

We Never Sleep
Pinkerton's national detective agency; US, from 1850 – when its first office was opened in Chicago. Through its open-eye symbol, Pinkerton's may also have given us the term 'private eye'. *Nunquam dormio* [I never sleep] has been used as the motto of various organizations and was (at some later stage) put under the original open-eye logo of the London *Observer* newspaper (founded 1791). Compare CITI NEVER SLEEPS.

We Polked You in 1844, We Shall Pierce You In 1852
Presidential election slogan; US, 1852. Franklin Pierce was a 'dark horse' candidate who was not considered as the Democrats' candidate for the presidency until the *35th* ballot at the party convention. When he was selected on the *49th*, the slogan was inevitable, given that James Knox Polk had been the previous Democratic president.

We Really Move Our Tail For You
Continental Airlines; US, current 1975. In that year some of the airline's stewardesses threatened to sue over the 'bad taste' it had shown in selecting this slogan.

We're Getting There
British Rail; UK, current 1985. On the whole, it was believed that by using this slogan, British Rail was being economical with the truth.

We're Not Allowed To Tell You Anything About Winston Cigarettes So Here's A Stuffed Aardvark

Winston cigarettes; UK, 1983. A pointed response to the ever-increasing restrictions on cigarette advertising copy.

We're With The Woolwich

Woolwich Equitable Building Society; UK, current late 1970s – in response to the question 'Are You With The Woolwich?' in TV ads. From the accompanying jingle came the phrase **The Safe Place, With The Nice Face**, and the nice face had a peculiarly ingratiating way of saying 'Good Morning'.

We're Working To Keep Your Trust

Corporate slogan for Texaco; US, quoted 1976.

We Serve You Better – Not Just A Slogan: A Commitment

Air Siam; UK, quoted 1981. Unduly apologetic?

We Shall Not Be Moved

Protest slogan; US, 1960s. According to *Bartlett's Dictionary of Familiar Quotations* (1981), this came originally from a 'Negro spiritual' (echoing more than one of the biblical psalms): 'Just like a tree that's standing by the water/ We shall not be moved.' Later widely taken up as a song of the Civil Rights and labour movements, from the 1960s.

We Shall Overcome

Protest slogan; US, since the early twentieth century. It began as a part of a song in pre-Civil War times, was adapted (c.1900) by C. Albert Hindley as a Baptist hymn, 'I'll Overcome Some Day' and became famous in 1946 when Black workers sang it on a picket line in Charleston, South Carolina. Pete Seeger and others added verses. In the early 1960s, it became the main US Civil Rights anthem:

Oh, deep in my heart, I know that I do believe,
We shall overcome some day.

In the Spanish Civil War a Republican chant was *¡Venceremos!* which means the same thing.

We Take You In, So The Boys Will Take You Out
Unknown New York corset manufacturer; US, 1964. Quoted 1996.

We Try Harder
See WHEN YOU'RE ONLY ...

We Want Eight And We Won't Wait
Informal political slogan; UK, mid-1900s. In a speech at Wigan (27 March 1909), George Wyndham commented on the construction of Dreadnoughts (battleships): 'What the people said was, "We want eight, and we won't wait".' The policy of the Liberal Government had reduced defence expenditure to pay for the introduction of social services and the Welfare State. Construction of only eight new Dreadnought destroyers was to be spread over two years but news of the threatening German shipbuilding programme caused a popular outcry, encapsulated in the slogan. As is clear, Wyndham (who had briefly been in the Conservative Cabinet in 1902) was merely quoting it, not coining it.

We Want Watneys
Watneys beer; UK, during the Second World War. So recalled by Leslie Thomas in *This Time Next Week* (1964). Also remembered as **What We Want Is Watneys** on a poster as though it were graffiti. Neither of these is verified. See also WOT NO —.

We Want Wilkie
Presidential election slogan; US, 1940. At the Republican convention, the balconies were packed with supporters of Wendell Wilkie. They helped sway the nomination in his direction, but neither this slogan nor **Win With Wilkie** enabled him to unseat the incumbent president, Franklin D. Roosevelt.

In the 1940 election, the President had his own slogan for crowd repetition: **Martin, Barton And Fish**. Seeking to blame Republicans for US military unpreparedness, he cited three Congressmen – Joseph Martin, Bruce Barton (later of the advertising firm Batten, Barton, Durstine & Osborn), and Hamilton Fish. The speech in which this phrase arose was written by Judge Samuel I. Rosenman and Robert E. Sherwood, the dramatist. Crowds loved to join in the rhythmic line echoing 'Wynken,

Blynken and Nod'. Roosevelt would ask: 'And who voted against the appropriations for an adequate national defense?' The reply: 'MARTIN, BARTON and FISH.' (Safire)

We Won't Make A Drama Out Of A Crisis
Commercial Union Assurance; UK, since the early 1980s.

What Becomes A Legend Most?
Blackglama mink; US, current 1976. Headline from a series of press ads showing mink coats being worn by 'legendary' figures including Margot Fonteyn, Martha Graham, Rudolph Nureyev (all three in one ad), Shirley Maclaine and Ethel Merman.

What Is A Mum?
See SOMEONE'S MOTHER

What Is The Secret Of Schhh?
Schweppes tonic waters and mixers; UK, from c.1963. A phrase which caught on in a really big way. It was thought up, jointly, by Royston Taylor, copywriter, and Frank Devlin, art director, at the Mather & Crowther agency. Taylor recalled: 'Schweppes had largely been handling their own advertising, featuring Benny Hill on TV and Stephen Potter's whimsical copy in the press. The problem was, "What can we say instead of **Schweppervescence Lasts The Whole Drink Through**" ? Our idea grew very much out of the spy fever that was raging at the time. The James Bond films were just beginning, *Danger Man* was on TV (indeed, at one stage, we wanted Patrick Magoohan to appear in our ads). I came up with the idea of **Tonic Water By You-Know Who** ... – the sort of thing you might say confidentially out of the side of your mouth in a bar. Frank Devlin suggested "The Secret of Schhh ..." which accorded with the old copywriter's dream of not showing or even naming the product if it could possibly be avoided. We compromised, just using the first three letters of the brand name and half a bottle. The comedians soon picked it up. It "made" William Franklyn, who used to appear in various comic spy situations. I suppose you could say it took Schweppes advertising out of *Punch*-style whimsy and into another area of popular whimsy – substituting one form of obscurity for another!'

What Makes A Shy Girl Get Intimate?
Probably for Intimate perfume; US, undated. (Baker)

What One Loves About Life Are The Things That Fade
Film, *Heaven's Gate* (US, 1980). Words taken from the legend written on Michael Cimino's original screenplay. Also **The Most Talked About Film Of The Decade** – as, indeed, it was on account of it being one of the biggest loss-makers of all time.

What's The Difference Between A Male Policeman And A Female Policeman? Six Inches
Police recruiting slogan; UK, quoted 1981. Unverified. (Perhaps it should be pointed out that the ad was drawing attention to the varying height requirements of male and female applicants.)

What's The Good Word? Thunderbird
Thunderbird wine; US, from 1957. *The Dictionary of American Slang* (1975 ed.) describes how this exchange was taken up in 'mainly hipster use' by Blacks in Harlem – a jive-like rhyming answer to a greeting. The wine itself was 'cheap and supposedly potent'.

What's Yours Called?
Renault cars; UK, from 1985. In TV ads. An irritating catchphrase, while it lasted.

What The Well-Dressed — Is Wearing
General clothing and fashion journalistic slogan; UK/US, probably since 1900. Now an ironical subject like 'tramp' or 'cart horse' is inserted where once something like 'man about town' might have been in a tailor's or couturier's advertisement. Applied to any eccentric or scruffy choice of clothing, by the mid-twentieth century.

What We've Got Here Is A Failure To Communicate
Film, *Cool Hand Luke*; US, 1967. A line from the film where it is spoken as: 'What we've got here is ... failure to communicate. Some men you just can't reach.'

What We Want Is Watneys
See WE WANT WATNEYS

When Adam Delved And Eve Span, Who Was Then A Gentleman?
Political slogan; England, fourteenth century. Taken as the text for a sermon preached by John Ball to Wat Tyler's men at Blackheath during the Peasants' Revolt (1381), though it had been recorded about forty years before.

When Better Automobiles Are Built ...
See IT MAKES YOU ...

When It Rains, It Pours
Morton Salt Co.; US, from 1911. This phrase could apply to other products, but with the logo of a girl in the rain, sheltering the salt under her umbrella, it capitalized on the fact that the Morton grade ran freely from salt cellars even when the atmosphere was damp. In a small booklet describing the product, a copywriter used the phrase as a paragraph heading and the slogan developed from there. (Lambert) **When He Pours, He Reigns** was used to promote the film *Cocktail* (US, 1989) in which Tom Cruise played a bartender.

When It's Time To Re-Tire
See TIME TO RE-TIRE

When Nature Forgets ...
See KEEP 'REGULAR' ...

When Should A Blonde Give In?
See IS IT TRUE ...

When *The Times* Speaks, The World Listens
See TOP PEOPLE TAKE ...

When Was The Last Time You Had A Really Good Frock?
Unidentified garment manufacturer; US, 1950s. Said to have appeared in a Sunday *New York Times*.

When You Got It, Flaunt It
Braniff Airline; US, current 1969. Headline used over ads featur-

ing celebrities such as Sonny Liston, Andy Warhol and Joe Namath. Probably the line was acquired from the 1967 Mel Brooks movie *The Producers* in which Zero Mostel as 'Max Bialystock' says to the owner of a large white limo: 'That's it, baby! When you got it, flaunt it! Flaunt it!' Later in the film he says, 'Take it when you can get it. Flaunt it! Flaunt it!'

The idea was obviously very much around at this time. In an episode of BBC radio's *Round the Horne* (15 May 1966), these lines occurred: 'The physique of a young Greek god and profile of classical perfection ... Still, what I say is if you've got it, you may as well show it.'

When You're Only No. 2, You Try Harder. Or Else
Avis Rent-A-Car; US and elsewhere, from 1963. Avis had been in the red for fifteen years when, in 1962, the Doyle, Dane, Bernbach agency was hired to do its advertising. A $3 million loss in 1962 became a $3 million profit in 1963, despite warnings that admitting you were not No. 1 was 'un-American' and would merely provide chief rival Hertz with a free advertisement. Sometimes also used in the form **We Try Harder.**

Where's George? – He's Gone To Lyonch
Lyons Corner Houses; UK, current 1936. W. Buchanan-Taylor, advertising chief at Lyons, recalled (in *One More Shake*, 1944): 'I resorted to the unforgivable and invented "Lyonch" as a descriptive of lunch at Lyons ... then I heard a story within the office of how a man on the advertising staff of *The Times* called one day a little later than was his wont to pick up his pal, George Warner, the head of my studio. He was so much later than usual that when he looked into the room and asked "Where's George?" the artist replied, without looking up from his work, "Gone to Lyonch, you fool." I made a note on my desk pad ... and I sent one of the staff to Somerset House to tot up the number of registered Georges in the country.' When the count had reached more than a million, the slogan was adopted. It had to be carefully obliterated during the funeral of King George V in 1936.

Where's The Beef?
Wendy International hamburger chain; US, from 1984. A TV ad

showed elderly women eyeing a small hamburger on a huge bun – a Wendy competitor's product. 'It certainly is a big bun,' asserted one. 'It's a very big fluffy bun,' the second agreed. But the third asked, 'Where's the beef?' Later in the year, when Walter Mondale was seeking the Democratic presidential nomination he famously quoted the slogan to describe what he saw as lack of substance in the policies of his rival for the nomination, Gary Hart. A classic example of an advertising slogan turning into a political catch-phrase.

Where The Elite Meet To Eat
Fictional slogan; US, 1940s. From the American radio series *Duffy's Tavern*, starring Ed Gardner (also on UK radio, 1944 and in a film, US 1945). Later, it was spoken by Bette Davis in the film *All About Eve* (US, 1950). On British radio, *Duffy's Tavern* made a further appearance as *Finkel's Café*, starring Peter Sellers (1956). Hence, the headline from *The Wall Street Journal* (8 October 1981): 'FOR THE DEMOCRATS PAM'S [Pamela Harriman's] IS THE PLACE FOR THE ELITE TO MEET.'

Where There's Life There's Bud
Budweiser beer; US, by 1959. Also **Budweiser. King of Beers**; US, current 1981.

Where The Rubber Meets The Road
Firestone tyres; US, quoted 1976. (IBM's headquarters in Valhalla, New York, is jokingly known as 'Where the rubber hits the sky'.)

Where Were You In '62?
Film, *American Graffiti* (US, 1973). Later taken as the title of a 1950s/60s nostalgia and trivia quiz on BBC Radio 2 (1983–5).

Which Twin Has The Toni – And Which Twin Has The Expensive Perm?
Toni home perms; US, current 1951. A headline that asks a question, a slogan that contains the brandname, and an idea that was dotty enough to be much copied. The ads featured pairs of identical twins (real ones), who also toured doing promotional work for the product. One had a Toni home perm, the other a more expen-

sive perm – a footnote explained which was which. (During the 1970 UK general election, the Liberal Party produced a poster carrying pictures of Harold Wilson and Edward Heath and the slogan **Which Twin Is The Tory?**)

Whispering Baritone, The
See SINGER WITH THE SMILE ...

Whisky With The Fascinating Suggestion Of Peat Reek, The
Mackinlay's whisky; UK, undated. (Sunners)

Whiter Than White, (Washes)
Unidentified washing powder/detergent; UK, probably from the 1950s. There is a firm belief in advertising circles that this line has been used, but it remains unverified. From *Campaign* (3 January 1986): 'How Mrs Thingy discovered that Bloggo could wash her floor whiter than white'; (8 August 1986): 'It could have been something startling and whiter-than-white from Procter and Gamble'; (30 January 1987): 'The classic ad where started A.N. Other Housewife pulls the whiter-than-white shirt from her machine and gasps with cataclysmic delight when she finds that the baby sick has been washed clean away.'

The expression meaning 'of extreme purity, innocence or virtue' is of longstanding. Psalm 51: 7 has: 'Wash me, and I shall be whiter than snow.' Shakespeare in *Venus and Adonis*, l. 398 (1592) has: 'Teaching the sheets a whiter hew than white.' Precisely as 'whiter than white', the phrase was known by 1924. Later: 'TOWN THAT'S WHITER THAN WHITE' (*Guardian* headline, 19 March 1992).

Compare **Persil Washes Whiter**.

Who Dares, Wins
SAS (Special Air Service) regiment; UK, from 1950. Founded by Col. David Stirling in that year, its origins lay in the Second World War. The motto (with the force of a slogan) became famous after members of the crack regiment shot their way into the Iranian embassy in London, in May 1980, to end a siege (when wags suggested the motto should really be, 'Who dares use it [fire-power], wins'). A feature film about the supposed exploits of the SAS was

made, using the motto as its title in 1982 and the *Daily Mirror* labelled its 'Win a Million' bingo promotion 'Who Dares Wins' in 1984.

The motto appears to have been borrowed from the Alvingham barony, created in 1929.

Who Else But Nelse?
See NIXON'S THE ONE

Who's Absent? Is It You?
Recruitment slogan; UK, during the First World War. Ads also featured a picture of John Bull.

Who's Polk?
Presidential election slogan; US, 1844. James K. Polk, the first 'dark horse' candidate, took the Democratic nomination from ex-President Van Buren. As a compromise candidate he was little known (just as more than a century later Jimmy Carter initially gave rise to the cry **Jimmy Who?**). He campaigned with the expansionist slogan **54-40 Or Fight**, seeking to reoccupy the territory of Oregon, then jointly held by Britain and the US, up to a northern boundary with Canada at 54° 40'. The Democrats won the election but President Polk negotiated a compromise settlement at the 49th Parallel. Coinage of the phrase is credited to Samuel Medary, an editor from Ohio, though William Allen, a Democratic Senator from that state, used it in a speech before the US Senate.

Who Wouldn't Fight For A Woman ...
See MEAN! MOODY! ...

Why Does A Woman Look Old Sooner Than A Man?
Sunlight soap; UK, from c.1890. William Hesketh Lever (the first Lord Leverhulme) recorded in a diary of his tour studying American publicity methods (1888) that he bought this slogan from a Philadelphia soapmaker, Frank Siddal.

Why Not The Best?
See HE'S MAKING US PROUD AGAIN

Wigan Nightingale, The

Bill-matter of the British music-hall comedian George Formby senior (who died aged forty-five in 1921). Somewhat ironical, as Formby didn't have much of a voice at all. 'Coughin' well tonight' was his catchphrase and he had a convulsive cough, the result of a tubercular condition which eventually killed him. Clearly the bill-matter was modelled after **The Swedish Nightingale**, sobriquet of Jenny Lind (1820–87), the soprano from Sweden who found fame in Europe and America. As for Wigan, Formby was much associated with the Lancashire town. It was he who invented the joke about 'Wigan Pier', an imaginary landmark not at any seaside resort but on the Leeds-Liverpool canal.

Wilkes And Liberty

Political slogan; UK, 1764. Cry of the London mob in support of John Wilkes (1727–97), the radical politician, who was repeatedly elected to Parliament despite ministerial attempts to exclude him because of his scurrilous attacks on the government. He was a popular champion of parliamentary reform and of the cause of the colonies in the War of American Independence.

Wilkinson Sword – The World's Finest Blade

Wilkinson Sword razor blades; UK, current 1982.

Will Not Affect Your Throat

See FOR YOUR THROAT'S SAKE ...

Wilson's Wisdom Wins ...

See HE KEPT US OUT OF WAR

Wine That Grandma ...

See JUST LIKE MOTHER USED TO ...

Wings Of Man, The

Corporate slogan for Eastern Airlines; US, quoted 1981.

Winning In Politics Isn't Everything, It's The Only Thing

Informal slogan of the Committee to Re-Elect The President (Richard Nixon]; US, 1972. Look where it got them.

Winston Tastes Good Like A Cigarette Should
Winston cigarettes; US, by 1965. The slogan dealt a blow to standard usage ('as a cigarette should … ') In a jingle by 1976.

Win This One For The Gipper
See TIME IS NOW

With A Name Like Smuckers It Has To Be Good
Smuckers preserves; US, from c.1960. Lois Wyse of Wyse Advertising, New York, recalled (1981): 'Slogans come and go but "With A Name Like … " has become a part of the language. I wrote it for a company with an unusual name in answer to a challenge from Marc Wyse who said that he didn't feel our Smucker advertising differed from the competition. The real job, however, was not thinking up the slogan but selling it to Paul Smucker. The then sales manager said: "If you run that line, Paul, we'll be out of business in six months"! But it's still in use after twenty years.'

Within The Curve Of A Woman's Arm
Odorono toilet water; US, from 1919. James Young of the J. Walter Thompson agency wrote the original copy. Two hundred *Ladies' Home Journal* subscribers cancelled their subscriptions when the advertisement tackled 'a frank discussion of a subject too often avoided', but the deodorant's sales increased by 112 percent in that year.

Wodka From Varrington, The
Vladivar vodka; UK, from 1972–78. The unlikely positioning of Greenall-Whitley's distillery in Warrington, far from Russia or Poland, gave rise to a distinctive and enjoyable series of campaigns. The original coinage was by Len Weinreich at the Kirkwood Company. Also **Vladivar From Warrington. The Greatest Wodka In The Vorld.**

Woman Never Forgets The Man Who Remembers, A
Whitman's Sampler chocolates and confections; US, current 1954. Also **Give Whitman's Chocolates – It's The Thoughtful Thing To Do**, coined in 1933 to remind people that 'social graces had not been lost in the slump'. (Lambert)

Woman's Right To Choose, A
National Abortion Campaign; US, 1970s.

Woman Without A Man Is Like A Fish Without A Bicycle, A
Feminist slogan; UK and elsewhere since the mid-1970s. Elaine
Partnow's *The Quotable Woman 1800–1981* (1982) attributes this
saying to Gloria Steinem but gives no hint as to why it makes
such a very dubious attribution, though it is reasonable to
assume that the words must have crossed Ms Steinem's lips at
some stage. It is, after all, probably the most famous feminist slogan of recent decades. Bartlett's *Dictionary of Familiar Quotations*
(1992) lists it anonymously as a 'feminist slogan of the 1980s'. So,
if not from Steinem, whence came the saying? Mrs C. Raikes of
Moseley, Birmingham contributed it to BBC Radio *Quote ...
Unquote* (1977), adding: 'I felt you had to share in this pearl of
wisdom I found yesterday on a lavatory wall in Birmingham
University. Written in German, it translates as ... ' Indeed, the
chances are that the saying may have originated in what was then
West Germany where it was known in the form, *'Eine Frau ohne
Mann ist wie ein Fisch ohne Velo!'* Compare, however, what Arthur
Bloch in *Murphy's Law ...* (also 1977) calls 'Vique's Law': 'A man
without religion is like a fish without a bicycle.' In 1979, Arthur
Marsall contributed the interesting variant: 'A woman without a
man is like a moose without a hatrack.' In Haan &
Hammerstrom, *Graffiti in the Big Ten* (1981) is 'Behind every suc-
cessful man is a fish with a bicycle.'

Women Of Britain Say – 'GO!'
Army recruitment; UK, during the First World War. On posters.

Women Reclaim The Night (or, US, **Take Back The Night**)
Women's movement slogan; UK/US; by 1981. From the campaign
to make it possible for women to go out in the dark without fear
of attack or rape. The American slogan was promoted by Women
Against Pornography.

Wonder Of Woolworths, The
See NOTHING OVER SIXPENCE

Workers Of The World, Unite!

Political slogan; UK and elsewhere, since 1848. Latterly the slogan of Industrial Workers of the World. It is taken from *The Communist Manifesto* by Karl Marx and Friedrich Engels: 'Let the ruling classes tremble at a communist revolution. The proletarians have nothing to lose but their chains. They have a world to win. Working men of all lands, unite!'

World's Favourite Airline, The

British Airways; UK and elsewhere, from 1983. Created by the Saatchi and Saatchi agency, on the basis of usage and marketing surveys. BA's claim was justified on the grounds that the airline flies more people to more international destinations than any other airline.

A problem all airlines share is in projecting a distinct image when the nature of the service they offer can differ only in minor respects. They also seem bound to pretend that being thrust through the air at 39,000 feet, in a cramped metal tube, is somehow a glamorous, life-enhancing experience.

World's Finest Blade, The

See WILKINSON SWORD ...

World's Greatest Bookshop, The

W. & G. Foyle, London; UK, current 1959.

World's Greatest Entertainer, The

Bill-matter for the Russian-born American entertainer Al Jolson (1886–1950). Typically modest.

World's Largest Store, The

Macy's, New York City. Current 1981.

World's Most Perfectly ...

See YOU TOO CAN HAVE A BODY ...

World's Most Popular King Size ...

See BEST TOBACCO MONEY ...

Worth A Guinea A Box

Beecham's pills (for stomach disorders and headaches); UK, from 1859. This slogan appeared in the first advertisement Thomas Beecham ever placed in a newspaper, the *St Helens Intelligencer*, on 6 August 1859. Family tradition had it that the saying was inspired by a woman in St Helens market who approached Thomas and asked for another box, saying: 'They're worth a guinea to me, lad.' But in 1897 Thomas stated categorically that he had himself had 'struck out from the metal anvil that spark of wit which has made the pills a household word in every quarter of the globe'. A probably apocryphal story is it that an ad was inserted in a church hymnal which led a congregation one day to chorus:

Hark, the Herald Angels sing
Beecham's Pills are just the thing.
For easing pain and mothers mild,
Two for adults, one for a child.

Also used was the slogan **Beecham's Pills Make All The Difference**.

Wot A Lot I Got
Smarties; UK, from c.1958 to 1964. Anthony Pugh of the J. Walter Thompson agency recalled in 1965: 'For a long time we did dotty advertising which said that everybody likes Smarties. This was palpably untrue, because only kids did ... What we discovered was that children like collecting lots of little things – so we thought of the phrase "What a lot". Then I taped my own children playing with lots of Smarties, and they said "WOTALOTIGOT" and "WOTALOTUGOT" ... Then I thought, why don't we show the people who are supposed to be eating them, let's just get ordinary kids, not television children. The sales soared.' (Pearson)

At the end of the TV ads came the quirky tag **Buy Some For Lulu**.

Wot No —?
Informal protest slogan format; UK, from the early 1940s. The most common graffito of the past 50 years in Britain – apart from 'Kilroy was here' (with which it was sometimes combined) – is the figure of 'Chad', 'Mr Chad' or 'The Chad'. He made his first appearances in the early stages of the Second World War, accompanied by protests about shortages of the time, such as, 'Wot no cake?', 'Wot no char?', 'Wot no beer?'

The format was then used by Watneys London Ltd, the brewers, to promote their beer, sometime in the 1940s or 50s. The slogan Wot no Watneys? was shown written on a brick wall – or so everybody says. Possibly, however, they may be confusing this with the famous poster which showed graffiti on a brick wall declaring WHAT WE WANT IS WATNEYS or WE WANT WATNEYS. Alas, Watneys themselves have no copy of any of these adverts in their archives.

In 1933, at the end of Prohibition, Buster Keaton played in an American film farce with the title *What, No Beer?* As always, there's nothing new ...

Wouldn't You Rather Be Hemeling?
See GIVE HIM A RIGHT ...

Would You Be More Careful If It Was You Who Got Pregnant?
Health Education Council; UK, 1970. Created by Jeremy Sinclair
of the Cramer Saatchi agency, this poster ad showed an apparently
pregnant male, accompanied by the copy: 'Contraception is one of
the facts of life. Anyone, married or single, can get free advice on
contraception from their doctor or family planning clinic ...'

Would You Buy A Used Car From This Man?
Informal slogan; US, from the 1950s on. A slur which attached
itself permanently to the personality of Richard M. Nixon. A simple joke or folk saying to begin with, although it has been attributed by some to Mort Sahl and by others to Lenny Bruce. The cartoonist Herblock denied that he was responsible (*The Guardian*, 24
December 1975). As to when it first arose, this is Hugh Brogan,
writing in *New Society* (4 November 1982): 'Nixon is a double-bar-
relled, treble-shotted twister, as my old history master would
have remarked; and the fact has been a matter of universal knowledge since at least 1952, when, if I remember aright the joke,
"Would you buy a second-hand car from this man?" began to cir-
culate.' It was a very effective slur and, by 1968, when the politician was running (successfully) for President, a poster of a shifty-
looking Nixon with the line as caption was in circulation.

Now used of anybody one has doubts about. Reisner has the
graffito: 'Governor Romney – would you buy a *new* car from this
man?' In August 1984, the would-be car manufacturer John de
Lorean said of himself – after being acquitted of drug-dealing – 'I
have aged 600 years and my life as a hard-working industrialist is
in tatters. Would you buy a used car from me?'

Yanks Go Home

Anti-US slogan; wherever there was unwanted American military and/or business presence, after the Second World War. 'Yankee/Yanqui Go Home' was widely used throughout Latin America from 1950 on.

Yesterday's Men

Labour Party general election slogan; UK, 1970. David Kingsley said (1991) that this phrase 'came from the three of us in the [party advertising] team and we never could untangle precisely who created it' – perhaps as well, as it had to be dropped for reasons of taste during the 1970 campaign. A colour poster showing crudely coloured models of Conservative politicians (Edward Heath, Iain Macleod, Lord Hailsham and others) and the additional line 'They failed before' was judged to 'degrade' politics. In fact, Labour lost the election to 'Yesterday's Men' but the phrase continued to cause trouble. In 1971 it was used as the title of a BBC TV programme about the defeated Labour leaders and how they were faring in Opposition. This soured relations between the BBC and the Labour Party for a long time afterwards.

'Yesterday Man' had been the title of a hit record by Chris Andrews in 1965.

Yesterday The Trenches, Today The Unemployed

Unofficial political slogan; UK, 1923. This cry was heard in the aftermath of the First World War and prior to the first Labour election victory, under Ramsay MacDonald.

Yes! We Have No Bananas

See HAVE A BANANA

271

You Ain't Seen Nothin' Yet!

Presidential election catchphrase (with the force of a slogan); US, 1984. Ronald Reagan appropriated this phrase in his successful bid for re-election. He used it repeatedly during the campaign and, on 7 November, in his victory speech. Partridge/*Catch Phrases* has a combined entry for 'you ain't *seen* nothin' yet' and 'you ain't *heard* nothin' yet, in which 'seen' is described as the commoner of the two versions. Both are said to date from the 1920s. One could add that Bachman-Turner Overdrive, the Canadian pop group, had a hit with a song called 'You Ain't Seen Nothin' Yet' in 1974.

The 'heard' version is most famously associated with Al Jolson exclaiming it in the first full-length talking picture *The Jazz Singer* (1927). He was not just ad-libbing as is usually supposed. He was promoting the title of one of his songs. He had recorded 'You Ain't Heard Nothing Yet', written by Gus Kahn and Buddy de Sylva, in 1919, and had also used the words as a catchphrase in his act before making the film. So, **You Ain't Heard Nothin' Yet** also qualifies as a kind of slogan.

You Are What You Eat

Informal slogan; US and elsewhere, by the 1960s. This neat encapsulation of a sensible attitude to diet (known in the US by 1941) was used as the title of an 'alternative' American film that was first shown in Britain in 1969. The idea behind the phrase has been around for many a year, however. Compare: Brillat-Savarin in *La Physiologie du goût*: 'Tell me what you eat and I will tell you what you are' and L.A. Feuerbach: 'Man is what he eats *[Der Mensch ist, was er ißt]*' – in a review of Moleschott's *Lehre der Nahrungsmittel für das Volk* (1850). The German film chronicle *Heimat* (1984) included the version, *'Wie der Mensch ißt, so ist er* [As a man eats, so he is].'

You Can Always Get It At The Co-Op

Co-Operative Wholesale Society shops and stores; UK, probably current in the early 1950s. Also remembered as 'I Got It At The Co-Op' – which facilitates a joke told about the alleged Co-Op poster, bearing this slogan, which was displayed next to one bearing 'VD' in large letters.

You Can Always Take One With You
Informal slogan; UK, 1940. This was suggested by Winston Churchill when invasion by the Germans was threatened in 1940. Recalled by him in *The Second World War*, Vol. 2 (1949).

You Can Be Sure Of Shell
Shell motoring fuel; UK, from c.1931.

You Can Do It In An MG
MG motor cars; UK, current 1983. Ascribed to Mike Fox at the Cogent Elliott agency, London.

You Can Rely On The Lion
See GO TO WORK ON AN EGG

You Can Take A White Horse Anywhere
White Horse whisky; UK, from 1969. The campaign which featured a white horse (but which did not bother to communicate any product benefit to the consumer) was masterminded in its original form by Len Heath at the KMP partnership.

You Can't Beat Somebody With Nobody
Presidential election slogan; US, 1904. With it, Theodore Roosevelt was re-elected over the Democratic challenger, Alton B. Parker.

You Can't K-nacker A K-nirps
Knirps umbrellas; UK, 1981. Chiefly remembered as the punchline of a TV ad in which a man holding one of these German-made umbrellas walked through a carwash unharmed. The full selling line was 'You can break a brolly, but you can't K-nacker a K-nirps'. Credited to Dave Trott. Shortly afterwards the parent company and its British subsidiary went into liquidation.

You Can Trust Your Car To The Man Who Wears The Star
Texaco motor fuel; US, current 1961.

You Don't Have To Be Jewish To Love Levy's Real Jewish Rye
Levy's rye bread; US, current 1967. The point of this slogan was re-inforced by its being positioned under pictures of very obviously

un-Jewish people – American Indians, Frenchmen, and so on. Nobody had heard of the brand until the Doyle, Dane, Bernbach agency got to work on it. However, the phrase has a well established feel to it and may have been a Jewish saying before its ad use. Leo Rosten in *The Joys of Yiddish* (1968) writes at one point, 'You don't have to be Jewish to be a folks-mensch' – though perhaps he was influenced by the then current slogan. In the UK, it ended up as the title of a radio programme for (mostly) Jewish listeners on BBC Radio London (from 1971). Graffiti additions have been plentiful. They include: ' … to be offended by this ad'/' … to be called one'/' … to go to Columbia University, but it helps'/' … to wear levis'/' … to be circumcised'. (Reisner)

You Gave Us Beer, Now Give Us Water

Informal political slogan; US, 1933. The dustbowl farmers' plea. The year of the great drought, which destroyed crops and created dust-storms was, ironically, when Prohibition ended. (Flexner, 1976)

You Give Us —— Minutes, We'll Give You The World

Broadcasting slogan; US, by the 1970s. More than one all-news radio station in the US has used this slogan format. 'You Give Us Twenty Minutes …' was being used by KYW in Philadelphia in 1972. Ten years later, a US TV satellite news channel was declaring: 'Give us eighteen minutes. We'll give you the world.' In the film *Robocop* (US, 1987), the shout of a TV news team is, 'You give us three minutes, and we'll give you the world.'

You Know It Makes Sense

Road safety slogan; UK, 1960s. This was used as the pay-off line to all road safety campaigns from the Central Office of Information in 1968–70. However, the phrase had earlier been spoken with emphasis on the BBC TV programme *That Was The Week That Was* in 1963 which suggests that it had probably been used before this in other contexts.

You *Know* Labour Govermnent Works

Labour Party general election slogan; UK, 1966. After almost four years in power, the Labour Government went to the country in an effort to increase its majority. It used a slogan intended to reflect its credibility (it had previously been out of power for thirteen years). David Kingsley said (1981) that the slogan was 'largely my own creation, but it grew out of team-work with Dennis Lyons and Peter Lovell-Davis'. A version of its creation is that Lovell-Davis suggested 'Labour Government Works' and Kingsley added the 'You Know'.

You Know What Comes Between Me And My Calvins? Nothing!
Calvin Klein jeans; US, 1980. Brooke Shields, all of 15 years of age, said this and the line is remembered for its mild suggestiveness. Sometimes recalled as 'Nothing comes between me and my Calvins'.

You'll Believe A Man Can Fly
Film, *Superman – The Movie*; US, 1978.

You'll Be Safe In The Park/Every Night After Dark/With Lefkowitz, Gilhooley And Fino
Political slogan; US, 1961. A dotty local election ditty from New York. There was even a version in Spanish for the Puerto Ricans (who otherwise appeared unrepresented on this cosmopolitan ticket).

You'll Look A Little Lovelier Each Day / With Fabulous Pink Camay
Camay soap; UK, current c.1960. One of the catchiest phrases from the early days of British commercial TV. The jingle gave rise to a parody about a Labour politician on BBC TV's *That Was The Week That Was* (1963):

> You'll look a little lovelier each day
> With fabulous Douglas Jay.

The soap also boasted **Perfume Worth 9 Guineas An Ounce.**

You'll Wonder Where The Yellow Went / When You Brush Your Teeth With Pepsodent
Pepsodent toothpaste; US, current 1950s. An appeal to vanity

rather than health, but curiously memorable. From a David Frost/Christopher Booker parody of political advertisements (BBC TV *That Was the Week That Was*, 1963): 'You'll wonder where the George Brown went / When Harold forms his Government.' In South Africa, reportedly, 'yellow' was changed to 'dullness'.

You Never Had It So Good
See I LIKE IKE

You Press The Button – We Do The Rest
Kodak cameras; US, from 1889. 'It was literally edited out of a long piece of copy by George Eastman himself – one of the greatest of advertising ideas.' (Watkins) 'The Kodak became so popular that many people errroneously began to call all cameras Kodak, so, in order to prevent Kodak from becoming a generic name, Eastman soon also used the slogan **If It Isn't An Eastman, It Isn't A Kodak**.' (Flexner, 1982)

NEW KODAKS

"You press the button, we do the rest."

Seven new Styles and Sizes
ALL LOADED WITH *Transparent Films.*
For sale by all Photo. Stock Dealers.

THE EASTMAN COMPANY,
Send for Catalogue *ROCHESTER, N. Y.*

Your Country Needs You

Recruitment slogan; UK, from 1914. The most famous recruiting slogan of all – inseparably linked to the picture of Field-Marshal Lord Kitchener, with staring eyes and pointing finger. Kitchener was appointed Secretary of State for War on 6 August 1914, two days after the outbreak of what was to become known as 'The Great War'. He set to work immediately, intent on raising the 'New Armies' required to supplement the small standing army of the day, which he rightly saw would be inadequate for a major conflict. The poster was taken up by the Parliamentary Recruiting Committee and first issued on 14 September.

In fact, work on advertising for recruits had started the year before, with some success. Then, towards the end of July 1914, Eric Field of the tiny Caxton Advertising Agency (owned by Sir

Hedley Le Bas) received a call from a Colonel Strachey, who 'swore me to secrecy, told me that war was imminent and that the moment it broke out we should have to start advertising at once'. That night, Field wrote an advertisement headed **Your King And Country Need You** with the royal coat of arms as the only illustration. The day after war was declared, 5 August, this appeared prominently in the *Daily Mail* and other papers. The alliterative linking of 'king' and 'country' was traditional. Francis Bacon (1625) had written: 'Be so true to thyself, as thou be not false to others; specially to thy King, and Country.' In 1913, J.M. Barrie had included in his play *Quality Street*: 'If ... death or glory was the call, you would take the shilling, ma'am ... For King and Country.'

The appeal appeared in various forms but Kitchener preferred these first slogans and insisted on finishing every advertisement with 'God Save The King'. The drawing was by the humorous artist Alfred Leete and the original is now in the Imperial War Museum. (Margot Asquith commented: 'If Kitchener was not a great man, he was, at least, a great poster.')

The idea was widely imitated abroad. In the US, James Montgomery Flagg's poster of a pointing Uncle Sam bore the legend **I Want You For The US Army**. There was also a version by Howard Chandler Christy featuring a woman with a mildly come-hither look saying, **I Want You For The Navy**.

Your Courage, *Your* Cheerfulness, *Your* Resolution Will Bring Us Victory

Government morale-building slogan; UK, 1939. One of the first posters after the outbreak of war, printed in vivid red and white, this caused a bitter outcry from those who resented any implication of 'Them and Us'. The slogan was suggested by A.P. Waterfield, a career Civil Servant at the Ministry of Information. He wanted 'A rallying war-cry that will ... put us in an offensive mood at once.' (McLaine) But it was judged to have fallen well short of the necessary belligerent tone. *The Times* thundered: 'The insipid and patronising invocations to which the passer-by is now being treated have a power of exasperation which is all their own. There may be no intrinsic harm in their faint, academic piety, but the implication that the public morale needs this kind of support, or, if it did, that this is the kind of support it would need, is calculated to promote a response which is neither academic nor pious.'

You're Going To Like Us
TWA; US, current 1980. Earlier, in 1967, when TWA hinted that it might be on the point of quitting its New York agency, Foote, Cone & Belding saved their bacon by slipping over to California and buying sole rights to the Jim Webb song 'Up, Up and Away'. They proceeded to incorporate this in the airline's ads as **Up, Up And Away With TWA.**

You're Having It Good ...
See LIFE'S BETTER WITH ...

You're Never Alone With A Strand
Strand cigarettes; UK, 1960. The slogan of a classic ad which caught the public imagination but yet failed to achieve its purpose – selling cigarettes. Devised in 1960 by John May of the S.H. Benson agency for the W.D. & H.O. Wills tobacco company, the campaign was to launch a new, cheap filter cigarette called Strand. Wills had rejected the first plan put to them and so, at rather short notice, May thought up a new concept. This amounted to appealing to the youth market by associating the cigarettes not with sex or social ease but with 'the loneliness and rejection of youth'. 'The young Sinatra was the prototype of the man I had in mind,' May recalled (1965): 'Loneliness had made him a millionaire. I didn't see why it shouldn't sell us some cigarettes.' (Pearson)

And so a Sinatra-clone was found in the shape of a 28-year-old actor called Terence Brook, who was also said to bear a resemblance to James Dean. He was shown mooching about lonely locations in a raincoat and hat. In no time at all he had his own fanclub. Music from the TV ad, 'The Lonely Man Theme', became a hit in its own right.

But the ads did not work. Viewers revised the slogan in their own minds to mean: 'If you buy Strand, then you'll be alone.' However much the young may have identified with the figure they did not want to buy him or his aura. Or perhaps it was just not a very good cigarette. Either way, it has not been forgotten.

Your Friendly Neighbourhood —
All-purpose slogan format; US/UK, probably from the 1960s. 'Usually ironic or facetious', *The Oxford Dictionary of Current Idiomatic English* (1985) notes of this construction, and says it is derived from the slogan 'Your friendly neighbourhood policeman' in a police public-relations campaign of the 1960s. Compare SUPPORT YOUR LOCAL —.

Your Future Is In Your Hands
Conservative Party general election slogan; UK, 1950. The Conservatives lost the election by a small margin but were returned to power under Winston Churchill the following year. Churchill himself had used the idea in an address to Canadian troops aboard RMS *Queen Elizabeth* in January 1946: 'Our future is in our hands. Our lives are what we choose to make of them.' The slogan led to the inevitable lavatorial joke, as in Keith Waterhouse, *Billy Liar* (1959): '"No writing mucky words on the walls!" he called. I did not reply. Stamp began quoting, "*Gentlemen, you have the future of England in your hands*".' The male lavatorial graffito, 'The future of Scotland is in your hands' was included in *Graffiti Lives OK* (1979).

Also from the Conservatives in the 1950 election: **A Vote For The Liberals Is A Vote Wasted ... Make Britain Great Again**.

Your Home Is Your Castle – Protect It
Political election slogan; US, 1960s. A 'code-word' slogan, designed to appeal to White voters concerned that property values would decline if Blacks moved in. Used by various candidates in mayoralty and state elections. Lester Maddox won a narrow victory in the contest for the 1966 Georgia governorship with it. (Safire)

Your Money *And* Your Life!
Anti-smoking slogan; UK, 1981.

Your Mother Wouldn't Like It
See MOTHER WOULDN'T LIKE IT

Yours Faithfully
Trust Houses Forte (hotel chain); UK, 1980s.

You Should See Me On Sunday
Knight's Family Health Soap; UK, quoted 1941.

Yours To Enjoy in the Privacy of Your Own Home
Various products; UK, probably from the 1950s on. A parody from *The Penguin Private Eye* (1965): 'Now experience the first world war in the privacy of your own home.'

You Too Can Have A Body Like Mine
Charles Atlas body-building courses; US, current 1930s. 'Charles Atlas' was born Angelo Siciliano in Italy in 1894. In his youth he actually was 'a skinny, timid weakling of only seven stone', as the later ads said (or **I Was A Seven Stone Weakling**). 'I didn't know what real health and strength were. I was afraid to fight – ashamed to be seen in a bathing costume.' After watching a lion rippling its muscles at the zoo, he developed a method of pitting one muscle against another which he later called **Dynamic Tension**. In 1922 he won the title of **The World's Most Perfectly Developed Man** in a contest sponsored by Bernarr Macfadden and his *Physical Culture* magazine. He started giving mail-order lessons: 'Hey! Quit kicking that sand in our faces!' He died in 1972.

You've Come A Long Way Baby (To Get Where You Got To Today)
Virginia Slims cigarettes; US, from 1968. A slogan that reflected the feminist mood of the time in selling to women smokers – indeed, the phrase has also been used on Women's Lib posters. One such shows a woman giving a karate chop to a man's head. An article by Julie Baumgold with the title 'You've Come a Long Way, Baby' appeared in *New York* Magazine (9 June 1969). A song with the title followed in 1971. After the failure of the US Equal Rights Amendment in 1982, a T-shirt appeared bearing the informal slogan, 'I Haven't Come A Long Way'.

You've Got A Lot To Live
See COME ALIVE ...

You've Never Had It So Good
See LIFE'S BETTER WITH ...

You Want The Best Seats, We Have Them

Keith Prowse ticket agency; UK, from 1925 – until the company collapsed in 1991. However, *Punch* (29 October 1913) has a short comic piece about toadstools advertising for toads to sit on them (in a form of words which was not perhaps strictly original, but, like most of the jokes at which audiences laugh was none the worse for that): 'TO THE NOBILITY AND GENTRY OF TOAD-LAND. YOU WANT THE BEST SEATS WE HAVE THEM.' So, the phrase would appear to pre-date Keith Prowse.

You Will Feel Like You Are Looking At The World For The First Time

Polaroid cameras; US, 1960s. Lumpy line uttered by Laurence Olivier in TV ads. No wonder he insisted they not be shown in Britain.

Zubes Are Good For Your Tubes
Zubes cough sweets; UK, 1960s.

Sources

Names of sources have mostly been given in parentheses. Abbreviations for those most frequently cited are as follows:

Atwan	Atwan, McQuade, Wright *Edsels, Luckies & Frigidaires* (1979)
Baker	Samm Sinclair Baker *The Permissible Lie* (1969)
Boorstin	Daniel Boorstin *The Image* (1960)
Calder	Angus Calder *The People's War* (1969)
Day	Barry Day (ed.) *100 Great Advertisements* (1978)
Flexner	Stuart Berg Flexner *I Hear America Talking* (1976); *Listening To America* (1982)
Jones	Edgar R. Jones *Those Were the Good Old Days* (1979)
Kleinman	Philip Kleinman *Advertising Inside Out* (1977)
Lambert	I.E. Lambert *The Public Accepts* (1941)
McLaine	Ian McLaine *Ministry of Morale* (1979)
Mayer	Martin Mayer *Madison Avenue, USA* (1971)
Nicholl	David Shelley Nicholl *Advertising: its Purpose, Principles and Practice* (1978)
OED2	*The Oxford English Dictionary* (2nd edition, 1989, CD-ROM version, 1992)
Ogilvy	David Ogilvy *Confessions of an Advertising Man* (1980)
Packard	Vance Packard *The Hidden Persuaders* (1957)
Partridge/ Catch Phrases	Eric Partridge *A Dictionary of Catch Phrases* (2nd edition, edited by Paul Beale, 1985)
Partridge/ Slang	Eric Partridge *A Dictionary of Slang and Unconventional English* (8th edition, edited by Paul Beale, 1984)
Pearson	John Pearson and Graham Turner *The Persuasion Industry* (1965)
Polykoff	Shirley Polykoff *Does She ... Or Doesn't She?* (1975)
Reisner	Robert Reisner and Lorraine Wechsler *The Encyclopedia of Graffiti* (1974)

SOURCES

Safire	William Safire *Safire's Political Dictionary* (1980)
Sayers	Dorothy L. Sayers *Murder Must Advertise* (1933)
Sunners	William Sunners *Prize Winning Slogans* (1968)
Turner	E.S. Turner *The Shocking History of Advertising* (1952)
Watkins	Julian Lewis Watkins *The 100 Greatest Advertisements* (1959 ed.)
White	Theodore H. White *The Making of the President 1961/1964/1968/1972* (1962, 1965, 1969, 1973)